Healing with

Trauma-Focused

DBT

A Trauma Survivor's Guide to

Manage Intense Emotions

and Reclaim Your Life

with Polyvagal Theory and

Dialectical Behavior Therapy

KIRBY REUTTER, PhD

New Harbinger Publications, Inc.

NEW HARBINGER PUBLICATIONS is a registered trademark of New Harbinger Publications, Inc.

New Harbinger Publications is an employee-owned company.

Copyright © 2026 by Kirby Reutter
New Harbinger Publications, Inc.
5720 Shattuck Avenue
Oakland, CA 94609
www.newharbinger.com

All Rights Reserved

Cover design by Amy Daniel

Acquired by Jess O'Brien

Edited by Karen Schader

Library of Congress Cataloging-in-Publication Data on file

Printed in the United States of America

28   27   26

10   9   8   7   6   5   4   3   2   1   First Printing

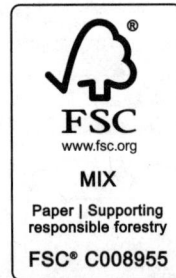

Contents

	Foreword	v
1	An Introduction to Trauma-Focused DBT	1
2	Dialectics for Trauma	19
3	Mindfulness for Trauma	41
4	Radical Acceptance for Trauma	67
5	Short-Term Coping for Trauma	85
6	Long-Term Balance for Trauma	105
7	Re-Engaging with Others	125
8	Building a Life Worth Living	147
	References	163

Foreword

Although dialectical behavior therapy (DBT) was originally created to treat borderline personality disorder, over the years research has demonstrated the efficacy of this treatment in managing emotion dysregulation more broadly, regardless of its cause. I myself have spent most of my career working toward the goal of making DBT more accessible for both clients and clinicians, teaching that these skills can be invaluable for a wide range of mental health problems, as well as for the more basic difficulties that arise for all of us in life: managing stress, grief, sadness, disappointment, anger, hurt, and so on. Many emotional difficulties are also rooted in trauma, and in recent years, many of us working in the trauma field have been using DBT alongside other tools and techniques to help people overcome the negative consequences of traumatic events they've experienced, including post-traumatic stress disorder.

Dr. Kirby Reutter's clinical expertise, academic knowledge, and real-world experience in both DBT and trauma therapy has perfectly situated him to author this book, *Healing with Trauma-Focused DBT*, a valuable resource for trauma survivors as well as the clinicians who work with them.

Trauma is universal and yet deeply personal, leaving an imprint on the mind, influencing our thoughts and emotions and physiology; in fact, we now know that trauma can even influence how our genes are expressed. Despite these very real and widespread consequences, trauma remains somewhat elusive: difficult to define, understand, and heal from. Fortunately, the field of psychology continues to evolve, providing us with increasingly sophisticated frameworks for understanding trauma and its effects. Among these, trauma-focused dialectical behavior therapy (TF-DBT) stands out as an indispensable approach.

In *Healing with Trauma-Focused DBT*, Dr. Reutter offers a ground-breaking synthesis of research, theory, and clinical wisdom, providing a guide that is both compassionate and highly practical. This book doesn't just explain trauma—it equips individuals and clinicians with the tools they need to work through it. By integrating core components of DBT with cutting-edge insights from polyvagal theory, neurobiology, and an understanding of dissociative processes, Dr. Reutter has written a guide that simplifies trauma and offers a structured path toward healing in a way that makes it accessible to readers. Translating complex concepts into language that is understandable and also deeply validating, Dr. Reutter approaches trauma and its consequences not as a problem to be "fixed," but as a lived experience—requiring empathy and curiosity, as well as, of course, evidence-based interventions. Dr. Reutter's psychoeducational approach ensures that readers will develop greater clarity and concrete strategies to address the fallout of trauma.

A crucial element of this book is its exploration of the neurobiology of trauma. Science has increasingly demonstrated that trauma is not just an event that happens to us, but an experience that fundamentally impacts our nervous system; therefore, the integration of polyvagal theory provides a vital perspective on how trauma affects our ability to feel safe, connect with others, and regulate our emotions. By understanding the role of the autonomic nervous system in activating survival responses, readers will gain powerful insight into why trauma symptoms manifest the way they do and, more importantly, how they can be addressed.

At the heart of *Healing with Trauma-Focused DBT* is a message of hope. Trauma certainly shapes us, but it doesn't have to define us. Through the principles of DBT, Dr. Reutter provides a road map for resilience and for moving toward posttraumatic growth and healing.

For clinicians, this book is a must-read, offering an integrative and structured approach to treating trauma with a balance of warmth and scientific rigor. For trauma survivors, it's a source of validation and empowerment, enabling them to make sense of symptoms that may have previously been experienced as incomprehensible and even further traumatizing. And for anyone seeking to deepen their understanding of trauma, it's an invitation to approach this work with compassion and courage.

In a world where trauma is often misunderstood or minimized or—even worse—stigmatized, *Healing with Trauma-Focused DBT* provides both the knowledge and compassion that will help readers find a greater understanding of themselves, of others, and of the capacity for healing that exists within us all.

—Sheri Van Dijk MSW
Author of *The Dialectical Behavior Therapy Skills Workbook for CPTSD*

An Introduction to Trauma-Focused DBT

Why another book on DBT? Why another book on trauma? If you're picking up this book right now, those are probably the first two questions you have. They're great questions, and they both deserve thoughtful answers.

What Is DBT?

Dialectical behavior therapy (DBT) was developed in the 1970s by Dr. Marsha Linehan to treat symptoms of what we call borderline personality disorder. A borderline personality is characterized by a fear of abandonment; chaotic relationships; chronic feelings of emptiness; reckless, impulsive, and self-injurious behaviors; and a constant roller coaster of emotions, including fits of rage. Before DBT came along, no approach seemed effective at treating these symptoms. At the time, DBT was revolutionary—there was finally a model that provided hope for emotional suffering (Linehan 1993).

So how was DBT able to accomplish what no other model could do? DBT works by teaching skills. DBT was, and still is, unique as a model of psychotherapy with its exclusive focus on skills work (Linehan 2014). Let's consider a silly example of why this was such a simple yet powerful concept. Assume you have a friend learning to swim in the deep end of the pool. He is currently kicking and screaming, flailing and floundering…and quickly sinking. It is *not* going so well for your friend. What's the best way to help? Well, if you wanted to use one approach to therapy, you could offer unconditional positive regard: "I believe in you! You've got this! You're doing a great job!" If you wanted to use another approach, you could explore his thinking errors and determine that he is most likely *catastrophizing*, or imagining the worst possible outcome. If you wanted to use yet another approach, you could help him analyze his prior experiences with water, including any recent dreams about drowning. Or if you prefer to pursue a more practical approach, you could try to shape better behaviors in your friend by reinforcing any movement that (sort of) resembles a swim technique. Is your friend still sinking? Let's try another approach: help your friend identify what gives his life meaning, especially since life is so fragile and finite.

I am being dramatic here, as all these approaches have their place. But right now, your friend does not need any of these interventions. Right now, what your friend needs is for someone to rescue him—and then teach the poor soul how to swim! That's what DBT does. It teaches people skills to use when they feel like they are drowning in the deep end of life. Only then will the other approaches to therapy be useful and make any sense.

DBT works by teaching five simple yet profound skill sets: mindfulness, distress tolerance, emotion regulation, interpersonal effectiveness, and dialectics. Each of these terms will be elaborated on in the following chapters, but let's introduce some basic working definitions to get us started. *Mindfulness* refers to awareness and acceptance of the moment. *Distress tolerance* refers to coping with a situation so that it does not become even worse. *Emotion regulation* refers to adopting a healthier lifestyle that will support healthier emotions. *Interpersonal effectiveness* involves how we deal with other people—communication, conflict, and all that drama. Finally, *dialectics* refers to looking at things from multiple perspectives and finding the middle path between two extremes (Linehan 2015).

Once the secret was out that DBT was effective in treating borderline personality disorder, people soon learned that DBT could be used to treat just about anything. Over the last few decades, DBT has been applied to pretty much anything that can be diagnosed: mood disorders, eating disorders, substance disorders, other personality disorders...you name it! (Ritschel et al. 2015).

Although never a substitute for appropriately prescribed medication, DBT has even been effective in mitigating organic disorders such as bipolar and schizophrenia. In other words, even with disorders in which there is literally something physically and chemically wrong with the brain, learning DBT skills can help people rewire their brain connections and find a more stable, healthier path through life (Van Dijk 2009; Mullen 2021).

This is good to know. Why? Because as you will learn, trauma is a disorder in which both the body and the brain are literally and physically thrown off balance. But unlike other disorders, there is no medication that can take away post-traumatic stress disorder (PTSD). There are some meds that can help reduce some of the symptoms of trauma, but there is no pill that can treat the trauma itself—so there better be some other options available!

So what about DBT? Is DBT effective in treating trauma symptoms? Well, of course. In fact, that's the whole point of this book! However, the full response is more nuanced than that. Later in this chapter, we will talk much more about the causes and effects of trauma. Since its development in the 1970s, there has literally been a half century of research on trauma that Dr. Linehan did not have access to. To give you some perspective: the first airplane was flown in 1903; the first space shuttle landed on the moon in 1969. Clearly, a lot can happen in fifty plus years! We now know so much more about how trauma impacts every aspect of human functioning—thoughts, feelings, awareness, reactions, relationships—than ever before.

What is truly amazing about original DBT is how effective it has been in treating the majority of trauma symptoms—even before we had the massive body of research that we now have. For example, DBT's emphasis on its five main skill sets directly targets many of the classic symptoms of PTSD related to avoidance, reactivity, self-blame, and dissociation. However, original DBT was never designed to treat symptoms of trauma related to reexperiencing the original trauma (such as nightmares and flashbacks).

In a nutshell, this is why DBT needs to be upgraded. This is why we need another book on DBT. And another book on trauma!

What Is Trauma?

Trauma affects every part of the body and every part of the brain. That's a lot of turf. There is still much that even highly trained professionals do not understand about how trauma affects a person, both physically and emotionally. What follows is an introduction to the causes and effects of trauma.

How is it possible for trauma to affect the entire body and the entire brain? At its core, trauma is a disorder of the nervous system. And since the nervous system is the bridge between the brain and the rest of the body, anything that assaults the nervous system will affect everything else.

More specifically, trauma directly assaults the *autonomic nervous system* (ANS), which is just the fancy medical way of saying the branch of the nervous system that operates automatically (whether we are thinking about it or not). This system regulates everything we do unconsciously, ranging from breathing to digesting to pumping blood. Within the ANS, there are two branches, or subsystems: the *sympathetic nervous system* (SNS) and the *parasympathetic nervous system* (PNS). Imagine these two branches as parts of a car: the SNS works like an accelerator, while the PNS operates like a brake.

Sometimes the sympathetic branch is referred to as the fight-or-flight system, while the parasympathetic branch is referred to as the rest-and-digest system. Depending on what is going on in the body or environment, sometimes the nervous system applies the brake, and sometimes it steps on the gas. Just like a car, the body needs both functions.

The PNS is also related to social interactions. When we trust someone and feel at ease in their presence, we feel warmth, empathy, and connection. We might even smile or laugh. This is a sign that the rest-and-digest system is currently activated. It is no wonder that in cultures all around the world, eating is a highly social event, especially during times of celebration. The system we use to digest food is also the system we use to connect with other people. But when we do not trust someone, we feel tense and on edge, poised to react at a moment's notice (Porges and Porges 2023). That's the fight-or-flight system.

We have all heard of fight or flight, but the nervous system actually has three basic instinctual responses to danger or crisis: fight, flight, and freeze. All of these responses are prevalent throughout the animal kingdom. In fact, many animals have a preferred default response. For example, bears fight, bunnies flee, and possums freeze. Humans, with all our sophistication, do all three. (In fact, humans even have a fourth trauma response—called fawning—that will be explained in a later chapter).

When humans are presented with danger, the first thing to happen is that the social part of the PNS—the car's brake—goes offline. In the face of a threat, we have no need for warmth, empathy, or connection. On the contrary, we need to be super alert and ready at a moment's notice to *dis*connect by either fighting or fleeing. In other words, the first thing our nervous system does when faced with danger is take our foot off the brake.

However, if the danger persists, then the SNS takes over. Remember, the sympathetic branch is the car's accelerator. This is the part of the nervous system that both energizes and mobilizes us to either fight or flee. This system is powered by the well-known body chemical adrenalin.

Whereas many animals have a set, preprogrammed default to either fight or flee, humans are endowed with many more brain cells, and therefore, we are equipped to make split-second choices between these options. In some cases, you will decide you have the strength and power to fight off the danger. In others, you will decide you are no match for the threat, and therefore, a mad dash would be a better use of adrenaline. Both fighting and fleeing are like slamming on the accelerator. Even though they may seem like opposite responses, fight and flight are very similar—both responses require superhuman surges of energy.

But what happens if you can neither fight off the threat nor flee the danger? Now what? Remember, we have both an accelerator and a brake. Just like we need both to drive, we also need both to survive. If you cannot avoid an accident by accelerating, then another option is to slam on the brakes. That's what the PNS does, and that's how you end up with the freeze response.

The freeze response includes many possible reactions, such as muscle paralysis, collapsing, fainting, or losing consciousness. Another common freeze reaction is *dissociation*. That's when you start to mentally disengage from the event. The situation may seem unreal, or like it is happening to a different person. For example, you might view the entire situation playing out from the perspective of a third-party observer. Or you may enter an alternate, imaginary reality (Van der Kolk 2014).

The practical benefits of the freeze response are simple: If you cannot effectively deal with a threat by either fighting it or fleeing it (in other words, you are stuck with the danger), then you might as well conserve your energy, minimize the pain, and contain the amount of physical damage done to your body. For example, a tense body experiences much more damage than a relaxed or limp body (Levine 2010), which is precisely why drunk drivers often survive their lethal car crashes, whereas their victims do not.

But here's the deal. If fight and flight work, you are much less likely to be traumatized, for two main reasons: First, because you were able to successfully deal with the threat by either fighting or fleeing. Second, because in the execution of fight and flight, you burned off all the extra energy produced by adrenaline (Levine 2010).

Yes, you will be rattled. Yes, your life may flash before your eyes. Yes, your heart may be pounding, your mind may be racing, and your lungs may feel like they are about to explode. But all of that will settle down as the adrenaline wears off and your SNS (the accelerator) is no longer glued to the floor. If anything, after the dust has settled, you will feel even stronger, even more empowered, and even more resilient than ever before. You faced the dragon…and lived to tell the tale!

But as soon as fight-or-flight responses are not viable options, and the freeze response kicks in, you are now much more at risk for becoming traumatized, for several reasons. First, the SNS is still active. All of the adrenaline, all of that fight-or-flight energy, is still cranking through your body; you are still "pedal to the metal." The main difference is that now the PNS (the brake) has also been activated to counteract this. In other words, the freeze response is not just the brake—it is both the brake *and* the gas at the same time (Levine 2010). You can imagine what that would do to a car. This is also not a good long-term strategy for the human mind or body!

In addition, the freeze response (although highly adaptive as a short-term, last-ditch effort) comes at a steep psychological cost. For example, people who survive the freeze response often experience intense feelings of guilt, shame, and self-blame. They often wonder, *Why didn't I fight more? Why didn't I try to escape?* The reality is—they couldn't!

And that's precisely why the freeze response automatically kicks in. This is not a conscious decision. In fact, once the freeze response is active, you are now *less* able to fight or flee, since the body literally becomes limp or even paralyzed. Furthermore, people who experience dissociation as part of their freeze response learn to quickly disengage from other aspects of their life as well. In short, many of the psychological effects of trauma come from this freeze response (Levine 2010).

However, just because you experience a freeze response does not mean you were or will be traumatized; it simply means that you are now at risk. If the body does its thing with both the accelerator and the brake, they are no longer glued to the floor, and both branches of the nervous system return to their normal functioning, then most likely you will rebound after some time—rattled for sure, but nonetheless better, stronger, and wiser.

Trauma happens when both the sympathetic and parasympathetic branches experience a permanent (or long-term) reset. Both systems get hijacked, and they stay hijacked, sort of like stomping on both the accelerator and brake at the same time. This results in a war between the two branches that can last for years or decades, or even a lifetime. The more the sympathetic branch steps on the gas, pumps adrenaline through the body, and ramps up all body systems for fight or flight, the more the parasympathetic branch slams on the brakes, attempts to shut it all down, and tries to freeze all this extra arousal (Levine 2010).

In fact, part of what gets "frozen" in the freeze response is this excess adrenaline. Since the adrenaline energy was never allowed to get fully released through the default fight-or-flight responses, and yet it continues to be produced, it remains stuck within the body, causing all manner of physical problems. This power struggle between the SNS and PNS drains the entire brain and body of much needed resources, all while the casualties continue to mount. Who is impacted by a war? Everyone! Therefore, all body systems are affected by the collateral damage (Levine 2010).

Since the nervous system regulates (or at least influences) every other system of the body, the effects of unresolved trauma can be catastrophic, including a myriad of medical issues. In fact, think of it this way: trauma *is* a medical problem. In my opinion, trauma is best conceptualized as primarily a medical disorder with mental health implications, rather than the other way around. Trauma is not a problem in the head that also affects the body. Rather, it is a problem in the body that affects all aspects of the body, including the brain.

To this day, many medical professionals do not fully understand or appreciate the physical impact of trauma on the nervous system (and therefore, the entire body). Since the nervous system interacts with all other body systems, many possible physical symptoms can result. These symptoms will be different for everyone, since we all have our own unique bodies with our own unique nervous systems. Unfortunately, these symptoms frequently elude precise medical diagnosing. Since everyone who has been traumatized ends up with their own personalized collection of sequelae, the symptoms you report to a medical professional may not match their criteria for specific medical disorders.

The way the brain generates the sensation of pain complicates this picture further. *All* pain is literally a sensation generated by your brain. Consider this example: Suppose you were hit over the head with a hammer; naturally, you would probably feel some pain. However, the hammer itself did not cause the sensation of pain; rather, your brain detected the assault caused by the hammer, and therefore emitted a pain signal to the body. The power of the brain to produce pain is even more amazing than that. Have you ever heard of phantom leg syndrome? Sometimes people with amputated limbs feel excruciating pain…in a limb that no longer exists (Stahl 2021)!

But what if your whole body is dysregulated? That's precisely what happens with trauma. Since both branches of the nervous system are affected, and since the nervous system interacts with every other system, there are plenty of other areas in your body that will be off-kilter in one way or another. The brain detects anomalies within the body itself and generates pain signals the same as it would with a foreign object—such as a hammer (Stahl 2021).

But here's the problem: If so many things are off in the body all at once, and these anomalies are so widely scattered, the brain cannot possibly generate precise pain signals for everything. Instead, you might feel diffuse, generalized pain throughout your whole body (that does not match the precise signs and symptoms your doctor is looking for), *or* your brain might even send pain signals for other parts of your body in which there is nothing medically wrong, sort of like the phantom limb we just talked about. But regardless, that pain is real.

The pain is telling you that your nervous system has been assaulted—and that message is *not* wrong (Stahl 2021).

So what ultimately causes the nervous system to get stuck in some people but not in others? This is a wide-open question within the trauma field. There are many plausible explanations, but at this point, there does not seem to be one single definitive factor that determines why some people become traumatized and others do not. A particular event may trigger the reset for some people, but not for others. And some people may experience a reset after a single occurrence of an event, while other people experience the reset only after many recurrences. Still others experience the reset after many occurrences of many different events.

Regardless, this much is clear: trauma is *not* defined by the event itself, but rather by the effect it has on the person. If both the sympathetic and parasympathetic nervous systems become hijacked, then you were traumatized...period (Levine 2010).

So far, you have learned about how trauma affects the nervous system in general. Sine the brain is literally the head of the nervous system, let's zoom in on two tiny parts of the brain that play a monumental role in both the causes and effects of trauma: the *amygdala* and the *thalamus*.

The amygdala is the alarm system for the entire brain and therefore the rest of the body. The amygdala is associated with both fear and anger. Both emotions inform of us of risk or danger, whether perceived or real. Fear tells us something bad *may* happen, while anger tells us something bad already *did* happen. This is the information the SNS needs in order to mobilize its fight-or-flight response.

But here's the deal with the amygdala: It is super good at remembering past threats. Therefore, anything that even remotely resembles a previous danger will fully activate the amygdala, which in turn reactivates *all* the other parts of the brain that were active during the prior danger (including sights, sounds, and smells). All of that launches a full mobilization of the fight-or-flight response, which may also trigger the freeze response…and now we are off to the races. This is exactly why trauma reminders are so triggering, sometimes resulting in rage, flashbacks, or fainting (Van der Kolk 2014).

The thalamus is the second tiny part of brain that plays a crucial role in trauma symptoms. The thalamus is the part of the brain that is responsible for integrating incoming sensory information (from all senses except for smell) and sending that data to other parts of the brain—including the amygdala—for further processing. When we are going through our normal daily routine in the absence of danger, the brain incessantly synthesizes a massive deluge of information. Once the information from the five senses (and other data points) are synthesized into a single, coherent message, that message is either regarded as relevant and stored in one of the memory folders, or disregarded as unimportant and quickly forgotten.

However, when we are presented with a threatening situation, for some reason the thalamus goes offline. The practical implications are enormous. When the thalamus is inactive, there is nothing to integrate all the incoming sensory information. That's precisely why, after surviving a crisis situation, we remember only fragments of what happened rather than the incident in its entirety. For example, you may remember the gunshot (sound), the attacker's face (sight), and the piercing pain in your foot (touch), but not the coherent, integrated sequence of what happened. So why is that a problem? Well, because the brain will file only complete, integrated memories into long-term memory—*not memory fragments*! That means many of the worst details of what happened are now stuck in your current ongoing awareness at all times. That explains the intrusive trauma memories of post-traumatic stress disorder (Van der Kolk 2014).

Here's a simple example to illustrate these concepts: The sensory details of what happen to you all day long are like pieces to a puzzle. The job of the thalamus is to put the pieces together to form some sort of coherent picture. Once the puzzle is complete, the picture gets stored in long-term memory, where it can be later retrieved if necessary. But during a threatening situation, since the thalamus is not working the way it normally does, the pieces to the puzzle do not get assembled—which also means they do not get stored in long-term memory. These unprocessed memory fragments remain at the front of your mind—both day *and* night.

When you sleep, the brain continues to sort through all the cognitive, emotional, and sensory information received while you were awake, and to connect these data points to other memories you already have. Much of this work happens in your dreams. When you sleep, the brain turns into a puzzle-solving machine. In fact, the brain might be working on hundreds of puzzles at once, with pieces from all of them! Now do you see why dreams can seem so random and bizarre? In the same dream, you might have a scene with Michael Jordan, Abraham Lincoln, your high school crush, and your lost gerbil. What do these things have in common? Nothing! Your brain is simply conducting its never-ending mission of organizing, classifying, and filing the gazillion data points it receives. But there's one glitch: it still does not know what to do with those pesky memory fragments from the traumatizing incident. These are the pieces that do not fit into any puzzle the mind is working on. And that's why those details keep coming up over and over again in nightmares.

Post-traumatic stress disorder, or PTSD for short, effectively means the "trauma after the trauma." This diagnosis should now make sense in light of everything you just read. When some sort of adverse event happens that is chronic or severe enough to hijack both branches of your nervous system, *and* the unprocessed memory fragments of what happened are forever present in the forefront of your mind (both day and night), *and* the amygdala randomly refires at the slightest trauma reminder...now you are traumatized.

Having your nervous system hijacked is now the new trauma. It is the trauma *after* the trauma—and in many senses, it is much worse than the original traumatizing event. Usually, the original event started but has ended (with the obvious exception of a current, ongoing threat). But a dysregulated nervous system just keeps going...

In summary, the flight, flight, and freeze responses were all meant to be short-term solutions to an unexpected situation. But when one of these responses persists beyond its original usefulness, it's like a hijacked Uber careening down the highway, causing one collision after another.

What Is Trauma-Focused DBT?

So far in this book, you've been introduced to DBT and trauma. Now let's connect the dots and explain why trauma-focused DBT is a great starting point for trauma work. In the previous section, you learned how trauma affects the nervous system. This explanation is called the *polyvagal theory*, and it provides the theoretical basis for trauma-focused DBT.

According to the polyvagal theory, trauma has an impact on both branches of the ANS. The SNS—the accelerator—is associated with physical and emotional activation (such as increased fear, anger, breathing, and heart rate); in the case of danger, this means fight or flight.

In contrast, the PNS—the brake—is associated with physical and emotional relaxation. In addition, the PNS has two branches of its own. One part (ventral) is associated with social engagement; the other part (dorsal) is responsible for rest-and-digest functions—and, in the case of extreme threat, freeze. Freeze occurs when the organism starts to physically shut down or mentally dissociate, or both.

When presented with danger, the various branches of the ANS are affected in a specific order. The first branch to be affected is the social engagement system. In other words, when presented with a threat, functions related to social connectivity—laughter, smiling, empathy, attunement, the ability to provide validation—go offline. This is like letting up on the brake.

If the danger persists, the accelerator is applied, which results in fight or flight. When neither fight nor flight can mitigate the threat, the brake is activated, resulting in freeze. The following actions summarize this sequence in slightly more technical language (Porges 2011):

1. Danger is sensed.

2. Social engagement goes offline (ventral PNS). This is like releasing the brake.

3. Danger persists.

4. Fight or flight is triggered (SNS). This is like slamming on the gas.

5. Danger cannot be mitigated through fight or flight.

6. Freeze response activates (dorsal PNS). This is like slamming on the brake while your foot is still on the accelerator.

When we drive, we need both the brake and accelerator to get to our destination safely. If the drive is smooth, sometimes we will gently accelerate and sometimes we will gently brake. The same process applies to our physical, mental, and emotional functioning. If the "drive" is smooth, our mind and body enjoy a gentle oscillation between accelerating and braking.

This flow is even reflected in our heart rhythm. A healthy rhythm is indicated by a consistently alternating repetition of fast-slow, fast-slow, fast-slow. The reason for this gentle pattern is so that the entire organism, at a moment's notice, can either accelerate further or brake further, as needed. A heartbeat that is either consistently fast, or consistently slow, or unpredictably fast and slow, is not a healthy rhythm.

Let's return to the driving analogy. If you are driving down the highway and a truck carelessly swerves right in front of you, you will probably demonstrate all of the reactions represented by the polyvagal theory. You may swear and flip a finger at the driver (social engagement goes offline); you may suddenly accelerate; or you may slam on the brakes. But after the danger is averted, you will most likely return to your baseline of gently oscillating between accelerating and braking as needed…until the next threat again requires more extreme action.

Now let's assume you have experienced so many highway hazards that you decide never to let down your guard. You are poised at every moment to yell and scream at other drivers, unpredictably accelerate, and unpredictably brake. If you are really frazzled, you may even attempt to accelerate and brake at the same time! Eventually, this becomes your new default driving style, regardless of the driving conditions: curse at everyone, suddenly accelerate, and suddenly brake. Do you see how this will lead to a wild ride? Even if the driving conditions would otherwise have been relatively smooth, they won't be anymore. And even if no danger would otherwise have been present, now there is.

This driving metaphor describes what happens to people who have experienced chronic trauma: too much accelerating, too much braking, and loss of social engagement. These dramatic shifts in the nervous system precipitate a long, complicated cascade of reactions in the brain and body (which are well beyond the scope of this book), but here's the bottom line: The end result of this domino effect is a variety of responses that are either too much or too little, resulting in a host of complications. This tendency toward too much or too little especially affects five domains: awareness, thoughts, emotions, reactions, and relationships. For each of these domains, it is possible to have either too much (overuse of the accelerator) or too little (overuse of the brake).

DBT is all about reconciling dialectical dilemmas (binary extremes resulting in dysfunction) by teaching specific behavioral skills to forge a middle path between those extremes. In particular, DBT teaches these five skill sets: mindfulness, distress tolerance, emotion regulation, dialectical thinking, and interpersonal effectiveness. These skill sets provide the middle path between each of the dialectical dilemmas mentioned above.

Domain Affected by Trauma	Too Much	Too Little	Middle Path
Awareness	Hypervigilance	Dissociation	Mindfulness
Thoughts	Rumination	Impulsivity	Dialectical thinking
Emotions	Feeling overwhelmed	Numbness	Emotion regulation
Reactivity	Increased crisis	Paralysis	Distress tolerance
Relationships	Aggression	Passivity	Interpersonal effectiveness

By practicing these skills, you learn to find a middle path in life, a path between the extremes. That's the essence of DBT...or what I like to call "developing balance therapy." The *dialectical behavior* in DBT is simply a really fancy way of saying *developing balance*. The rest of this book explores each of these middle paths in much more detail.

Once a person has stabilized by learning each of these middle paths, many, if not most, trauma symptoms will start to resolve. The purpose of these middle paths is to restabilize the nervous system, which is a huge feat in and of itself. But there's a caveat here: even after the nervous system has restabilized, it is quite possible for the brain and body to still have those memory fragments that the thalamus never integrated. Standard, traditional DBT was not designed to deal with those intrusive memories and recurring nightmares. But trauma-focused DBT is! This theme will be addressed in the final chapter of this book.

As long as people are existing and operating at the extremes of life, it is extremely difficult for them to do even basic counseling—much less trauma work (or the rest of life, for that matter). That is why DBT as a treatment model is entirely skills focused. In particular, trauma-focused DBT teaches the foundational skills you need to optimize counseling, stabilize for trauma work, and then thrive in life—"building a life worth living," in the words of Dr. Linehan (2020).

Chapter 2

Dialectics for Trauma

In chapter 1, you learned that DBT stands for dialectical behavior therapy. In particular, you learned that the concept of dialectics refers to the idea of bringing together opposites and seeing things from different perspectives. You also learned why this concept is so important for trauma work. Trauma is an extreme situation that forces us to react in extreme ways. For example, trauma causes us to press too hard on the accelerator (fight or flight), slam on the brakes (freeze)— and often both at the same time. This leads to a series of reactions that are either too much or too little. Dialectics is all about finding a middle path between those extremes. Let's unpack this concept in more detail.

The term "dialectics" has a long, rich history in philosophy, going back to the ancient Greek philosopher Socrates. Socrates either coined the term himself or popularized the concept through his teaching method. He was famous for his teaching style: instead of giving his students answers, he asked them questions. He taught this way in order to challenge their thinking, expand their understanding, and inspire them to find their own answers. In fact, Socrates was so effective at this strategy that he could get a student who passionately supported viewpoint A to just as passionately advocate for opposing viewpoint Z…simply by asking questions (Farnsworth 2021)!

Ever since Socrates, dialectics has remained a key concept within philosophy. In the 1600s, a German philosopher named Hegel made the term even more popular, at least within academia. Hegel reached some major insights that still characterize the term "dialectics" to this day. He realized that it was not just philosophy students who learned to think dialectically; rather, *all* human knowledge tends to evolve in very predictable, dialectical patterns. He became famous for identifying the specific sequence in which this process tends to unfold: thesis, antithesis, and synthesis (McTaggart and McTaggart 2016).

Thesis refers to any current, prevailing theory or paradigm. This is simply what most people believe and take for granted. But inevitably, someone comes along and makes a discovery that does not fit the current theory. Therefore, this person (or someone else) comes up with another theory to account for the new observations. These data points, which once seemed to be outliers, now become much more credible, because they have a theory of their own. Hegel called the new theory the *antithesis*. The only problem: there are now two opposing and competing theories in circulation.

So of course, someone else comes along with an epiphany. This person realizes that some aspects of both theories are correct, and therefore combines elements of both, and reworks them into a brand-new way of thinking, which Hegel called the *synthesis*. And guess what? The synthesis becomes the new prevailing paradigm…until, of course, someone else comes along and notices some new outliers that do not fit the current model, then this process just repeats indefinitely. In this sense, all human knowledge tends to evolve dialectically.

If you are struggling to believe this description of dialectics, just read any research journal. Research studies contradict themselves all the time! Have you ever shaken your head at a pattern like this? A study on wine is conducted and comes to the definitive conclusion: "Wine is good for you." Then you come across another study on wine that also comes to a definitive conclusion: "Wine is bad for you." Now you're confused. Which is it? Is wine good for you…or is it not? Well, inevitably, someone else will eventually do a *meta-analysis*—that is, review hundreds of studies—and come to the very definitive conclusion that wine is both good for you and bad for you, since the outcome depends on many variables, such as the age, weight, metabolism, and sex of the person, not to mention the quantity, frequency, and type of wine consumed. This is dialectics in action!

Now let's fast-forward from Socrates and Hegel to the late 1970s, when Marsha Linehan was busy developing a treatment model. Dr. Linehan reached another revolutionary insight: it's not just philosophers and scientists who learn to be dialectical—this is how all healthy human adults think and process information! In fact, a breakdown in the ability to deal with life dialectically is precisely what Dr. Linehan saw as a defining feature of mental illness (2015).

Whether we realize it or not, we use dialectics all the time. Think of a productive work meeting. Everyone at the meeting has an opportunity to share a different perspective, and yet, by the end of the meeting, the group comes to a consensus, agrees on a few action items moving forward, and identifies a few other items that need further clarification. Maybe the group agrees to disagree on some items. But regardless, dialectics are in action. In fact, just to decide what to have for lunch today, you will need to use your dialectical skills: in a split second, you will rifle through the pros and cons of heating up left-overs, the pros and cons of grabbing fast food, and maybe even the pros and cons of skipping lunch altogether to keep reading this book! (Please do not do that.)

Dialectics allow us to do what psychologists call *executive functioning*: thinking about things like pros and cons, cause and effect, short-term versus long-term…and ultimately, thinking about thinking itself. Since life is so complex with so many variables and so many moving parts, we need to constantly analyze situations from these various angles. Can you imagine what life would be like if we did not know how to be dialectical?

As you read earlier, dialectics is a term borrowed from philosophy. Within philosophy, this concept draws from several basic assumptions about the universe itself. In a bit, you will see how each of these assumptions applies to trauma work.

The first assumption states that the universe is full of opposites. That should be fairly obvious. Opposites are part of our daily experience. For example, think of summer and winter, male and female, or day and night. But are these so-called opposites really as opposite as they seem? Let's unpack the last example a little bit more.

Day and night certainly seem like very obvious, concrete opposites, don't they? In fact, in English we even use the expression "as different as day and night" to describe a set of complete opposites. But let's think about this in a little more detail. Does complete day literally turn into complete night in a split second? Or does total night instantly morph into total day in a single moment? Of course not! There is an entire chunk of the twenty-four-hour cycle called evening, in which day gradually fades into night. And then there is an entire chunk of the same cycle called dawn, in which night incrementally slips into day. In other words, there is a large intermediate gray zone (literally) between the two extremes.

Furthermore, just because it is day for you, does that mean it is day for everyone? No! Whenever it is day for you, that simply means it is *not* day for literally half the planet. And furthermore, would someone from the equator have the same understanding of day and night as someone from the North Pole? No, they would not! At the equator, day and night are almost always evenly split by twelve hours. At the North Pole, day and night are almost always evenly split by... six months.

Let's now assume you are not even on planet Earth. You are sitting on a comet far, far away, observing the solar system with your favorite pair of galactic binoculars. Would you even notice things like day versus night or summer versus winter? No! Instead, you would simply notice the earth's rotation on its axis and revolution around the sun. In other words, you would notice what *causes* the perception of night and day or summer and winter from an earthling's perspective, but not the actual effect that we experience.

Point for point, this night-and-day example explains many of the key concepts of dialectics. Yes, the universe is full of apparent opposites. But when you take a closer look at things, many of these opposites may actually be a matter of degree or perception or perspective. And if you have enough perspective, you may not even perceive any opposites at all. Trauma is notorious for causing us to fixate on the opposites of life: life versus death, good versus evil, friend versus foe, safe versus unsafe, us versus them. Dialectics helps us understand that life is much more nuanced than those polarities.

Another assumption of dialectics states that everything in the universe is interconnected and interrelated. In other words, the universe is a dynamic system in which everything affects everything else. For example, according to physicists, every single atom in the universe has the potential to affect every other atom (Scott 2021). In short, there is no such thing as a lone ranger in this universe!

This is also an important concept because trauma causes us to overly fixate on how other people have affected us. This fixation in turn can cause what psychologists call learned helplessness or a victimstance. Yes, of course it is true that other people have and can and will impact us. But the universe is not linear. You are also an agent of change in the universe. You can learn the skills not only to heal but also become empowered to make the universe a safer, better place for both yourself and others.

Another assumption of dialectics states that the only constant in this universe is change. In other words, this infinitely complex system, teeming with apparent opposites, is also in constant flux. Regardless of what universe we have in this second, it is a different universe the next second. As one ancient Greek philosopher famously stated, "No man ever steps in the same river twice—for it's not the same river, and he's not the same man" (Heraclitus and Kahn 2008).

This is another important concept for healing from trauma. Trauma causes us to fixate on what the universe was like when we were traumatized. On one hand, that universe was real; on the other hand, it is a different universe now. Healing cannot take place in the past for the simple reason that we cannot go back in time. Healing must take place in the universe we have right now. Not only is the universe constantly changing, but we can (and must) be part of that change.

Once we understand these basic assumptions of the universe, our lives become much more manageable. We start to mold our beliefs and expectations to how the universe really is, as opposed to how we think it should be. What good is a screwdriver if it is not the right shape or size for the screw? The more we understand that the universe is full of paradoxes, that everything in the universe is interconnected, and that the universe is constantly changing, the more we can accomplish the following.

First, we start to see things from different perspectives. Not only do we start to see things from other people's viewpoints, but we even start to look at things from multiple angles within our own heads. We also start to think more in the middle, not just the extremes. We start to see more shades of gray, and less black and white. In addition, we become more flexible and less rigid, not only in our thinking but also in our behaviors and decisions. And finally, we can start to change how we think when presented with new information. All of this helps us let go of blame, release the past, and press forward on a new path toward healing.

I realize that this discussion so far may seem really abstract, so I would like to share two widely circulated stories that helped me better understand the concept of dialectics. The first story goes something like this:

Many centuries ago, there was an old Chinese farmer who had a very loyal workhorse. Because of this horse, the Chinese farmer was successful and prosperous. One day, however, the workhorse just up and left. All the villagers came running to the farmer and exclaimed, "Oh my, this is very, very bad luck!" The farmer simply shrugged his shoulders and said, "Maybe." But then, a few weeks later, the loyal horse wandered back…along with fifty wild stallions. This old farmer had just made a fortune! So, once more, all the villagers came running back to the farmer. This time they exclaimed, "Oh my, this is very, very good luck!" The farmer simply shrugged his shoulders and said, "Maybe."

A few days later, the farmer's strong, handsome, hardworking son was out in the corral, trying to tame one of the wild stallions. Tragically, he fell off and broke his leg. So all the villagers came running back to the farmer and once again exclaimed, "Oh my, this is very, very bad luck!" By now, you already know the farmer's response: he simply shrugged his shoulders and said, "Maybe." But wouldn't you know it—a few months later, war broke out in the region, and all of the young, able-bodied men were obliged to go and fight for the king. Sadly, many young men lost their lives in that battle. But guess who was exempt from the war?

The story could go on and on, but I am sure you get the point by now. And the point is this: The villagers were *not* very dialectical, since everything seemed either very, very good or very, very bad. As a result, the villagers reacted strongly to each situation. That's exactly how trauma causes us to think and operate. The old farmer, in contrast, was much more dialectical. Why? Because he understood that there was potential good and potential bad in every situation. Unlike the villagers, the farmer did not become ruffled. He simply accepted life, adapted the best he could, rolled with the punches, and enjoyed the ride.

The second story concerns a man who was stuck in traffic, waiting his turn to pay his toll to cross the Golden Gate Bridge. He noticed that all the tollbooth attendants were monotonously going through the motions of their job—with the notable exception of one quite animated attendant, who seemed to be having the time of his life. He was dancing, he was singing, and he enthusiastically greeted each of his customers as if they were royalty. The driver decided to change lanes and see what was going on with this particular attendant.

As the driver pulled up to the tollbooth, he rolled down his window and said, "Wow, I couldn't help but notice that you really seem to enjoy your job." The tollbooth attendant grinned and replied, "Well of course I do. This is the best job on the planet! For starters, I have a four-window office suite. Do you know of a single CEO that has a *four*-window suite? And just look at this view. This is what I get *paid* to look at all day long. This is the best view in the whole city! And not only that, but someday I want to be a professional singer. And here I am, getting *paid* to sing and dance *all* day!" The driver replied, "Wow, it's great that you have such a positive attitude. But it doesn't look like your coworkers share your enthusiasm." The toll-booth attendant responded, "Oh, you mean those guys over there? The ones working in their stand-up coffins?"

This story illustrates the power of dialectics, of seeing things from different perspectives. As you go through life and face various situations, do you see your "tollbooth" as a stand-up coffin? Or do you see your tollbooth as a four-window executive suite with the best view in the city?

There is a reason we are not always as dialectical as the Chinese farmer or the Golden Gate Bridge tollbooth attendant, and the reason for that is what psychologists call the *negativity bias*. There are a few ways this plays out. One aspect of the negativity bias is that the brain tends to favor false alarms over no alarms. Consider the following example: You are walking through the woods, and you see a stick— but you think it's a snake, and one that may be lethal. You will certainly experience an intense rush of anxiety…but you will live. False alarm! Now let's assume you are walking through the woods, and you see a snake—but this time you think it's a stick. You don't even react…and you die. No alarm! Do you see the difference between a false alarm versus no alarm? Can you also see how it is adaptive to have false alarms over no alarms at all? While the occasional false alarm seems annoying (and it is!), do you also see how this is what keeps you alive?

Just in case you are struggling to believe this whole idea of a negativity bias, think of it this way: How many insults does it take to undo many compliments? Just one! How many compliments does it take to undo one insult? Many! Researchers have actually attempted to quantify this ratio. For example, Dr. Gottman and Dr. Gottman are a husband-and-wife team who are both psychologists and world-renowned marriage experts. After decades of research, this team found that successful couples manifest approximately twenty positive interactions to every negative interaction. Even during times of conflict, effective couples still share five positive exchanges to every negative exchange (Gottman and Gottman 2015).

Another way in which we have a negativity bias is that the brain learns really quickly (and permanently) from negative events, but does not learn nearly as quickly from neutral or positive events. In fact, this tendency alone can explain so much of what we call PTSD. After a single negative event, the brain will often permanently learn (and perhaps overlearn) the event to the point where now you can't forget about it—even if you want to! The negative event now randomly pops into your head, dominates your memories, causes nightmares, and may even trigger flashbacks. In fact, you may have noticed that the more you try to avoid thinking about the negative event, the more you end up thinking about what you are trying hard not to think about!

Once again, this tendency is adaptive. When something negative happens, it could be potentially lethal. Therefore, when presented with danger or crisis, the brain will often deeply imprint that situation—very quickly and very permanently. If this situation is truly a matter of life and death, this might be your only chance to learn the lesson. So you had better learn it now, learn it well, and learn it permanently!

In contrast, we do not tend to overlearn positive events quickly and permanently. Our response to positive events is quite different: After the initial thrill, we quickly start to acclimate, habituate, and desensitize to the positive event. In other words, we get used to it, and the positive event starts to lose its luster. That's why, as humans, we are never completely satisfied and continuously want more and more of a good thing. Unlike a negative event, we do not have intense, vivid memories, dreams, and flashbacks of a positive event years or decades later. We tend to learn positive or neutral events only from lots of repetition. As humans, we only seem to get post-*traumatic* stress disorder, not post-*triumph* stress disorder!

In short, the negativity bias causes you not only to overfocus on the negative but even on the potentially negative—and then never forget it. In other words, the brain is actively amplifying the "negativity neurons." This explains a great deal of PTSD symptoms that are related to anger, anxiety, depression, paranoia, self-blame, and hypervigilance. The brain then feels overwhelmed by so much negativity, and so it tries to shut down the negativity overload through avoidance: avoidance of external triggers (such as people, places, and things related to the negative event) and even avoidance of internal triggers (thoughts, feelings, and memories related to the negative event). As you can see, this negativity bias causes quite a stir!

Automatic Negative Thoughts

Once you know what to look for, it is fairly easy to identify the negativity bias in other people. (It is always much harder to notice it in yourself!) Let's look at some common *automatic negative thoughts*—or ANTs (Reutter 2019). Think about how each of these ANTs is related to trauma and the negativity bias we just discussed.

- **All-or-nothing thinking** is when your brain is stuck at the extremes, and you cannot see shades of gray.

- **Overgeneralizing** is when you take something negative in your life and think it applies to everything.

- **Mental filtering** is when you fixate only on the negative and can't see anything positive at all.

- **Disqualifying the positives** is when you initially recognize something as positive, but then you decide it's actually more negative than positive…so that card gets ejected from the game.

- **Making assumptions** is when you presume the worst-case scenario. You can do this either through mind reading or fortune-telling.

- **Mind reading** is when you assume other people are thinking something negative about you. Mind reading is often a projection of our own negativity onto other people.

- **Fortune-telling** is when you already "know" how terrible something will turn out, even before it happens, which often results in a self-fulfilling prophecy.

- **Magnifying** is when your brain makes a small problem seem much bigger than it actually is.

- **Catastrophizing** is when you react as if something is life-and-death, even when it isn't.

- **Minimizing** is when you make a big problem seem like it's no big deal.

- **Denial** is when you have a huge problem on your hands, but you completely ignore it.

- **Emotional reasoning** happens when you see your feelings as facts—and actually, the *only* facts you are willing to consider, regardless of any other data points.

- **Should-ing** happens when you beat yourself up with unrealistic expectations and endless negative judgments.

- **Labeling** happens when you define yourself (or someone else) in terms of a single trait, often negative. (It is worth noting that even positive labels can be extremely damaging.)

- **Personalizing** is when you take something personally that was not directed at you at all.

Did you recognize any of these ANTs in yourself? You may have noticed that all these ANTs are interrelated and tend to overlap. If you have one ANT, you probably also have at least five of its cousins! The reason all these ANTs are so similar is because they have all descended from the same common ancestor: they are all a breakdown in dialectics.

People who have been traumatized tend to have five more ANTs: hindsight bias, self-blame, and the three Ps (permanent, pervasive, and personal). Let's assume you leave a work party early because you are feeling a little nauseous. When what you thought was your ride-share finally arrives, three people jump out and you are violently mugged. You are now at risk for the following five trauma ANTs. As with the other ANTs, you will notice they all closely related cousins.

You might notice the hindsight bias, in which you beat yourself up with everything you *should* have or *should not* have done to somehow magically prevent the trauma you didn't know was going to happen. For example: *I should have left sooner. I should have left later. I should not have left at all. I should not have gone to the party in the first place. I should have known why my ride was taking so long.* In fact, you can think of the hindsight bias as "should-ing" applied to the past. You can also think of the hindsight bias as fortune-telling applied to the past: on the day of the trauma, you should have been able to predict what was going to happen. The problem with this line of reasoning is that trauma, by definition, is an atypical event that *nobody* can predict!

As you can see, hindsight bias is closely related to self-blame. It is very common for trauma survivors to excessively blame themselves following a traumatic event. In fact, this is one of the official diagnostic symptoms of PTSD. There are many theories for why people blame themselves even for events they had absolutely no control over. One possible explanation is the just-world theory, which basically implies that good things happen to good people and bad things happen to bad people. Even though this theory is clearly not true, we often bow to this belief because we feel psychologically safer believing the world is a just place (Hafer and Sutton 2016). But maintaining that belief comes at a huge psychological cost: if something bad happens to me, that must mean I deserved it.

Another possible explanation for disproportionate self-blame is the psychological need to feel like we have more control than we actually do. Of course, a traumatic event, by definition, is something that was out of your control. But if you can blame yourself for at least part of the trauma, that helps you maintain the illusion that you did have some control.

Children are especially vulnerable to self-blame. They have even more of a psychological need to believe that the world is safe and that adults know what they are doing. Even in the case of extreme abuse or neglect, children will often believe it was their fault. This helps them preserve their belief in caring, competent adults. This is called a *fantasy bond*. Children need attachments to survive. When a child cannot form an attachment with their caregiver as they are, they will form an attachment with an imaginary, idealized version of their caregiver (Firestone 1987). Once again, this fantasy bond comes at the steep psychological cost of self-blame.

In addition to the hindsight bias and self-blame, you may also notice the three Ps: personal, pervasive, and permanent. In fact, by definition, trauma *is* personal, pervasive, and permanent. For example, getting mugged by fake Uber drivers was personal; it happened to you—*your* body was attacked. In addition, this event was pervasive: it affected every aspect of your life. It did not affect just your physical body; it also affected your thoughts, your emotions, your reactions, and your relationships. And furthermore, it was even permanent, in the sense that you cannot be unmugged, and you will likely carry this memory for the rest of your life.

But remember, PTSD is the trauma *after* the trauma. The three Ps take on more power than they should when the traumatic event remains personal, pervasive, and permanent at the front of your mind, as opposed to getting stored in long-term memory. The three Ps also become overempowered when all negative events start to seem much more personal, pervasive, and permanent than they really are.

Regardless of your particular ANTs, you have lost your dialectical balance. You are stuck at the extremes; you have lost the shades of gray. You see only how the world has impacted you, and not how you can also influence the world. You have become overly rigid in your approach to life. And even when all the evidence keeps piling up to suggest your current approach is not effective, you stay the course anyway. You keep doing what you already know is not working. You need your dialectics back! You need to harness your inner Chinese farmer or the tollbooth attendant with an executive four-window office. So how do you do that?

Becoming Mindful of Your Thoughts

I would like to conclude this chapter with a few simple, practical exercises to help you become more dialectical. Before you can change your thought process, you first need to know what you are thinking. The first series of exercises will focus on becoming more mindful of your thoughts. As you will learn in the next chapter, simply observing something changes what you observe.

To start, identify a thought that is distressing to you—one of your ANTs. This could be a thought about a specific trauma, but it does not have to be. Now say that thought out loud. In fact, say it repeatedly, over and over. Now change the volume. Shout your thought, whisper your thought. Now change the speed. Say your thought really slow or really fast. Say your thought in the voice of your favorite movie characters. Sing your thought. Exaggerate your thought even more. Or write your thought on paper—over and over again.

This exercise may seem silly, but there is a lot going on psychologically with this simple intervention. First, it helps you see thoughts for what they are: simply words running through your head. This is an important concept. When you listen to the radio, you understand that some of the words are probably true and some may not be. However, we tend to assume that the words in our head represent absolutely reality, which is not the case.

Second, it helps provide some distance between you and your thoughts. This is another important concept. When we listen to the radio, we do not feel connected to the words we hear, but we tend to have a different relationship with the words in our heads. Not only do we assume the words are true, but we also assume the words define us: we become fused to our thoughts (Hayes et al. 2012).

Third, this exercise also shows that you can learn to regulate your thoughts. For example, by changing the volume or speed of your thoughts, you are also learning to modulate their intensity. And fourth, these exercises also help you become habituated to your thoughts through exposure and repetition. In other words, the more you repeat these thoughts over and over again, the less intense they become, and eventually, they just seem like a bunch of sounds. In short, just by becoming more mindful of your thoughts through these simple exercises, you have already learned to change them.

Dancing with TOM

Now that you have identified some of your intense thoughts through mindfulness practice, you are ready to dance…with your thoughts. In particular, you are going to learn a three-step dance with TOM—Thought, Opposite, Middle. (Do you see how TOM is simply the more down-to-earth version of Hegel's thesis-antithesis-synthesis model?)

This is how the dance works. First, select one of the intense thoughts you have already identified from the mindfulness exercises. Let's assume your intense thought is: *I am worthless and will never amount to anything.* The next step is to think of the complete opposite of that thought. When you do this, try to exaggerate and embellish as much as possible. For example, your opposite thought might be: *I am the most valuable specimen of humanity that has ever graced the face of this planet. In fact, no human will ever surpass me in knowledge, talent, or skill.* Now try to think of something more in the middle; for example: *I have met some of my goals in life, but not all of them. Just like everyone else, I am a work in progress.*

Here is what's going on psychologically with this simple exercise. First, did you notice how unrealistic and unreasonable your opposite thought was? We are usually very good at recognizing how much we embellish the opposite thought, but rarely do we realize this is exactly what we have done to the original thought. For example, we quickly recognize that "I am the most valuable specimen of humanity" is an embellishment—but we do not so quickly realize that "I am worthless and will never amount to anything" is also an exaggeration!

Second, did you notice how quickly you can shift your thinking simply by identifying the opposite and then coming up with something more in the middle? You accomplished this without psychoanalyzing your original thought. You did not have to refute it, dispute it, dissect it, challenge it, or diagnose it as irrational and illogical. All you had to do was identify the two extremes and then something more in the middle. Too easy!

Did you also notice that among the three options (thought, opposite, middle), the middle thought is probably the most accurate? Whereas the two extremes tend to be exaggerations of some grain of truth, the middle thought tends to contain the grain of truth from both perspectives, but without the embellishment.

Finally, did you notice the intensity of your emotions go down as you shifted your thinking from the original thought to the middle thought? When you bring your thinking more to the middle, you will easily detect changes in emotions as well. Let's put this to the test: What emotion do you feel when you fully believe the original thought?

On a scale of 1 to 100, how intense is that emotion? Now let's assume you fully believe the middle thought. How intense is that emotion on a scale of 1 to 100? Let's assume your emotional intensity shifted from a 90 to a 50. If the temperature outside dropped that much, would you notice? Of course!

Now granted, just because you identified a middle thought does not mean that you will forevermore believe the new thought 100 percent of the time, while completely erasing the original thought from your brain. But's here the deal: Since you were the one to identify your own middle thought, part of you does believe it. After all, those words came from your head. At the very least, your original thought no longer has a monopoly; there is now some competition in this market! And furthermore, having two competing beliefs in your head at the same time is precisely what psychologists call ambivalence or cognitive dissonance (Miller and Rollnick 2013). The human brain does not like contradictory beliefs, and therefore feels very motivated to change your thinking for you. Go, TOM!

Responsibility Pie

Dancing with TOM is great, but will not always be enough to shift your thinking when it comes to feeling responsible for your own trauma. Remember that one of the symptoms of PTSD is self-blame? When you feel responsible for your own trauma, it is time to bake your first Responsibility Pie.

Here's the recipe: First, draw a circle. Second, identify all the people you feel are responsible for the trauma. Third, assign a percentage of responsibility to each person. Fourth, create a pie chart, with each person getting a slice of the pie corresponding to the percentages you just assigned. Take a long look at this Responsibility Pie, and then ask yourself these questions:

- Who got the biggest piece? Why?

- Who got the smallest piece? Why?

- Did you ask for the trauma?

- Did you want the trauma?

- Did you demand the trauma?

- Was the trauma something you had scheduled for that day?

- Would you have prevented the trauma if you could have?

- What would you tell your best friend if they experienced the same trauma?

You may have noticed that the technique I just used here was the Socratic method, mentioned at the beginning of this chapter. My goal was to see if you can start to see the trauma from different angles, simply by asking you lots of questions. After you have answered these questions, see if some of your percentages have changed. If the percentages have shifted, bake another Responsibility Pie. With the help of a trusted friend or counselor, keep repeating this exercise until you no longer feel inappropriate responsibility for a trauma that you were not responsible for!

It is very common for people who have been abused to blame themselves for the abuse more than they blame their abusers. As explained earlier in this chapter, this tendency is even more pronounced in children. Recognizing and overcoming self-blame is a critical component of trauma work. According to research, when people blame themselves for the trauma, it is much harder to overcome their PTSD symptoms. One theory for this observation is that when people blame themselves for the trauma, they think they deserve to suffer, and therefore, they deserve their PTSD symptoms. In fact, they may even have an unhealthy need for the symptoms, in order to feel a sort of psychological penance (Unthank 2019).

Fortunate-Unfortunate

Here's how this intervention works: Create an outline of your life. If you want, you can even chronicle your life as if it were a fairy tale. For example, you can start off with "Once upon a time…."

Next, write down something fortunate about your life, followed by something unfortunate that happened to you. Then write down something fortunate that resulted, followed by another unfortunate event. Keep narrating your life story in this way, alternating between "fortunately" and "unfortunately," until you are satisfied with the ending. Your fairy tale does not need to end with "happily ever after," but it should end with a final "fortunately." The final "fortunately" can be something fortunate that has already happened, or that you hope will happen.

This little exercise can help you understand that life is full of both highs and lows. In fact, you may even see that some of the bad things in your life ultimately turned out good, while some of the good things turned out bad. That's life! You are now well on your way to becoming a Chinese farmer…

Playing Your DS

I will wrap up this chapter with one final intervention I call Playing Your DS. I am probably dating myself, but way back in the early 2000s, Nintendo created a videogame device called dual screen, or DS for short.

What an analogy for dialectics! Dialectics is all about creating a dual screen for real life. Having a second screen to look at is especially helpful when your negativity bias has been hijacked. You will know that you are too entrenched in your negativity bias when the majority of the adjectives you use to describe yourself, others, or the world sound overly negative. If you notice that happening, it is time to play your DS! In this case, DS stands for dialectical synonyms. Here is how the game works.

Since the English language borrows from so many other languages (both existing and extinct), it has an enormous vocabulary. As such, English has gobs of synonyms—many ways to say the same thing. Even though synonyms basically mean the same thing, some words tend to sound more positive, while others tend to sound more negative. Here are some basic examples: stingy versus frugal; skinny versus slender; childish versus youthful; and stubborn versus determined. For each of these pairs, were you able to identify which synonym sounded lovely versus lousy? The next time you notice too many lousy-sounding adjectives in your sentences, try playing your DS: with your dual screen, say the exact same thing, but using words with a more positive connotation. And then you will be a gamer for life!

In conclusion, consider the following quote from Dr. Wayne Dyer (2007): "If you change the way you look at things, the things you look at change." Based on everything you have learned in this chapter, why do you think this is?

Chapter 3

Mindfulness for
Trauma

As you may recall from previous chapters, trauma causes a paradoxical effect, or a dialectical dilemma, in which we end up with both too much and too little of something. Each of the next few chapters will focus on a specific pair of extremes caused by trauma, as well as the middle path between those extremes.

For example, people who have been traumatized experience both too much awareness and not enough. The clinical term for excessive awareness is *hypervigilance*, while the technical term for diminished awareness is *dissociation*. Hypervigilance occurs when you and your senses are on high alert and you are poised to react at a moment's notice. Dissociation, in contrast, happens when you completely check out and don't even remember something significant taking place. Often the trauma survivor will do some combination of both, in which you obsess over minor details (overfocus) while completely ignoring major issues (underfocus). While both hypervigilance and dissociation serve important functions in helping you to survive the original trauma, these reactions can cause gobs of issues with other aspects of your life.

For example, let's assume you're at your ten-year-old's piano recital. The auditorium is packed with people. Your attention starts to focus on the large crowd. You remember a time when you were humiliated in front of a large group of people, with no escape. You start to scan the room for the closest exits. You notice that your heart beats faster and your hands get clammy. You start to panic...precisely about having a panic attack! Your mind knows exactly what to do next: to avoid creating a scene, you completely check out. And in the process, you miss the entire piano recital. As a result of hypervigilance and dissociation, you were not mindfully present. Due to your trauma history, your mind overfocused on some details while underfocusing on everything else.

The middle path between these two extremes is a state of mind called mindfulness. The concept of mindfulness has been around for thousands of years. Mindfulness simply refers to paying attention for an intentional purpose, in the present, without judging (Kabat-Zinn 2023). Each of these components is essential to the definition of mindfulness. For example, you could pay attention to something randomly or by accident or obsessively—but that's not mindfulness, since mindfulness, by definition, is intentional. Or you could intentionally focus your attention on something that already happened or something that may happen—but that's still not mindfulness, since mindfulness, by definition, refers to awareness of the present. Or you could try really hard to concentrate on something happening right now in this moment (such as reading this book), but instead end up focusing much more on your judgmental thoughts about the book than on the book itself (such as *This book is too long; I am never going to get through all of this; Mindfulness is so boring.*) None of those scenarios would be mindfulness.

A great example of mindfulness is children playing. Healthy children (and especially children at play) are naturally mindful. In fact, they are mindfulness machines—and it's contagious! Think of a group of children playing at recess. Are they worried about the test they will take after lunch? Are they fretting about the scuffle they had yesterday? Are they incessantly judging their quality of play? No, they are not! Without any external prompting, they are mindfully engaged in the present moment. And even if there is a distraction or disruption (such as an annoying teacher with too many rules), what do they do? They get back in the game as quickly as possible! And that, my friend, is what mindfulness is all about.

Each of the components of mindfulness is critical for trauma recovery. Due to the polar processes of hypervigilance and dissociation, your brain has learned to focus on just about everything *except* the present moment. With hypervigilance, your brain—like a sniper—is acutely trained to scan the environment and zero in on any data point that resembles a prior danger, which your brain interprets as a present or potential threat. Your brain also focuses much more on your cognitive, emotional, and physical reactions to the situation than on the actual situation itself.

Therefore, hypervigilance is not *uber*mindfulness—it is *pseudo*mindfulness! Point for point, hypervigilance does not meet the criteria for true mindfulness. Hypervigilance is a reaction, and therefore not intentional. Hypervigilance focuses more on connecting the dots between prior and potential danger than on the present reality. In addition, hypervigilance focuses more on judgments (negative assessments or interpretations) of the situation than on the actual situation. Even worse, once dissociation gets triggered, mindfulness is completely out the window. Therefore, mindfulness practice is critical for relearning a middle path between these two extremes.

In Sanskrit, an ancient language, there were three separate words to describe what have all become clumped together into our current English word "mindfulness" (Gethin 2011). Each of these concepts is significant in its own right.

- One of the original words for mindfulness referred to a concentrated focus; in other words, focusing your attention on just *one thing at a time* (for example, noticing your breathing)—even if only for a few moments.

- Another word for mindfulness referred to sustained focus; in other words, learning to keep your focus going *over a stretch of time* (for example, intentionally noticing your breathing for a full five minutes).

- A third word for mindfulness was used to denote yet another concept: awareness of the mind itself, including when the mind is able to focus, and also when the mind wanders.

Each of these components is critical for trauma recovery. In order to overcome the extremes of hypervigilance on one hand and dissociation on the other hand, a great starting point is learning to focus on just one thing at a time. With hypervigilance, your brain wants to focus on too many things at once; and with dissociation, your brain doesn't want to focus on anything. Since both hypervigilance and dissociation become deeply entrenched default settings, occasionally focusing on just one thing at a time will not be enough to reprogram your brain. Therefore, you will also need to practice focusing your attention on just one thing at a time and for extended periods of time. This will help establish another default setting for your brain: a middle path between the two extremes.

So does that mean once you have practiced training your brain to focus on just one thing at a time, and even for extended periods of time, that your brain will never, ever revert back to patterns of hypervigilance or dissociation? Of course not! The last component of mindfulness is probably the most important of the three. Remember, the third form refers to mindfulness of the mind itself. That means, over time and with lots of practice, you will better notice when your mind is staying on track but also when your mind is drifting over to one of the two extremes. Mindfulness is *not* about always paying perfect attention at all times (since that is impossible, even for the Zen Buddhists of the world). On the contrary, mindfulness is much more about learning to observe the mind itself (both when it behaves and does not behave), and learning to gently bring the mind back to the middle path.

The Power of Observation

So how and why does mindfulness work anyway? Well, even the best scientists on the planet cannot fully answer that question. (In fact, no one can even define the mind itself, much less mindfulness). But it is possible to explain the power of mindfulness in one simple concept without needing to understand the infinite complexity of the human brain. And that is the power of observation.

It is a basic fact of life that whatever we observe as humans, we change. Just think of a few simple examples. What happens when a principal walks by a room full of unruly students? Without a single word, just by her popping her head into the room, the classroom dynamics will shift instantly. What happens when a police officer parks at a busy intersection? Even if he does nothing more than sit and observe, the traffic patterns will change. Now obviously, sometimes a principal might need to issue a detention or three, and sometimes a police officer might need to bestow a well-deserved citation. Clearly observation does not change everything, and further intervention is often required, but here's my point: observation can change an awful lot—all by itself.

This concept explains not only what mindfulness is, but also why it works. In short, we change what we observe simply by the act of observing it. And that applies to the mind itself. As soon as we observe the mind, the mind starts to behave differently. So does that mean mindfulness will fix all our problems? Of course not. But mindfulness is a great start. And none of our problems will get fixed without it.

Getting Started with Mindfulness

So what does mindfulness practice even look like? When you're just getting started, these tips can help. First, select an activity that you enjoy doing. That way mindfulness will be inherently self-rewarding. After all, why wouldn't you want to be more fully present with an activity that you enjoy? (Eventually you will need to learn to be mindful of less enjoyable experiences as well, but that will come later.)

Second, select an activity that you are already doing on a regular basis. This has several advantages. For example, if you pick something that you already do, (1) you will not need to remember to schedule it, (2) you will also not need to block off extra time, and (3) you will not need to spend extra money.

Once you have selected an enjoyable activity that you already do on a regular basis, the next step is to be intentional about dedicating at least a portion of that activity to mindfulness practice: learning to focus exclusively on that activity alone, and on as many details of that activity as possible. As your mind wanders to other internal or external distractions (and it most certainly will), simply notice those distractions, notice any judgments you have about those distractions, and then gently refocus your attention back on the enjoyable activity.

Mindfulness of the Body

When we're learning to become more mindful, it is usually best to follow this sequence: mindfulness of physical experiences (that is, the body), mindfulness of internal experiences (that is, the mind), and then mindfulness of external experiences (that is, everything else). Thus, the first phase of mindfulness practice refers to becoming more mindful of your physical body. This includes awareness of the five senses (sight, sound, smell, taste, and touch) plus all other somatic sensations (such as pressure, pleasure, temperature, balance, hunger, thirst, or physical symptoms).

You can practice mindfulness of the body by intentionally paying attention to each of your five senses. For example, take five minutes every day to view your favorite scene (such as the sunrise); appreciate your favorite sound (such as soothing music); savor your favorite aroma (such as a burning candle); relish your favorite flavor (such as gourmet coffee); or snuggle with your favorite object (such as a comfy blanket). If you can mindfully engage each of your five senses per day, that is already twenty-five minutes of mindfulness practice!

You can also learn to pay more attention to your body simply as you go through life: as you walk, dance, exercise, stretch, breathe, brush your teeth, or make love. If you mindfully attune to just five activities per day, for five minutes per activity, that's another twenty-five minutes of mindfulness practice. You are well on your way to becoming a mindfulness machine!

Mindfulness of the body is essential for healing from trauma for a variety of reasons. First, your body is constantly communicating with you. Every single sensation (both pleasant and painful) is your body's attempt to send you a message. The more you ignore your body's messaging system, the more it just may need to scream at you!

Furthermore, as previously explained, unresolved trauma gets trapped in the body through the freeze response. When faced with danger or crisis, the body unleashes high levels of very powerful chemicals (adrenaline, dopamine, and cortisol) in order to execute fight or flight. When fight or flight is not possible, the body continues to pump these powerful chemicals, while at the same time slamming on the brake to contain them. Thus, the body gets locked into an endless war in which both sides continue to escalate (fight or flight versus freeze), resulting in a myriad of physical symptoms in potentially every single body system. In short, you cannot possibly heal from trauma without learning to notice your own body.

Mindfulness of the Mind

The second phase of mindfulness practice refers to becoming more mindful of your psychological experiences, such as your thoughts, beliefs, feelings, moods, memories, urges, or cravings. Mindfulness of the mind is also essential for healing from trauma. Many of the official diagnostic symptoms for PTSD have to do with what's going on in your mind, such as memories of the trauma, intense emotional reactions, and negative beliefs about yourself and others, to name just a few. There are many ways to practice mindfulness of the mind. Here are two of my favorites: stream of consciousness and the Balanced Mind.

Stream of Consciousness

Imagine that your mind is like a river. You are sitting along the bank of this river, just watching the boats as they float by. Each boat represents something happening in your mind. You might notice the thought boat: *I missed breakfast and I was too busy for lunch.* You might notice the memory boat: *The last time this happened, I almost passed out.* You might notice the feelings boat: *I am already feeling hangry. Not a good sign!* You might notice the urge boat: *I am craving a triple whopper with double bacon and cheese, extra mayo.* The key to this exercise is to simply notice each of these boats—not to act on or react to them!

Now let's repeat this same exercise with a more trauma-specific example. Once again, imagine yourself sitting along the bank of the river, observing the boats as they float by. Each boat represents something happening in your mind. You might notice the feelings boat: *I am starting to feel really panicky, and I don't even know why.* You might notice the thought boat: *That man seems vaguely familiar.* You might notice the memory boat: *The man looks just like the guy who abused me.* You might notice the urge boat: *I feel like puking.* Once again, the key to this exercise is to simply notice each of these boats—not to act on or react to them!

As you can imagine, it takes much more intentional effort to *not* react to events happening in your mind than to act on them. In order to just notice (without reacting), you may need some additional skills that are collectively called *distress tolerance*, which you will learn about in chapter 5.

The Balanced Mind

Part of your mind does the thinking and part of your mind does the feeling. In other words, you have a Thinking Mind and a Feeling Mind. The gift of the Thinking Mind is that it is verbal. You can think of thoughts as the lyrics of a song. In contrast, the gift of the Feeling Mind is that it is nonverbal. You can think of emotions as the music of a song.

Because of the Thinking Mind we have language, which is undeniably one of the most complex tools we use as a humans. And because of language, we have culture and civilization. But even with all our linguistic sophistication, humans still communicate more nonverbally than verbally!

We clearly need both parts of the mind, and one part is *not* more important than the other. In fact, research clearly shows that we cannot make good decisions unless both parts of the mind are active and working together (Pham 2004). Lyrics can send powerful messages, even without the music. And music can be very inspiring, even without the lyrics. But the mind is always at its best when its playlist includes songs with both lyrics and music.

However, since we constantly have both verbal and nonverbal messages running through our minds, we need another part of the mind to make sense of all this information. This part is called the Balanced Mind. The job of your Balanced Mind is to notice your thoughts and feelings, assess those thoughts and feelings, and upregulate or downregulate them, as necessary. Think of the Balanced Mind as both thermometer and thermostat. The Balanced Mind not only constantly reads the temperature in the other two minds but also knows how to set the temperature. And finally, the Balanced Mind also knows how to make wise, dialectical (that is, balanced) decisions. The Balanced Mind relies heavily on both the Thinking Mind *and* the Feeling Mind, as well as other important sources of information, such as prior experience, intuition, and spiritual inspiration (Linehan 2015).

When we have been traumatized, our Balanced Mind has been hijacked, and instead of performing these functions, it is reprogrammed for the extremes of hypervigilance and dissociation. While hypervigilance and dissociation are great for emergency measures, these functions were not designed to balance thoughts and emotions or make balanced decisions.

This new default leads to all kinds of issues with both the Thinking Mind and Feeling Mind. Sometimes the Thinking Mind will overthink (for example, ruminating obsessively), and sometimes it will underthink (for example, making impulsive decisions). Sometimes the Feeling Mind will become overloaded, and sometimes it will become completely numb. Furthermore, chaos in the Thinking Mind triggers chaos in the Feeling Mind, while chaos in the Feeling Mind triggers chaos in the Thinking Mind. This escalating dysregulation results in decisions that trigger even more chaos!

You can literally think of the Feeling Mind, Thinking Mind, and Balanced Mind as different structures within the brain. For example, for most people, the left hemisphere is the more logical, linear, and linguistic region of the brain (the thinking part) while the right hemisphere is the more creative, spontaneous, and intuitive sector of the brain (the feeling part). And the Balanced Mind comes into play when both hemispheres are working together.

Another way the brain is compartmentalized into thinking versus feeling is the prefrontal cortex (which, as the name implies, is located in the front part of the brain) versus the limbic system (which is one of the inner brain regions). The prefrontal cortex is designed for thinking, while the limbic system is programmed for emotional reactions. So what is the Balanced Mind? When both are working together!

The whole point of mindfulness practice is to restore the role of the Balanced Mind. That's where recovery will happen. Whether you are triggered or not, three really good questions to start asking yourself are:

- What is my Thinking Mind telling me?

- What is my Feeling Mind telling me?

- What is my Balanced Mind telling me?

Mindfulness of Everything Else

The third phase of mindfulness practice refers to becoming more mindful of everything else in your life, such as your behaviors, reactions, environments, and relationships. This is the last phase because you cannot possibly be mindful of everything else in your life until you are first and foremost mindful of what is happening in your body and mind. For example, the five senses are your window to the outside world. So how can you possibly be mindful of the outside world if you are not even mindful of the window itself? Furthermore, your emotions are an amazing interpretive summary of everything happening in your body and mind in any given moment. In short, your body and mind are mindfulness machines…so pay attention to them!

Once you have developed more mindfulness of your body, more mindfulness of your mind, and more mindfulness of other things in your life, you are on the path to insight. Think of anything in your life that you can become more mindful of. Insight happens when we start to connect all those dots and see how they are all interrelated.

Consider this example. It's great if you can become more aware of physical reactions in your body, such as *My chest feels tight*; or *I feel a knot in my gut*; or *I feel like puking*; or *I feel lightheaded*. It's great if you can start to notice psychological states, such as *I feel panicky*; or *I feel a sense of dread*; or *This seems like a déjà vu*. And it's great if you can become more cognizant of what's happening outside your mind and body, such as *That man looks just like the guy who assaulted me. His mustache and sunglasses look almost identical!* But wouldn't it be even better if you could connect the dots and see how all these data points are interrelated? That's when insight happens!

On one hand, we must first be mindful of each of these data points before we can connect the dots and form an insight. On the other hand, what would be the purpose of only becoming more mindful of these various data points in isolation, but never understanding how they all connect? Some people make mindfulness the be-all and end-all of life and miss the entire point. Mindfulness is a means to an end, not the end itself. The goal we are striving for is better insight into our symptoms, and ultimately healing from our trauma. We need mindfulness to get there.

Exercises You Can Build On

The rest of this book is devoted to applied mindfulness of your thoughts, feelings, reactions, and relationships. To get you started on that path, I would like to introduce several exercises that you can build upon as you progress through this journey.

Keeping a Diary Card

Create a table with eight columns. The first column is for whatever you want to start noticing or tracking more in your life. This column could include:

- PTSD symptoms, such as various trauma-related triggers, reactions, memories, nightmares, or flashbacks;

- intense thoughts and emotions;

- levels of anxiety and depression;

- your general mood;

- physical aches and pains;

- fluctuations in sleep and appetite;

- any other signs, symptoms, and sensations worth noting.

The next seven columns are for the days of the week—and now you have a place to track each of these items on a daily basis. The goal is not necessarily to do anything with this information (unless, of course, one of your data points is life threatening). Rather, the goal at this point is simply to become an expert on your own body and mind through mindfulness practice—by noticing, monitoring, and tracking.

Making a Mindfulness Action Plan

Sometimes mindfulness practice will be more challenging than you anticipated. With some activities more than others, you may notice that your mind wanders, you get distracted, or you just want to give up. (Well, as you have already learned, just noticing these tendencies is already being mindful!) If you keep getting detoured on your path to mindfulness, you may need a MAP—a mindfulness action plan—to stay grounded in the present. This map includes six reference points to keep you on track (Hayes et al. 2012).

Simply complete the following sentences starting with these prompts:

I am… (Insert identity or role relevant to the mindfulness exercise.)

Here now… (Focus on the present moment.)

Accepting… (Acknowledge the challenges of mindfulness in this moment.)

Noticing… (Apply your observation skills.)

Committing to… (Make a decision to remain mindful.)

What I care about… (Make this decision in light of your priorities and principles.)

Let me share a personal example of how this works. My favorite mindfulness exercise is playing with my kids. As previously mentioned, kids are mindfulness machines, and their mindfulness is contagious. But even when I really want to be mindfully present as I play with my kids, sometimes it is difficult, and my mind starts to drift to other competing commitments in my life. That's when I remember my MAP!

I am *a father.*

Here now *playing with my kids.*

Accepting *the fact that other commitments I have will need to take a back seat.*

Noticing *the tension in my chest as I think about everything else going on in my life.*

Committing to *playing with my kids, regardless of what other commitments I have.*

What I care about: *Family is more important to me than career and other priorities.*

Think of a situation in your life where you have found it challenging to stay engaged in the present and would like to be more mindful. What is your MAP?

At http://www.newharbinger.com/55848, you'll find a tool you can use to create your own MAP.

RAIN Check

RAIN Check is applied mindfulness at its best. This tool is especially useful for dealing with trauma reactions that show up as intense emotions. The RAIN Check is not just an acronym; it is also a metaphor. Just as a rainstorm can come on suddenly, we must learn to manage emotions that emerge in a moment. Instead of fearing the storm, allow it to pass, knowing it is only temporary. The more you fight with your emotions, the more they fight back. We fight with our emotions by judging, suppressing, or trying to control them. In contrast, RAIN Check is a four-part storm response that involves the following steps: **R**ecognize, **A**llow, **I**nquire, and **N**urture.

Here's an example of how to apply this skill to a very common emotion: anger.

> First, start by learning to **recognize** your anger—and especially where you notice it in your body (for example, your jaw is clenched).

> Next, give yourself permission to **allow** your anger (instead of judging or resisting it, which will only make it more difficult to manage in the long run).

> Then learn to **inquire** about your anger—approach it with curiosity, empathy, and maybe even humor. After all, fear and anger are neurologically incompatible with empathy, curiosity, and humor (Kershaw and Wade 2012).

> Finally, engage in some sort of **nurturing** (that is, self-soothing) behavior to release the anger in an appropriate way (such as taking a long walk through the woods or reorganizing your apartment).

What are some ways you might practice the RAIN Check in your daily life? Think of some emotions that you might struggle with, such as anger, sadness, or worry. Journal or reflect on how this technique can help you work through these feelings with compassion instead of judgment.

Pattern Wheel

A very common symptom of PTSD is a fascinating concept called *reenactment*. You may find yourself in certain situations over and over again—and each time, you wonder, *How in the tarnation did I end up this mess…again?* There are many explanations for why people engage in reenactment, almost always subconsciously. Perhaps the main reason is that reenactment provides an opportunity to "redo" the traumatizing situation, thus helping the trauma survivor potentially reach a place of resolution or closure. Unfortunately, however, the process of reenactment often has the opposite effect of exposing the person to even more traumatization (Levine 1997). The purpose of this mindfulness exercise is to start to notice these recurring patterns. Here's how to do it:

Draw a circular flowchart with the following boxes: Prompting Event, Interpretations, Reactions, Action Urges, Behavior, Consequences, and ANTs. You can also download a copy of this flowchart at http://www.newharbinger.com/55848.

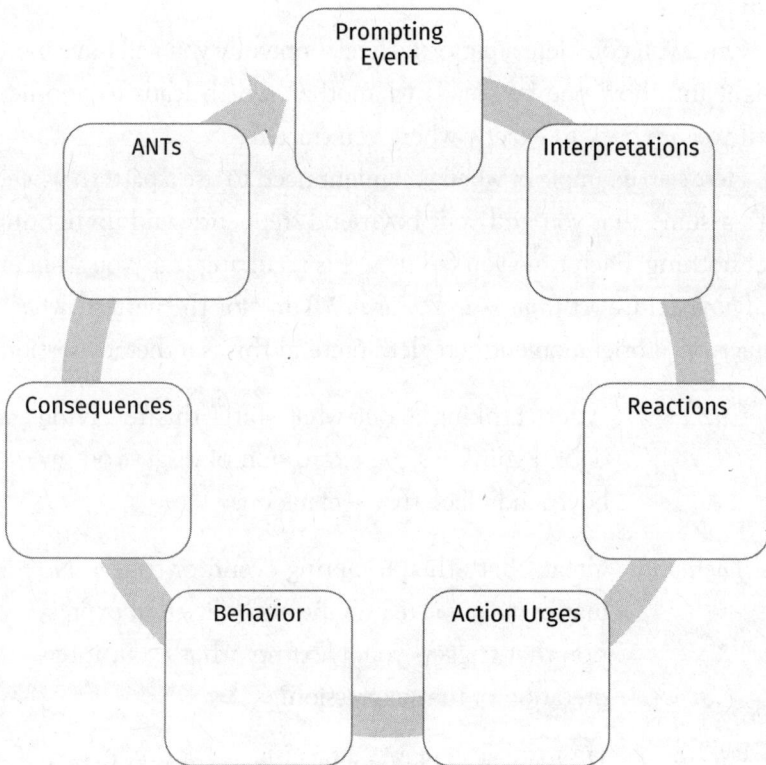

Prompting event refers to the situation that starts this whole cyclical effect (that is, the trigger). Interpretations refer to your perceptions or assessment of that situation. Reactions refer to what you feel (both physically and emotionally) once you have been triggered. Action urges refer to what you feel like doing after being triggered, whereas behaviors refer to what you actually end up doing. Consequences refer to the aftermath of your behaviors. For example, now that have you just done what you just did, what are the real-world implications? In particular, how do the consequences of your behaviors make you even more vulnerable to the same situation repeating all over again? And finally, the ANTs: As you have already learned, the ANTs are your automatic negative thoughts. Do you have any ANTs about any of these boxes that are making things worse rather than better?

Once you complete a pattern wheel, hopefully you will have more insight into how one box leads to another, which leads to another, until you are back to exactly where you started.

Here's an example of when you might need to use a pattern wheel. Let's assume that you and your boyfriend frequently end up fighting over nothing. Each time you fall into this recurring trap, you wonder, *And how did we get from A to Z...again?* Time for the pattern wheel! In fact, for a brief moment here, let's pretend this is a therapy session:

Client: After thinking about what starts this revolving door, I think it's the expression of disgust on my boyfriend's face that sets me off.

Therapist: Great, that's the prompting event, or trigger. No matter what you're arguing about, it's that expression that triggers you. Next up: what's your interpretation of that expression?

Client: He hates me. He's going to leave me. This relationship will never work.

Therapist: Nice work! So now what are your physical and emotional reactions?

Client: I feel rage. I feel like the blood vessels in my head are going to pop.

Therapist: Awesome self-awareness. So now what are your action urges? In other words, regardless of what you end up doing, what do you feel like doing?

Client: I feel like hugging my boyfriend really tightly around the neck.

Therapist: Wonderful insight! So what do you actually do? Do you act on your urge, or do you end up doing something less lethal?

Client: Partner strangulation is illegal in my state, so no, I don't do that. Instead, I yell and scream and throw things.

Therapist: Great self-control…compared to the alternative. So what are some of the implications of this behavior?

Client: Well, now my boyfriend is more focused on dodging unidentified flying objects than whatever we were trying to argue about.

Therapist: Fantastic. And how do these consequences set you up for this same situation to happen all over again?

Client: Well, now my boyfriend has even more of that expression I despise.

Therapist: Lovely insight! And finally, can you think of any ANTs you might have throughout this process that only make it worse?

Client: Well, this whole time I'm thinking I'm such a klutz. I'm probably overreacting. Also, I need to improve my aim when I throw things.

As you read through this highly theatrical script, do you notice all the times and ways this sequence could be interrupted and redirected? If so, you are clearly rocking Mindfulness 101!

Building Your House

Draw a four-story house, including the foundation, a front door, a chimney, and even a billboard in the front yard. If you prefer, you can download a template of a house at http://www.newharbinger.com/55848.

On the foundation of your house, make a list of your most important values (such as faith, family, and friendship). On the first level, jot down the major issues in your life you want to work on (for example, getting sober and recovering from your divorce). On the second level, make note of any emotional challenges you may have (such as rage, panic attacks, and loneliness). On the third level, identify any less intense, everyday issues you would like to address (for example, finding a better job and paying off the mortgage). On the fourth level, make a list of your goals, plans, and dreams for the future (such as getting your master's degree, buying a house, and finding a life partner).

On the walls of your house, jot down your main supports in your life (for example, your pastor and your dog). On the roof, make note of who or what protects you (such as your friends and God). On the door, identify what you keep hidden from others (for example, how you were abused as a child). On the chimney, describe how you blow off steam (such as bowling, fishing, and hunting). Finally, on the billboard, write down whatever you are most proud of about yourself (for example, your resilience, your sobriety, and your two beautiful children). This "house" will serve as your visual treatment plan as you work through the rest of the book. Refer back to this house often, and especially every time you start to wonder, *And why am I reading this book again?*

Satisfaction Scale

Let's create another table. (You can create your own or download a template at http://www.newharbinger.com/55848.)

This table will have four columns:

The first column is for all the major areas in your life that you would like to rate. This could include things like your career, your finances, your relationships with various people, your physical health, your emotional health, and so on.

In the next column, write down your level of satisfaction with each of these areas on a scale of 0 to 10. A 10 means everything is perfect in that area, and there's nothing that could possibly be improved. In contrast, a 0 would indicate the perfect storm in which nothing could possibly go more wrong. Next, put a star next to whatever area(s) of your life you would like to improve. This could be an area that already has a high rating, but you would like an even higher score. Or it could be an area in which you are completely tanking. What's most important is that you select areas that you truly want to work on.

In the third column, for each of the areas you starred, write down what your life could look like if it were already a 10 in that domain.

And since you are really smart, take what you have just written in the third column and rewrite it as a SMART goal in the fourth column. A SMART goal is one that is specific, measurable, achievable, relevant, and time-bound. For example: "I want to be healthier" is a great goal, but it is not yet a SMART goal. Even though it is relevant to what you want to accomplish, and perhaps achievable, it is not yet measurable and does not have a time limit. "I will run three marathons and lose forty pounds by tomorrow" is relevant, measurable, and time-bound, but certainly not achievable. You get the point. A SMART goal would sound more like: "I will walk five miles a day until I lose ten pounds or until I can fit into my favorite dress—whichever comes first!"

And voila. Now you have another treatment plan to guide you through the rest of this book.

Acceptance and Change

Time for another table! Since we're on a roll, let's make four columns again (or download at http://www.newharbinger.com/55848). The title of this table will be any problem behavior you want to work on. "Problem" behavior here refers to any issue *you* identify as a problem, not necessarily what other people think is a problem. For example, you could choose one of the domains that you gave a low score to on your satisfaction scale.

Label the first column "pros" and the second column "cons." In the first column, write down all the advantages of your problem behavior. That's right, you read that correctly. If you keep doing a problem behavior over and over again, there must be *something* good you're getting out of it, so we might as well figure out what that is.

In the second column, make a list of all the disadvantages of your problem behavior. Now let's compare the two columns. This will be a nice, old-fashioned cost-benefit analysis. Are there more pros than cons? More cons than pros? As you do your comparison, remember that all not all pros and cons have the same weight. For example, when you do this exercise, you may end up with numerically more pros than cons, but then realize that the few cons you have greatly outweigh the many pros.

We are rarely motivated to change problem behaviors until we are truly convinced the cost outweighs the benefits. Now that you have determined this is a behavior worth changing, let's proceed to the next two columns.

Label the third column "external causes" and the fourth column "internal causes." Under external causes, identify the main details of whatever is going on *before* the problem behavior starts. This should include the classic staples of journalism, including who, what, when, and where. In other words, before the problem behavior occurs, who are you usually with? What are you doing? When does this scenario tend to take place? And where are you? Under internal causes, describe whatever you are usually thinking and feeling before the behavior happens. Remember, feelings are both emotional and physical: what you are feeling emotionally, and where in your body you physically feel that emotion.

Congratulations! With the completion of the last two columns, you have just identified your triggers. Triggers are whatever tends to happen before a problem behavior occurs. An efficient way to start changing a problem behavior is to start changing the triggers. Eliminate them, avoid them, reduce their frequency, or find ways to manage them.

Mindfulness Reflections

Now that you have a few mindfulness exercises under your belt, it is time for some mindfulness reflections. In fact, it's a good habit to ask yourself the following self-reflective questions each time you practice your mindfulness:

- What did I notice when I was mindful?

- What was different about this experience?

- How does what I learned relate to my symptoms?

- How does what I learned relate to my life goals?

You may have just mindfully noticed that each of these questions is basically an example of mindfulness—about mindfulness itself! Talk about becoming a mindfulness machine...

Let me provide an example of how this exercise works by featuring a former client as a case study. Several years ago, a young woman presented in therapy with complaints of panic attacks that were getting in the way of her goals for her career and dating life. As I got to know the client and her panic symptoms, it was clear that she would benefit from some basic mindfulness training. After a little brainstorming, we quickly determined that riding her bicycle would be an excellent mindfulness exercise, since this was something she did on a regular basis, and also something she enjoyed doing. When she came back for her next session, I asked her these four questions to see what she learned from her mindfulness practice.

When I asked what she noticed about mindfully riding her bicycle, she replied: "I noticed my breathing increase, I started to sweat more, my heart rate also increased, and I also noticed some of my muscles became more tense." (You may have just realized that what my client noticed while mindfully riding her bicycle were precisely the symptoms of a panic attack!)

I continued with the next question: "Very good, great observations. And how was mindfully riding your bicycle different from how you normally go on your bike ride?" Her response was fairly typical: "Well, when I normally ride my bike, my mind just wanders, and I don't really pay attention to those things." I validated her insights: "So when you are mindful, you notice what is going on in your body, but not so much when you are not mindful. Is that correct?"

I then proceeded to the third question: "So how does what you learned from this little exercise relate to your symptoms?" This was the moment I had been waiting for! I could see the wheels turning in her head. "Hey," she stammered, "so...so that's exactly what I feel when I am having a panic attack!" "Exactly," I responded. "But you didn't have a panic attack. Why not?"

"Because I was exercising!" she exclaimed. "You're *supposed* to have those 'symptoms' when you exercise." This was my golden opportunity. "Exactly! So you're telling me it is possible to have all the symptoms of a panic attack, but still not have the panic attack. Because ultimately it's your interpretation of the symptoms that cause the attack and not the symptoms themselves. Is that correct?"

I could see her wheels still turning, so I proceeded to the fourth and final question: "How does what you learned relate to your personal and professional goals?" This is when my client finally grasped the connection between the mindfulness practice, her symptoms, and her goals. She agreed that it would be great if she could learn to recognize the symptoms of panic—whether at work or while on a date—*but not have the panic attack!* And with some additional relaxation techniques, she got there. But it all started with mindfulness.

My clients do not always reach such dramatic insights when we do mindfulness reflections. When I ask how the mindfulness practice went, a more typical response is: "I'm terrible at this. My mind constantly wandered." That's when I counter with: "That's amazing. So you're starting to notice some of your judgments. You're even starting to notice how your mind works. You've already started on the path to mindfulness!"

And my excitement when I make these statements is completely sincere. Because chances are, these negative judgments and struggle with focus are precisely what have been causing their symptoms and getting in the way of their life goals. Even when clients feel like they have bombed a mindfulness exercise, it is completely the opposite. The only way to fail a mindfulness exercise is to enter a clinical coma.

Remember the definition of mindfulness from the beginning of this chapter? Mindfulness is about paying attention, for a purpose, in the present, without judging. As my client learned, there is indeed a purpose for mindfulness practice. Every time you do a mindfulness exercise, ask yourself, *How does this exercise relate to my symptoms? And how will this exercise help me meet my life goals?* If you do not understand the purpose of mindfulness practice, then you probably will not do it.

Awareness, Acceptance, Action

This entire chapter (and really, the entire book) can be summarized in just a few words: awareness, acceptance, and action. Mindfulness is not just about awareness of the moment—that would be too easy. It is also about acceptance of the moment, which is a lot harder. Remember, mindfulness is paying attention, for a purpose, in the present, *without judging*. This chapter focused mostly on the awareness component of mindfulness. The next chapter will focus much more on acceptance.

It is easy to be mindful (aware and accepting) of something we like or enjoy. But when we intentionally attune to and accept something we emphatically do not like, now that's another story. That's why awareness plus acceptance is *already* taking action. And sometimes, once we are aware and accepting, we need to take *even more* action. And that's what the rest of the book is about. Stay tuned!

Chapter 4

Radical Acceptance for Trauma

Pain has always been a part of the human experience. For thousands of years, poets and philosophers have voluminously reflected on the purpose of human suffering. But in contrast to the modern concept of avoiding pain at all costs, ancient thinkers taught their students to embrace suffering rather than reject it. What? Why?!

One ancient philosopher (the Buddha) gave the example of two arrows. Anytime something painful happens to you in life, it is like getting shot by an arrow. Now, of course, nobody likes getting shot by arrows. But as soon as you do not accept the arrow, you get shot by a second one—the arrow of nonacceptance. According to this thinker, human suffering results much more from the second arrow than from the first one. His point was simple yet profound: Life already flings enough arrows at us, and those arrows are already plenty painful. Do we really need more arrows? And yet, that is precisely what we do when we refuse to accept a painful situation—we increase the pain even more. Life causes us pain, but we cause our own suffering when we are not willing to accept the pain. We have no control over the first arrow, but we do have control over the second one (Jordan 2016).

Jesus taught very similar concepts, but instead of using an arrow analogy, he used the example of a cross, which was the symbol of execution in the ancient Roman world. On one hand, he taught his students: "But when they persecute you in this city, flee ye into another" (Matthew 10:23 [King James Version 1611]). In other words, do not seek out pain just for the sake of pain. But on the other hand, he also taught his students *to take up their cross* (Matthew 16:24 [KJV 1611]). In other words, some pain cannot be avoided—and that's precisely the pain you need to accept and embrace.

Keep these concepts in mind as I introduce what DBT calls *radical acceptance*. Think of radical acceptance as accepting the first arrow so that you do not have to deal with the second one. Think of radical acceptance as taking up your cross in some situations, while fleeing to another city in others.

At its core, radical acceptance means seeing something as it is—no more and no less. After a trauma, we sometimes see situations as much worse than they really are (which would be catastrophizing) or much better than they really are (which would be denial). Both extremes are the opposite of radical acceptance. Read through the following statements about radical acceptance, and then we will unpack each concept in more detail (Linehan 2015).

- Normal acceptance means that you accept something you already like.

- Radical acceptance means that you accept something you do not like.

- Radical acceptance does *not* mean to approve of or to agree with.

- Radical acceptance *does* mean to acknowledge and embrace.

- Radical acceptance is the opposite of denial.

- Radical acceptance is active, not passive.

- Pain + radical acceptance = healing.

- Pain − radical acceptance = suffering.

- Pain is required, suffering is optional.

- Radical acceptance is the first step out of hell.

Radical acceptance means something very different from how we normally use the term "acceptance," and that is part of the reason this concept can be so difficult to grasp. When we normally use the term "acceptance" in everyday English, we tend to imply that we like or want or agree with whatever we are accepting. For example, if I give you a gift or share an opinion, and you accept it, you are implying some level of assent.

Radical acceptance means the exact opposite of that. Radical acceptance, by definition, refers to accepting something that you emphatically do *not* like—and that is precisely what makes it radical. Just to be clear: Radical acceptance does not mean you approve of something—simply that you are willing to acknowledge it or embrace it. For example, we all know it's possible to hug someone we do not like. In a similar way, it is possible to emotionally embrace something you did not sign up for.

When we use the term "acceptance" in everyday English, we also often imply some sort of passive avoidance, such as condoning, looking the other way, or sweeping something under the rug. For example, "Just accept it" is often synonymous with "Don't rock the boat" or "Don't upset the apple cart." Once again, radical acceptance is the opposite of that. In fact, radical acceptance is *never* about passive avoidance. On the contrary, radical acceptance is all about facing the facts just as they are—and then dealing with those facts. Radical acceptance is the opposite of denial or minimizing. Radical acceptance is all about accepting what cannot be changed precisely so that you can free up your time and energy to address what can (Linehan 2015).

Why is radical acceptance such a big deal for trauma work? Healing cannot happen until we first understand and accept that we have been traumatized, and that trauma affects us in many ways: physically, emotionally, mentally, relationally, and spiritually. After all, denying reality does not change reality—and no reality can be changed until it is first accepted. Reflect on this quote from social activist James Baldwin (1962): "Not everything that is faced can be changed, but nothing can be changed until it is faced."

Marsha Linehan famously called radical acceptance "the only way out of hell." Radical acceptance is not just the realization that we have experienced a personal hell; it is also the active, intentional decision to leave that hell. Granted, the healing process will still require plenty of hard work even after we leave hell. In fact, when you first start to accept reality, things may seem even worse than you imagined. That's okay. It's better to see the facts as they are, not as we want them to be. Accepting may increase sadness at first, but then leads to peace and freedom (Linehan 2015).

When we radically accept something painful in life, the pain becomes less painful, which puts us in a much better position to face and deal with the painful situation. In contrast, when we do not accept something painful, the pain becomes more painful, and the original situation only gets worse. That's why pain plus radical acceptance leads to healing, whereas pain without radical acceptance leads to suffering.

Let me give you a personal example of this concept. I have had eye problems for my entire life. In fact, I used to wear an eye patch when I was a kid, and my classmates used to say I was the son of a pirate. (Another theory was that I had lost my eyeball while falling off the jungle gym.) When I was in my twenties, I noticed that both eyes were starting to get blurrier, and especially the left one. Instead of facing the facts and dealing with the issue, I made one excuse after another: "I'm a grad student. I'm too poor for a doctor. Plus I'm reading too much and sleeping too little, so of course my eyes are blurry." Meanwhile, my vision just kept getting worse and worse.

One day, I finally decided to update my glasses prescription, thinking that would solve all my eye problems. The optician helping me took one look at my eyes and told me there was no prescription that could fix my issue, and immediately referred me to a specialist. At the specialist's office, for the first time in my life, I could no longer read the big E on the eye chart. (I knew it was an E because it's always an E, but I wisely decided that, at this point, the gig was up.) To make a long story short, I was forced to undergo an excruciatingly painful cornea transplant, which left me with sixteen stitches in my left eye. It took a full year and a half for all sixteen stitches to be removed.

Here's my point: Pain without radical acceptance leads to more pain. If I had simply accepted and dealt with my blurry eyes when I first noticed them, this could all have been avoided. Nonacceptance does not bypass pain; it only creates more.

Remember the two arrows? Pain is required, since pain is a basic fact of life. We don't have a choice with the first arrow. But suffering is optional, in the sense that we do not have to add nonacceptance to the mix. For me, it is useful to distinguish between "clean" pain and "dirty" pain. Clean pain refers to pain that you are willing to face, whereas dirty pain refers to pain you have decided not to deal with. Think of unnecessary suffering as dirty pain.

Many modern languages still reflect this distinction between original pain versus secondary, ongoing pain. For example, in Spanish the word *sentir* means "to feel," whereas the word *resentir*, which literally means to "refeel," can also be translated as "to resent." Therefore, to resent something literally means to refeel it…over and over again. We all feel the first arrow. It hurts. It is painful. That is clean pain. But when you resent the first arrow, you refeel it, perhaps hundreds or thousands of times. Even if you were shot with the first arrow only once, the second arrow has an infinite potential to keep shooting you for the rest of your life. If the first arrow was painful, why would anyone want to keep refeeling it?

Obviously that was a facetious rhetorical question. Nobody wants to keep reliving something painful. But as you read earlier, that is precisely what trauma does to us. Due to the negativity bias, we cannot forget the trauma, even when we want to and even when we try to. The trauma continues to live in our thoughts, memories, reactions, and nightmares. Sometimes the second arrow is a conscious decision to keep reliving the trauma (such as deliberately nursing a grudge), and sometimes the second arrow represents automatic processes that we cannot control on our own (such as nightmares).

There are three basic life scenarios that require radical acceptance: events from the present that cannot be changed; events from the past, which can never be changed; and events from the present that *can* be changed. Can you think of any arrows that life has hurled at you from any of those categories? For example, think of a situation from the past that is no longer occurring. The bad thing started and stopped. And yet, now you are continuing to suffer, perhaps more from an inability to accept what happened than from what actually happened. The first arrow is long gone, but now you are clinging to the arrow of nonacceptance.

Now think of a current, ongoing situation that also cannot be changed. Are you suffering more from the situation or from an inability to accept the situation? Finally, think of a current, ongoing situation that really *can* be changed—but you haven't changed it yet, since you have not fully accepted that it's a problem!

Radical acceptance is *not* easy. But here's the deal: nonacceptance is even harder. In each of those three scenarios, the arrow of nonacceptance makes things more painful, not less. The second arrow does not solve any problems; it only creates more!

All this blather about acceptance may sound really abstract, so let's look at a concrete example. Imagine it's 2:00 a.m. and your two-month-old baby is screaming her head off. You have a few options at this point. For example, you could scream back at the baby. Or you could totally ignore the baby. Now granted, neither option is advisable. Both options may seem like a viable quick fix, but they will only make things much worse—both in the short run and over the long haul. And yet, that is precisely how we deal with so many things in life: we either scream at them or completely ignore them. And here's my point: neither option is radical acceptance.

So what's a better response when your baby is screaming her head off at 2:00 a.m.? Embrace your baby! That will be the best way to calm your child and get her back to sleep. (Of course, whether *you* get back to sleep or not is another story.) But regardless, embracing the baby will still be the best way to get through the night. Radical acceptance is also the best way to get through life.

Once I was in session with a young mother who was experiencing some postpartum depression. Part of her depression included lots of negative self-talk. One day she brought her baby to session, and I could not help but notice how she gazed at the baby in absolute awe and admiration. I decided to use this as a teachable moment. "So why do you even love this baby so much?" I asked. "She can't do anything right," I continued. "She can't walk. She can't talk. She can't feed herself. She can't use the bathroom. She can't even sleep through the night."

That's when my client's gaze turned into a puzzled stare as she retorted, "Yes, but she's perfect!" "Exactly," I said. "You know your baby can't do anything right—yet—but you already see her as perfect. Don't you think maybe that's how you need to see yourself?"

Think of radical acceptance as just that: compassionately embracing yourself the same way you would embrace a screaming, imperfect baby as if she were already perfect. Radical acceptance is not just a harsh, stoic acceptance of the cold, cruel facts. It is so much more than that!

Here's another example: Imagine you are planning a barbecue in your backyard, and you invite all your friends. But on the day of your get-together, someone shows up who was definitely *not* invited: your neighbor Jeff. Jeff is annoying, he smells, and he talks way too much, so you decide to throw Jeff out of the party. But as soon as you are back with your friends, guess who shows up again? Once again you expel Jeff from the party, but this time you decide to make sure he does not sneak back in. You stand guard at your gate like a vigilante to preemptively eliminate any more Jeff appearances. And in the meantime, you are missing the whole party...

Then you realize that you are literally letting a single person ruin the entire barbecue. So now you decide to rejoin your own party and make the best of it. You will no longer waste your time and energy guarding the gate or trying to kick out your neighbor Jeff. Not only are you enjoying the party, but you also start to realize some things about Jeff you never realized before. Yes, he is still annoying, but now that he is free to come and go, he becomes less annoying. In fact, you start to notice some of Jeff's quirks are (mildly) amusing, and he even has a dry sense of humor (although it's buried pretty deep).

Do you see how this analogy relates to radical acceptance? Think of your neighbor Jeff as anything in your life that you wish never existed: a past trauma, an overwhelming emotion, a diagnosis, a supervisor, you name it. The more you expend your resources on *not* accepting the situation, the more you miss out on the rest of your life. While radical acceptance certainly requires energy, nonacceptance is an absolute energy drain.

Radical acceptance is all about choosing to allocate your time and resources toward what matters the most to you—whatever gives your life purpose and meaning. Not only is this a much better investment for your life, but the painful situation becomes less painful and more bearable. In contrast, when you invest all your energy into *not* accepting something, it only gets worse. What a waste! If this were a fiscal investment, your financial advisor would *not* be pleased.

How will you know if there is something in your life that you currently need to radically accept? Take some time to honestly reflect on the following questions: On one hand, is there anything that you are constantly lying about? Or trying to minimize? Or avoiding? Is there anything that you keep making lots of excuses for? Or something you are forever trying to cover up? Is there something you keep blaming other people for? If you answered yes to some of these questions, you may be experiencing some denial.

On the other hand, is there anything that you constantly obsess, ruminate, or worry about? Something that you cannot stop thinking about, day or night? Whether it's denial (underthinking) or obsessive rumination (overthinking), that is precisely what needs to be radically accepted in your life.

So far you've read some definitions and examples of radical acceptance, and you've learned about its importance. But how do you actually put this stuff into practice? Let's do that now.

Everyday Acceptance

A great place to start with radical acceptance is everyday acceptance. As the name implies, everyday acceptance refers to learning to become more accepting of the ordinary, everyday frustrations, irritations, and setbacks that happen to all of us. This can include things like getting stuck in traffic, losing your phone, or dealing with annoying coworkers.

Getting in the habit of everyday acceptance helps you deal with little problems before they become huge problems. Everyday acceptance is also really good training for radical acceptance. Every time you practice everyday acceptance, you are teaching your brain to become more accepting of life in general. Everyday acceptance can be as simple as opening your hands or kneeling down in prayer. Whenever you physically assume an open, surrendering body posture, your mind is likely to follow suit (Linehan 2015).

Willingness vs. Willfulness

How will you know when you are becoming a more accepting person? You will notice it in your attitudes and behaviors. *Willingness* refers to acceptance in action, whereas *willfulness* is what your actions look like without acceptance. Both willingness and willfulness are acts of the will, which means that they lie within your conscious control (Linehan 2015).

Willingness is doing whatever it takes to get the job done, whether you like it or not. Think of willingness as "smart stubbornness." It takes lots of determination to keep persevering at something, especially when you would rather give up. But that's the effective kind of stubbornness. In contrast, think of willfulness as "stupid stubbornness." It takes just as much persistence to keep doing the same thing over and over again, even when it is not working, and especially when the only person you are hurting is yourself. Physicist Albert Einstein is often credited with saying: "The definition of insanity is doing the same thing over and over and expecting a different result." This is the kind of stubbornness that is not effective.

Therefore, stubbornness is not the problem, but rather how you use it. As you start to radically accept life, you will notice your behaviors become more willing (effective) and less willful (ineffective). Once you understand these concepts, you have a decision to make every time you face a challenging situation. Will you be willing or willful? Think of each challenge in life as a fork in the road. Which way will you turn your will?

Understanding Pain

Another strategy that can be quite helpful with radical acceptance is to change your relationship with pain itself. In order to have a relationship with a real person, you first need to understand that person. The reality is, we need pain. Pain is a warning sign that something needs your attention. And that is precisely why pain is so, well, painful. You need pain to learn, grow, and heal.

Congenital insensitivity to pain is a rare genetic disorder that prevents people from feeling physical pain. This may seem like a good problem to have, but trust me, it is not. Many of the children born with this disorder never make it past age three, much less to adulthood (Shin et al. 2016). In my case, something I did not have as a child was basic fear. Since I was constantly doing really crazy things, kids in my neighborhood used to make bets about what age I would die at. For example, I would stand on the back pegs of my bike (with no hands on the handlebars) and rush down long, winding driveways onto the road without looking for oncoming traffic. Antics like this resulted in many near crashes with vehicles, and several dangerous tumbles in which I leapt off the bike at the last moment. Fortunately,

I did have pain—especially the time I flipped over the handlebars and smashed my collarbone upon impact with the pavement. Without pain, I highly doubt I would have survived my childhood.

Once you understand that the purpose of pain is to get your attention for your own good, you can learn to recruit pain as an ally, instead of seeing it as your archenemy. Since pain is doing you a favor, learn to listen to it rather than ignore it. In fact, learn to listen to your pain even when it whispers. Otherwise, since the whole point of pain is to get your attention, it will have to raise its voice in order to do its job. But, if you learn to accept and befriend your pain, it can do its job without screaming at you.

Letting Go

Another way to practice radical acceptance is a skill called *letting go*. Let me give you two examples to better understand this concept. First, imagine that you and a ferocious monster are involved in a tug-of-war, a contest to the death. A bottomless pit stretches between the two of you. If you win the tug-of-war, the monster will fall to its demise, and you will finally be free. But if the monster wins the tug-of-war, your fate has been sealed. The harder the monster pulls, the harder you pull. And the harder you pull, the harder the monster pulls. The more you engage in this tug-of-war, the more intense it becomes, and the more you are at risk of losing everything, including life itself. Of course, the most obvious solution would be to let go of the rope.

Think of ways this example applies to your life. What is the monster in your life? What is the tug-of-war? What is the rope? What would make more sense for you: to keep fighting the tug-of-war or to let go?

Here's another example: To catch a monkey, you simply make a hole in a coconut and then slip some fruit into the hole. You want to make sure the hole is big enough for the monkey to slip in his hand, but small enough so that the monkey cannot extract his hand once he is grasping the fruit. Apparently monkeys are so intent on grasping the fruit that their hand is now literally stuck inside the coconut, which makes them much easier to catch. In order to be free, the monkey simply needs to...*let go!*

Once again, think of ways this example applies to your life. What is the coconut in your life? What is the fruit? What would make the most sense for you: To keep grasping the fruit? Or to let go?

Finding Meaning

In my experience, one of the most powerful ways of achieving radical acceptance is to find meaning in whatever arrows life has hurled at you. Pain without purpose leads to suffering. In contrast, pain with purpose can lead to healing and transformation. In my opinion, we are all philosophers and theologians. Humans are very distinct from plants and other animals due to how our brains are programmed: we are meaning-making machines.

Dr. Viktor Frankl was a Jewish psychiatrist who survived Auschwitz and several other concentration camps during World War II. Based on his own personal experiences and observations, Frankl wrote *Man's Search for Meaning* (1992), an amazing psychological analysis of what it takes to survive a concentration camp. In his book, Frankl explains that people can survive insane amounts of adversity as long as they can find a purpose in what they are experiencing. But the day people no longer see a purpose for their hardship, they commence what Frankl described as a psychological death, which in a concentration camp setting, soon resulted in physical death as well. Frankl even described in detail the predictable symptoms and medical collapse he observed in people as soon as they lost any sense of meaning.

In order to find a purpose for what you have experienced, learn to channel your inner philosopher or theologian by asking yourself some of the deep questions of life: What has this trauma taught me that I could not have learned otherwise? What forms of strength and resiliency were developed in me precisely because of this trauma? How can this trauma be redeemed for something positive? How can I use this trauma to educate others? How can I leverage this trauma to leave this world a better and safer place than I found it?

Finding purpose in pain is not just naïve, pie-in-the-sky, Pollyannaish thinking. There is a robust and growing body of research on a phenomenon called *post-traumatic growth*. You'll learn more about this concept in the final chapter, but for now, consider this: When you heal from trauma, your life can become richer, deeper, and more meaningful than it would have been without the trauma. There is indeed purpose in pain, as long as we look for it.

Grief Counseling

So far in this chapter, you have learned tips for radical acceptance that you can start practicing on your own. But the reality is that radical acceptance is not something you do in isolation. You absolutely need the help of other people to radically accept the "slings and arrows of outrageous fortune," as Shakespeare's Hamlet poetically called the disappointments of life. Sometimes we need the help of a best friend, a spiritual leader, a trusted mentor, or a life partner. And sometimes we need the help of a professional therapist. The last two strategies included in this chapter both require professional intervention.

In 1969, psychiatrist Elisabeth Kübler-Ross published her monumentally influential book, *On Death and Dying*. In this book, Dr. Kubler-Ross explains how people do not immediately jump to a state of complete acceptance when faced with a terminal illness. Instead, they tend to progress through predictable phases of denial, anger, bargaining, and depression prior to reaching a place of accepting reality. This insight was so revolutionary because it applies not only to the processes of death and dying but also to anything in life that can be difficult to accept.

Rarely in life do we immediately accept all of the arrows flung at us. We often experience intense emotions and reactions. All of these phases (denial, anger, bargaining, and depression) are normal, healthy, and adaptive—as long as they are conduits toward acceptance. The phases often overlap, you can go through the same phase multiple times, and not everyone goes through all these phases, or in this exact sequence. Sometimes, however, we may camp out in one of these phases for too long—in which case, these phases can become roadblocks to acceptance rather than stepping stones. Keep these concepts in mind as you learn about each phase.

Denial: When you initially receive shocking news, your brain knows you cannot handle it. That's why your brain gives you a huge shot of a psychological anesthesia called denial. (Think of denial as the dissociative escape from reality discussed in the first chapter.) While you are in state of shock or denial, both the thinking and feeling parts of your brain have been numbed. In a literal, physical sense, taking a numbing agent during a medical procedure is highly adaptive—but persisting with a completely numb body years later would not be. Do you have any denial in your life that has outlived its usefulness?

Anger: Once a painkiller wears off, you feel the pain. Once your denial wears off, you feel the anger. Anger provides an extremely useful function in that it energizes and mobilizes you to aggressively combat an adverse situation. Whereas denial is like a numbing agent, anger is like a steroid. During the anger phase, the feeling part of your brain has been activated. You need to feel and express the anger in order to heal. But what if no amount of anger can change the situation? And what if constant, ongoing anger is now causing even more problems? Do you have any anger in your life that has outgrown its usefulness?

Bargaining: Once the two powerful chemicals (the painkiller and the steroid) have run their course, the problem-solving part of your brain takes over. During the anger phase, the feeling part of your brain was in overdrive. Now the thinking part of your brain has been hijacked. This is when you morph from boxer to lawyer. Isn't the brain such an amazing organ! If raw emotions could not solve the problem, maybe thinking can. This is the phase in which you obsess, ruminate, perseverate, strategize, and negotiate every possible way out of the challenge. But what if no amount of problem solving can solve the problem? Are you stuck in your head? Do you have any overthinking in your life that has outlived its usefulness?

Depression: When neither boxer nor lawyer can undo the damage, that's when we enter a phase of despair characterized by helplessness and hopelessness. And if these symptoms are severe enough, we call this depression. Depression happens when both your Thinking Mind and Feeling Mind are overactive. We tend to think of depression as a mood disorder (and it certainly is), but depression is just as much a cognitive disorder. Our overactive, overly negative thoughts and feelings mutually trigger each other, sending us further and further into a deep tailspin. While depression may feel like the worst of these phases, it is also the closest to acceptance. In fact, the main reason we feel so depressed is precisely because we are now mourning our loss. Not only do we finally see the loss for what it is, but our overactive Thinking and Feeling Minds may even overshoot the mark and see the loss for worse than it is.

Acceptance: I do not need to say much about acceptance here, since that is what this entire chapter is about. But let me just reiterate: We cannot always get to a place of acceptance all on our own. We may need a skilled professional to help us see what is keeping us stuck; someone who can gently, compassionately guide us through these phases.

Trauma Processing

Due to the fight-flight-freeze responses discussed throughout this book, trauma often becomes literally stuck throughout our bodies and brains, and then randomly resurfaces as automatic, intrusive, unwanted, involuntary thoughts, emotions, reactions, nightmares, or flashbacks. These symptoms usually require the intervention of a skilled trauma specialist.

Up to this point, you may have formed the impression that radical acceptance is entirely a matter of the conscious will. That is incorrect. No matter how hard we try to accept a trauma, many of these symptoms will persist anyway. But here's the good news: a skilled trauma therapist can help us release the trauma that is still stuck, and from there, the mind very often spontaneously comes to a place of acceptance on its own. Acceptance is not just the path to healing—it is also the sign that we have arrived. Acceptance is the evidence of a healthy mind that has re-engaged with life.

In conclusion, pain is a basic fact of life and cannot be avoided. When we ignore our pain, it only gets worse and turns into suffering. In addition, denying reality does not change reality—and no reality can be changed until it is first accepted.

Reflect on the following quote: "The secret of change is to focus all of your energy, not on fighting the old, but on building the new" (Millman 2006). What do you think?

Chapter 5

Short-Term Coping for Trauma

By now, you have heard repeatedly that trauma forces us to extremes. Our fight-or-flight response to danger or crisis is like throwing down the accelerator, while the freeze response is like slamming on the brakes. To either fend off or escape a situation that is life-threatening or that greatly exceeds our own strength requires superhuman energy. This energy comes in the form of powerful chemicals such as adrenaline, cortisol, and dopamine. These chemicals empower us to act in ways that would not be possible under normal circumstances.

When the accelerator does not do the trick (fight or flight), the next best option is to slam on the brakes (freeze). But if tremendous energy is released through fight or flight, just imagine how much energy must also be expended in order to counteract or contain all of that adrenaline, cortisol, and dopamine. Remember that with the trauma response, we slam on the brakes while the accelerator is still pedal to the metal. The freeze response is no passive endeavor!

Once both pedals have been hijacked, someone who has been traumatized ends up with two polar responses to life: either overreacting or underreacting—or both. While both overreacting and underreacting are highly adaptive ways of dealing with extreme situations, they are not effective ways for dealing with the rest of life. Our patterns of either overreacting or underreacting (or both at the same time) often cause many more issues than the actual situation that triggered us. Remember the driving analogy? If you are careening down the highway and just randomly pounding the accelerator or slamming on the brakes, your driving style itself is now what's dangerous!

By now in this book, you have also learned that DBT was designed to reconcile polarities: in other words, to forge a middle path between two extremes. Trauma-focused DBT, in particular, is a unique adaptation of original DBT to provide a middle path between the extremes caused by trauma. In this chapter, we will focus on *distress tolerance*, which refers to short-term coping in the moment. Distress tolerance is the middle path between overreacting and underreacting.

There are two definitions of distress tolerance. One definition is surviving the moment without making it worse. In other words, distress tolerance is not necessarily about making a situation better. Why not? Well, for a couple of reasons. First, you cannot make a situation better while you are still actively making it worse. And that's exactly what overreacting-underreacting behaviors are doing. And second, it's precisely your attempts to make the situation better that are actually making it worse! In other words, your "solutions" to the problem are often much more problematic than the problem itself.

Think of distress tolerance as damage control, containment—or what the mental health field likes to call *harm reduction*. Distress tolerance skills are not designed to solve all the world's problems; they are simply short-term coping skills designed to stop the bleeding. The idea is to replace impulsive, reckless, self-injurious, addictive, or suicidal behaviors (in other words, any behavior that will cause even more of a crisis) with more effective coping strategies.

Another definition of distress tolerance is turning unbearable pain into bearable pain. In other words, distress tolerance is not about taking away pain (since that is impossible, as we learned in the previous chapter). Instead, distress tolerance is all about finding different ways to relate to your pain so that it becomes more manageable to deal with.

In summary, distress tolerance is basically a collection of coping skills. As you will learn in this chapter, both the body and the mind are coping machines. You just need to learn how they work! You will also learn a wide variety of specific coping behaviors.

Coping with the Body

No matter how poor or rich you think you are, there is one resource you always have with you at all times—your body. In the following paragraphs, you will learn specific ways to use your physical body as a coping device.

Self-Soothing with the Senses

In a previous chapter, we discussed the importance of mindfulness of your body as an essential starting point for healing from trauma. In particular, we discussed the five senses as a great way to get started with mindfulness practice, and especially mindfulness of the body. Now that you have learned to become more mindful of your five senses, you can also co-opt them as a powerful coping mechanism. In fact, that's what all of distress tolerance boils down to: using mindfulness as a way to cope.

One way to use your body to cope is by identifying something from each of your five senses that will have an immediate calming, grounding effect on you: something you can look at, something you can listen to, something you can taste, something you can smell, and something you can feel with your skin. Once you have identified at least one coping mechanism for each of the five senses, there are three more steps to take:

1. Find a way to have immediate access to each of these activities throughout your day.

2. Incorporate these items into your daily schedule, so that you are engaging your five senses whether you are triggered or not.

3. Practice visualizing each of these experiences. That way, in the event you cannot access one of these items for whatever reason, you at least have the activity stored in your memory bank.

TIPPing the Balance

Since trauma (and trauma reminders) will cause you to either overactivate or underactivate your body, sometimes you will need to cope by relaxing your body, and sometimes you will need to cope by engaging your body. Over the next few paragraphs, you will learn the TIPP skill to mobilize the body and the REST skill to calm the body. Even though they seem like opposites, these strategies are similar in that both are ways to use the physical body to cope.

These skills are also similar in that both tap into the mind-body connection. Because of this connection, one of the quickest ways to change your emotional state is to change something in your body. TIPP refers to four ways of "tipping" your body chemistry in order to quickly shift your mood: Temperature, Intense physical activity, Paced breathing, and Progressive muscle relaxation (Linehan 2015).

Changing your temperature is easy. Drink something hot. Drink something cold. Take a hot shower. Take a cold shower. Turn the thermostat up. Turn the thermostat down. You get the point. Changing the temperature is probably one of my favorite DBT skills, and I use it every single day. For most of the day, I alternate between sipping ice-cold water and steaming hot coffee or tea. I also love to take boiling hot showers. And when I'm stressed while driving (especially when I'm stuck in traffic), I crank up the air conditioner to full blast.

In fact, I learned to cope by changing my temperature long before I knew anything about DBT. There was a time in my twenties when just about everything in my life was out of control. I knew I desperately needed to cope, so I got a membership at a local gym—but I rarely went there. The reason I chose this particular gym was because that membership gave me unlimited access to the pool, sauna, and Jacuzzi of a local hotel. Every time I needed one of my coping sessions, I went to the hotel and simply rotated between the pool, sauna, and Jacuzzi for about an hour, or until I felt better. I would leave my temperature-changing sessions a completely new, recharged human. Now just to be clear: there was absolutely nothing I changed in my life…except my temperature! And yet, that simple change alone was enough of a reset for me to face the myriad of challenges assaulting my life.

Intense physical activity refers to any exertion that gets your heart to pump, your blood to circulate, and your brain to release those beautiful, blissful endorphins. Runner's high is real. If I go for several weeks without a runner's high, I feel it all over my mind and body. But don't worry, you don't need to actually run anywhere to get a runner's high. Just get your body in motion doing *something*. The human body was never designed to be as sedentary as it has become in modern times.

Paced breathing refers to deep belly breathing. You probably know the basics: Inhale through your nose, exhale through your mouth. Inhale slowly and exhale even more slowly (if possible, twice as long). Use your diaphragm to breathe, not your chest muscles. When you are breathing correctly, you will notice your abdomen expand like a balloon as you inhale and deflate when you exhale. We will talk more about breathing later in this chapter.

Progressive muscle relaxation refers to systematically tightening, then relaxing various muscle groups throughout your body. You can tighten and then release each respective muscle group in succession. Or you can tense your whole body all at once and then sequentially relax one muscle group at a time. Something else you can try is doing your paced breathing and progressive muscle relaxation at the same time. Here's how it works: as you inhale, tighten your muscles, and as you exhale, relax your muscles (Linehan 2015).

Here's the beauty of the TIPP intervention: each of the four skills is effective all on its own, and many times you will be able to tip your body chemistry (and therefore shift your mood) with just one of the four. But if you can combine the skills, all the better. In fact, there are many activities in which you can accomplish all four at the same time (such as swimming, dance, or yoga). My personal favorite way to do a full TIPP is by going for long bicycle rides.

Find Some REST

As the name implies, and in contrast to the previous intervention, REST—**R**estrictive **E**nvironmental **S**timulation **T**herapy—is all about relaxing your body. The idea is to eliminate as much ambient activation as possible (such as noise, light, smell, and pressure) as a way to quiet the body, which in turn will help quiet the mind. The mind is constantly processing, analyzing, organizing, storing, or discarding the never-ending barrage of sensory input. If we decrease sensory input, we can also reduce our mental workload. This could include taking a warm bath in the dark with your phone in another room, engaging in intentional meditation, or taking a nap (Speer 2023).

Heart-Focused Breathing

Like other skills in distress tolerance, heart-focused breathing is very simple. Here's how to do it: Focus your attention on the area of your heart. Imagine your breath is flowing in and out of your heart or chest area, while you intentionally breathe a little slower and deeper than usual. It's really that simple!

Let's explore why such a simple intervention is so effective. First, the heart is surrounded by the lungs, and these two organs are in constant communication with each other. The lungs are the first organ to receive blood from the heart, and the heart is the first organ to receive oxygen from the lungs. Therefore, these two organs constantly affect each other. If one organ is off, the other will be off as well.

As you've read throughout this book, when all is calm and well, the entire body enjoys the gentle oscillation of a fast-slow rhythm. Remember the driving analogy? Remember that the SNS is like an accelerator and the PNS is like the brake? The two organs that are probably most affected by both systems are the heart and lungs. No organ follows the fast-slow pattern more than the heart. And no organ is more affected when that pattern is disrupted. When all is calm and well, the heart beats in a rhythm that is consistently fast-slow, fast-slow, fast-slow. Anything other than this pattern both reflects and causes a lack of balance throughout the entire nervous system.

For example, when we are anxious, the heart deviates from this pattern by only beating fast. When we are depressed, the heart strays from this pattern by only beating slow. When we are angry, the heart veers from this pattern by going completely haywire—in other words, the rhythm (or rather, arrythmia) becomes unpredictable. That's why finding ways to quickly restore the heart to its natural fast-slow default pattern can be a game changer (Childre et al. 2000).

In addition, the heart is an extremely intelligent organ. It is constantly monitoring the quantity and quality of oxygen it receives from the lungs. If the heart detects inadequate levels of oxygen, it starts to panic and beat faster. Why? Because the heart knows nothing in the brain and body can function without oxygen. Without oxygen, everything will start to shut down in minutes. Therefore, the heart starts to frantically pump the little bit of oxygen it detects as quickly as possible. But each time it does that, it sends intense warning signs to the brain: Danger! Danger! Danger! This only further exacerbates the panic cycle (Childre et al. 2000).

Not only do the heart and lungs have a really tight relationship, but so do the heart and the brain. These two organs are also in constant communication. However, unlike the relationship between the heart and lungs, the relationship between heart and brain is much more one-sided—but not in the direction you would think. For every nerve connection between the heart and brain, *four* of those connections go from heart to brain, and only *one* goes from brain to heart! Therefore, the heart wields tremendous influence over the brain. If the heart is out of whack, the brain will be out of whack, and soon your entire body will be out of whack (Childre et al. 2000).

All of this explains why heart-focused breathing is so effective. As you do your paced breathing, especially while focusing on your chest, more oxygen is transported to your heart. And as more oxygen arrives, it has a calming effect on the heart; regardless of its current rhythm (or lack of rhythm), the heart starts to resume its default setting of fast-slow, fast-slow, fast-slow. This in turn signals to the brain that all is well. And once the brain knows that all is well, the rest of your body will relax too (Childre et al. 2000).

Take at least one week to practice your heart-focused breathing, even if for only five minutes a day. Once you are in the habit of focusing on your heart as you do your breathing, there are more interventions you can add to the mix. Take an entire week to practice each of these interventions:

1. Practice heart-focused breathing while imagining your favorite place, activity, or memory. Notice the positive emotion associated with this experience. Pay particular attention to where you physically notice that emotion in your body.

2. Next, practice heart-focused breathing with that emotion present in your body. If you need to imagine your favorite place, activity, or memory to access that emotion, no problem. But eventually, try to get to the point where heart-focused breathing is automatically associated with that positive emotion. Reaching that point may take lots of repetition.

3. As you do your heart-focused breathing, imagine that you are radiating that positive emotion toward someone you love.

4. As you do your heart-focused breathing, imagine that you are radiating that positive emotion onto a mirror and back to yourself.

5. Continue to do heart-focused breathing as part of your normal daily routine, whether you feel triggered or not. But then when you are triggered, be quick to use heart-focused breathing as one of your first interventions. Heart-focused breathing is especially effective for panic attacks.

6. Once you are really advanced in the skill of heart-focused breathing, consider trying this next intervention. As you do your heart-focused breathing, imagine that you are radiating that positive emotion toward someone you cannot stand—maybe even someone who has hurt you. The point of this exercise is emphatically not to excuse or condone what that person did to you, but rather to decrease the sense of distress you feel whenever you are reminded of that person and the harm they caused.

Coping with the Mind

Both the mind and body are very powerful coping machines. You have just learned a variety of ways of using your own physical body to cope. And why not? You always have your body on you! Now you will learn a few ways to cope with your mind. And why not? You always have your mind on you as well. You will learn three examples of what the mental health world calls *imagery*, or visualization.

Containing Your Trauma Memories

The container exercise is invaluable for trauma work. If you are currently in therapy for trauma, you may have encountered this exercise. Its purpose is to help you "contain" trauma memories so that you do not feel overwhelmed by them. Since PTSD consists of intrusive thoughts and memories of the trauma, it is extremely helpful to learn to feel some level of mastery over these intrusions.

Here's how it works. Imagine any sort of container. This could be a physical container, such as a chest, vault, safe, or trunk. This could also be any sort of electronic or virtual container, such as a computer file, cloud storage, flash drive, or secret account. Regardless of what you choose, you are the only human who has access to this container, the only one with the key, the combination, the password, or the secret code.

Practice depositing anything in your mind that is too distressing into your imaginary container. And if you need to put your container into another container, or bury it deep in the ground, that is completely fine. You can be as creative as you want! Since you are the only one with access to your container, only you have control over deciding if or when to open it.

Your therapist may guide you through this exercise to contain other trauma memories to help you focus on just one memory at a time. Your therapist may also lead you through this exercise to contain an entire session, so that you do not have to think or worry about what was discussed in session during the rest of the week.

Here's an example of the container exercise in action. Bethany, a forty-two-year-old woman who received a PTSD diagnosis after a lateral collision with a drunk driver, was flooded with memories of the accident anytime she got into a car. After months of physical therapy she was physically able to drive again, yet she was psychologically unable to do so. When she was introduced to the container exercise, she remembered she had a special shoebox she had decorated when she was a waitress, where she kept all of her tips. She decided to bring her shoebox with her the first time she felt ready to go on a practice drive. Anytime she recollected something about the accident, she imagined herself depositing the memory into that special box, which helped her drive again.

Your Safe Place

Think of a setting that for you would be the most secure, most beautiful, most tranquil place imaginable. This could be a well-known location, a secret location that only you know about, or a completely imaginary location. For many people, their safe place is somewhere in nature: a beach scene, a mountaintop, a waterfall in the middle of a forest…whatever invokes a sense of serenity for you.

After you identify your safe place, immerse yourself in every sensory detail possible. What do you see in your safe place? What do you hear? What do you smell? What can you feel with your skin? Is there a taste associated with your safe place? Take a moment to mindfully savor each of these details. The more sensory information you can visualize, the better.

Now focus on your emotional state. What positive emotions are invoked as you relish your safe place? And most importantly of all, where in your physical body do you notice that positive emotion? In your chest? Your stomach? Your head? Congratulations…you have just learned that your "safe place" is right in your own body—at all times!

If your safe place also happens to trigger negative emotions (such as sadness or loneliness), you may need to find a different safe place. There is nothing wrong with negative emotions, and we need them just as much as we do positive emotions. But there will be enough negative emotions with trauma processing. The whole point of the safe-place exercise is to use your own mind and body as a resource to quickly access positive emotions, especially when you need them the most.

Riding the Wave

This coping skill is all about visualizing your intense feelings (either emotions or urges) as a wave, and then learning to interact with them the same way you would deal with a real wave. If you are at the beach and a big wave is coming, you always have a couple of options. One option is to simply get out of the water, if you have enough time. But if that is not possible, another option is to just ride the wave. Yes, it will feel uncomfortable. Yes, it will feel like you are losing control. But what you do not want to do is fight the wave. That will only make matters worse!

When people panic at the beach, their first instinct is to control the wave by fighting it—kicking and thrashing. The problem is that you cannot control a wave, no matter how much you kick and thrash—but a wave can certainly control you! Here's the paradox: the more you try to control a wave, the less control you actually have, and the more *you* are the one who gets controlled. And if a wave really controls you, you might even get caught in the undertow, which is a really scary experience—not to mention dangerous.

All of these concepts apply to intense feelings (both emotions and urges). Sometimes if you notice an intense wave coming, you can simply get out of the situation that is causing the wave. But if you cannot, your next best option is to simply ride the wave. Yes, you will feel uncomfortable. Yes, you will feel like you are losing some control. But just like a real wave, you cannot control feelings anyway. And just like a real wave, the more you try to control feelings, the more they will control you.

And just like people try to control a real wave by kicking and thrashing, people try to control their intense feelings through judgments. You may think, *I should not feel this way. This is stupid. I hate depression.* And if you judge your feelings too much, you just might end up in the psychological undertow, which will drag you through all kinds of emotional rocks and cognitive seaweed. Think about it: if you are angry, and you judge yourself for being angry, you may just feel angry at the anger, or guilty about the anger, and then anxious about the guilt…

Your anger problem just got even worse—not better! When you are caught in the psychological undertow, negative emotions both amplify (increase in intensity) and multiply (increase in number). That's why it's always better to ride the wave than to fight it.

Acting Opposite

In the previous paragraphs, you learned to imagine your intense feelings (either emotions or urges) as if they were waves, and then you learned to visualize riding out those feelings just like you would surf a real wave. You especially learned *not to fight the wave*. But what if that wave is a tsunami? You certainly cannot fight it…but you also cannot surf it! So now what? *Acting opposite* is an extremely effective skill when the waves are simply too dangerous for surfing.

Before we dive into how this skill works, let me provide some basic background. As you've already read, we all have intense feelings (emotions and urges) that come and go in waves. Often we can learn to surf those waves. But sometimes these emotions and urges feed off each other, causing both waves to go even higher, all while creating even more waves of their own. The result? We end up with a psychological tsunami!

How does this happen? Intense emotions are often associated with intense urges. For example, feeling depressed is, by definition, associated with urges to withdraw, isolate, sleep beyond what your body needs, overeat, and ruminate about death. And guess what? The more you withdraw, isolate, sleep too much, overeat, and ruminate about death, the more depressed you will feel! In other words, the more you experience some intense emotions, the more you feel the intense urges that go along with them. And the more you act on those urges, the more you feel the intense emotion. This can be a dangerous vortex. This is no longer a surfing wave. This is a wave in which you *must* act opposite!

Acting opposite means doing the opposite of what your urge is telling you to do. So for example, instead of isolating, reach out to your besties. Instead of oversleeping, set a firm curfew and wake up to an alarm. Instead of overeating, follow a meal plan with balanced portions. Instead of ruminating about death, plan a dream vacation. And so forth. The more you act opposite to your intense urges, the less intense—and more manageable—they become.

There are many ways to act opposite to intense, destructive urges. You can act opposite with words: if you feel like cursing at someone, give them a compliment instead (or at least compliment someone else). You can act opposite with your body: if you feel like clenching your fists and giving someone the finger, relax your body and give a friendly wave. You can act opposite with your behaviors: if you feel like bingeing on junk food, hit the gym instead. You can act opposite with emotions themselves: if you feel really sad, watch a hilarious movie that will make you laugh. You can even act opposite by simply visualizing the opposite of your urge.

Acting opposite is a simple skill to understand but extremely difficult to apply. Why? Because nobody wants to do what they don't want to do! Remember willfulness versus willingness from the previous chapter? Willfulness refers to doing whatever you want (such as acting on intense urges) even if you only make matters worse, especially for yourself. Willingness, in contrast, refers to doing whatever it takes to get the job done, whether you like it or not. In other words, it takes willfulness to keep acting on destructive urges even when you already know it's not going to help. On the flip side, it takes a heavy dose of willingness to try the opposite of what you feel like doing.

And of course, trying any new behavior (such as learning to skate or drive a stick shift) never feels natural at first. That's okay. You've likely heard the expression "Fake it till you make it." It's completely okay if acting opposite feels a little fake at first (or even a lot). That's why it's called *acting* opposite!

...And Even More Coping Strategies

Now that you have learned to cope with your body (using the TIPP skill), cope with your mind (using the container skill), and cope with your behaviors (by acting opposite), let's review some additional tried-and-true coping strategies that fall under those three categories:

Journaling. This skill refers to any kind of written expression....and doesn't even have to be verbal. You may prefer to draw or scribble.

Memorizing. Commit to memory your favorite quotes, lyrics, prayers, poems, or passages from sacred literature. Use phrases that you know by heart as your personal mantras, especially when you are triggered.

Helping others. Volunteering can be a powerful way to take your mind off your stressors. You'll feel productive helping someone else. However, if you are already codependent (that is, you have a pathological need to be needed), then maybe you should act opposite and do self-care instead.

Triggering a different emotion. Do something to automatically trigger a different emotion from the one you are feeling. Ideally, this will be a positive emotion, but this skill can still work by triggering a different negative emotion. For example, watching a horror movie can trigger feelings of terror, which may give you a break from depression.

Using humor. Watch something that will make you laugh. Laughter is associated with every positive neurotransmitter in the human brain: dopamine, serotonin, endorphins, and oxytocin. No psychiatric medication can compete with that! Laughter really is the best medicine (Yim 2016).

Making a gratitude list. Make a list of all the things you are thankful for and then count your blessings!

Praying or meditating. Take some time to pause and reflect on the spiritual dimensions of life.

Working on one thing at time. Make a list of everything that needs to get done, prioritize the list, and then work on *one thing at a time!*

Taking a minivacation. Go to the movies, go for a walk, treat yourself to a nice meal out—or whatever break you need to take—until you are in a better frame of mind. Do something to pamper yourself. You deserve it. Or at the very least, you need it!

Smiling. If you cannot literally produce a full smile, then don't fret—try at least a partial smile! Due to the mind-body connection, any change in facial expression will start to trigger a change in mood.

Looking back or forward. Think of a time in the past when you were not dealing with this issue, or a time in the future when you will no longer be facing this particular challenge.

Self-validating. Remind yourself: It is okay to feel this way. It is normal to feel this way. This feeling will eventually pass.

The Coping Card

Now that you have learned a wide variety of coping strategies, you need to commit to using them. One way to make sure these various skills get applied is to create a coping card. Of course, nowadays there are a gazillion ways to have electronic reminders and notifications, especially through smartphone applications. However, it is still a really good idea to have a tangible reminder of your favorite coping skills, one that you can loop on your key chain, tape to your mirror, or carry in your purse. But regardless of whether your coping card is hard copy or virtual, these same basic principles apply:

- Since you will not always be in your Balanced Mind, you need to have a backup. Your coping card can be that backup. Make sure all your coping resources are easily accessible. If you can't find your coping card, that means you have lost *both* your minds...which no one can afford to do!

- Remember, all of these coping strategies work for someone, but none of these strategies work for everyone. Be patient with yourself as you learn and practice these various skills. If one skill is not your thing, simply move on and be willing to try another one. That's precisely why there are so many options. In fact, think of all these distress-tolerance skills as a long buffet table for you to choose from.

- Just because you now have a coping card does not mean you will always want to use it. When you least want to use it is precisely when you need it the most! (Remember the acting opposite skill?) Therefore, another feature you should consider including on your coping card is a simple pros-and-cons chart. In fact, make two of them. First, make a list of the pros and cons of using one of your coping skills. Next, make a list of the pros and cons of defaulting to whatever your typical reactions are. The next time you are triggered and feel tempted to slide back into old habits, take a quick peek at your pros-and-cons charts and see if that helps you make a better decision.

- Finally, think of an effective coping card as a living document, in both senses of the word. First, an effective coping card is a living document in the sense that it may very well be the lifeline that keeps you alive, especially if you are feeling suicidal. Second, an effective coping card is also a living document in the sense it is never set in stone. The more you try out and practice various coping skills, the more you will learn what works (or does not work) for you. Therefore, your coping card will always be a work in progress.

In this chapter, we covered the topic of distress tolerance, which refers to short-term coping—surviving the moment without making it worse. You learned a wide variety of coping strategies with a wide variety of applications. For example, you learned that sometimes effective coping might mean mobilizing your body, while at other times it might require relaxing your body. On some occasions, effective coping might involve engaging your five senses, while on other occasions, it might include reducing sensory stimulation. You even learned that some forms of coping might work better for smaller waves, but other forms of coping might be better suited for tsunamis.

Since trauma forces us to the contradictory extremes of either too much or too little, it is no surprise that effective coping would also seem paradoxical. If you are walking a tightrope and you start to falter toward the left, you will need to make rightward-leaning corrections to nudge you back to the middle. Or if you start to waver toward the right, you will need to make leftward-leaning adjustments to inch you back to the same centerline.

But regardless of how you have lost your balance, and regardless of which skill is best suited in any given moment, all distress-tolerance skills have these two characteristics in common: they all require mindfulness, and they are all designed to bring you back to the middle path of balance.

Chapter 6

Long-Term Balance for Trauma

In the previous chapter, we covered the topic of distress tolerance, which refers to short-term coping—surviving the moment without making it worse. But what about long-term change? That's where emotion regulation comes in. In contrast to distress tolerance, emotion regulation refers to an entire lifestyle adjustment that will support healthier and more balanced emotionality. These two concepts—distress tolerance and emotion regulation—are intricately connected. Once you have more effective patterns of short-term coping, and once effective coping becomes part of your daily life (whether or not you are triggered), you are already on the path to long-term change. In short, distress tolerance lays the foundation for emotion regulation—which is the focus of this chapter.

So far in this book, you have learned that trauma refers to anything that assaults the nervous system enough to result in a long-term reset of both the sympathetic (accelerator) and parasympathetic (brake) branches of your nervous system. This new baseline results in a series of reactions, responses, and behaviors that are either too much or too little. Trauma-focused DBT offers a middle path between each of the extremes caused by trauma.

In a previous chapter, you learned about the Thinking Mind, the Feeling Mind, and the Balanced Mind, which is a combination of both (yet another dialectic). The Thinking Mind is verbal (like lyrics) while the Feeling Mind is nonverbal (like music); however, the Balanced Mind is both (the entire song).

Clearly life, and especially trauma, can knock both the Thinking Mind and Feeling Mind out of whack, which ultimately results in a Balanced Mind that has lost its balance. This is especially true in light of the negativity bias that we learned about in chapter 2. For example, the Thinking Mind may either overthink (obsessive rumination) or underthink (impulsive decision making)—or both. In addition, the Feeling Mind may either overfeel (emotional overwhelm) or underfeel (emotional numbness)—or both. Furthermore, dysregulation in the Thinking Mind triggers reactivity in the Feeling Mind, and vice versa.

Think of mindfulness as the main tool for accessing and bolstering the Balanced Mind. After all, you will certainly need mindfulness to know what you are thinking and feeling in the first place. Remember, mindfulness is the middle path between overawareness (hypervigilance) and underawareness (dissociation). When you are either hypervigilant or dissociative, you do not have an accurate read on your thoughts and feelings.

Think of distress tolerance as the main tool to recalibrate an unbalanced Balanced Mind as quickly as possible. Remember, distress tolerance is the middle path between overreacting (classic fight-or-flight responses) versus underreacting (classic freeze response). When you either overreact or underreact, once again you do not have an accurate read on your thoughts and feelings. Think of distress tolerance (effective coping) as applied mindfulness to get you back into a Balanced Mind state.

Both the Thinking Mind and Feeling Mind are truly amazing. And despite all the hype on how different they are, they actually share some quite similar functions. For example, the Thinking Mind is wired to help us connect, communicate, motivate—both ourselves and others. And how does it accomplish that? With words. Words are an incredible tool (understatement here!) that enable you to connect with others *and* connect with yourself; to communicate with others *and* communicate with yourself; to motivate others *and* motivate yourself.

But guess what? The Feeling Mind is also wired to help us connect, communicate, and motivate—both ourselves and others. And how does it accomplish that? With emotions. Emotions are also an incredible tool (another understatement!) that enable you to connect with others *and* connect with yourself; to communicate with others *and* communicate with yourself; to motivate others *and* motivate yourself.

Clearly, we need both tools, and therefore we need to take care of them, just like we do with any tool. Even once we are in a Balanced Mind state, we need to actively (and *pro*actively) cultivate wholesome habits to ensure both a healthy Thinking Mind and a healthy Feeling Mind. Dialectical thinking is the path to developing a resilient Thinking Mind. If you can train your Thinking Mind to think more like the old Chinese farmer from chapter 2, you are well on your way to fostering healthy thought patterns. So how do you cultivate a healthy Feeling Mind? Well, that is what this entire chapter is about. In fact, since by now we have all been inspired by the Chinese farmer, let's continue the theme of cultivation.

Cultivating a Healthy Feeling Mind

The secret to maintaining a healthy Feeling Mind is really as simple as this: treat your emotions the same way you would treat flowers. Throughout this chapter, we will use an extended garden analogy to learn five basic emotion regulation skills. Point for point, each way that you would take care of a garden of flowers is also the way you need to care for your garden of emotions.

Let's assume you have a garden of flowers. Would it make any sense to blame, shame, control, coerce, or manipulate your flowers? How about yelling and screaming at them? Or ignoring them? Or burying them deep underground? Of course not!

Emotions are just like flowers. If those strategies would not work for flowers, then why would they work for your emotions? What emotions need most of all is to be cared for. By the end of this chapter, you will be a much better gardener. In particular, you will learn how to (1) plant the right seeds, (2) check the soil, (3) do some weeding, (4) get some pest control, and (5) fertilize.

Planting the Right SEEDS

The first thing you need to do in a real garden is plant the right seeds. For example, if you want a garden of flowers, then please do not plant vegetables! The same applies to your emotions. In this case, planting the right seeds means taking care of your physical body. The SEEDS acronym stands for Symptoms, Eating, Exercise, Drugs, and Sleep.

Symptoms. Do you have any aches and pains? Is there anything going on in your body that requires medical attention?

Eating. Are you getting enough to eat? Are you eating too much? What is your diet? Are you getting enough nutrition?

Exercise. Are you engaging in enough physical activity?

Drugs. Are you taking the prescribed medications you need for your body to function? Are you ingesting other chemicals that were not prescribed?

Sleep. Are you getting enough shut-eye? Do you follow a sleep schedule?

As explained in the previous chapter, humans have a very strong mind-body connection. What happens in one directly affects the other. If something in your body is out of whack, your emotions—if they are doing their job—will surely let you know. Therefore, the first thing you need to do to take care of your emotions is to take care of your body.

Unfortunately, due to the freeze response, people who have experienced trauma become quite good at *not* knowing what is going on in their bodies. As you tune into your body, you will become more aware of the adjustments you need to make in order to feel better, both physically and emotionally. I often ask clients to provide a quick SEEDS report at the beginning of a session. I always reassure them that there is no such thing as a *bad* SEEDS report; any SEEDS report is a good one, since the whole point of this intervention is to start paying more attention to what is going on in your body.

Greg's Story

Greg is a thirty-two-year-old truck driver who was chronically abused as a child. He has a variety of trauma symptoms, including panic attacks, fits of rage, and irritability. Greg takes great pride in his job hauling large loads across the country.

He also has some chronic health issues. He is moderately overweight with chronic back pain. In addition, he chain-smokes all day while consuming a constant flow of coffee, energy drinks, and other caffeinated beverages with high sugar content. His only intake is whatever fast food or junk food he picks up at truck stops. After a long day on the road, Greg tries to unwind in the evenings over a few beers, but struggles to get to sleep and stay asleep.

What did you notice about Greg's SEEDS? First, the obvious: He has chronic back pain; his eating habits are less than ideal; exercise is not part of his life; he has lots of chemicals passing through his body; and he doesn't get enough restorative sleep between rides. But do you also see how each of these domains affects each of the others? For example, his weight, caffeine intake, and chronic pain are certainly not conducive to a good night's rest. And do you see how unhealthy patterns in each of these areas are certainly not going to help him stabilize his emotions?

That's why at the beginning of every session, Greg was asked to provide a quick rundown of each of these areas: symptoms, eating, exercise, drugs, and sleep. Over time, he started to become more aware of how these domains all affected each other, and how they impacted his emotions. Greg eventually realized that when he started to make some basic lifestyle changes in these areas, he started to feel much better—both physically and emotionally. Greg was learning to plant the right SEEDS. By taking care of his physical body, he was also taking steps to stabilize his emotions.

What seeds are you planting in your garden of emotions? What is *your* SEEDS report?

Checking the Soil

Something else every gardener knows is that you need the right soil for the right plants. After all, a tropical palm tree needs a different type of soil than a desert cactus. The same is true for your emotions. Emotions will react to whatever information they have, regardless of whether or not that information is accurate. Of course, emotions always respond best when they are grounded in the right information.

The purpose of this exercise is to use your Thinking Mind to make sure your Feeling Mind is grounded in the best available information. Here are ten simple questions you can start asking yourself whenever you face a triggering situation:

1. What are the facts of the situation?

2. What do I know to be true and what do I know to be false?

3. What information am I missing?

4. What is the worst-case scenario?

5. On a scale of 0 to 10, how likely is the worst-case scenario?

6. Is the worst-case scenario a matter of life and death?

7. How can I cope with the worst-case scenario?

8. What is the best-case scenario?

9. What is the most likely scenario?

10. How can I cope with the most likely scenario?

When facing a triggering situation, you first and foremost need to make sure you know the facts. The facts of a situation refer to whatever can be verified and confirmed. Sometimes we invest more emotional energy in conjecture or speculation about things we don't even know for sure, while neglecting what we do know for sure. As you identify the facts of a situation, you will start to realize some of what you are reacting to is either false or missing information. Reacting to erroneous information will obviously not make matters any better. And reacting to missing information can also create quite a stir, for two reasons.

First, psychologists have long noticed that the brain tends to focus more on incomplete tasks than completed tasks. This is called the *Zeigarnik effect*. For example, servers at restaurants tend to remember customers who do not leave tips much more than customers who do (MacLeod 2020). Think of the last time you took a big test. Afterward, what did your mind fixate on more: the forty-five questions you nailed, or the five you weren't so sure about? Probably the five you weren't so sure about. Or think about the last time you fired off five urgent text messages. What did your mind obsess about more: the four texts that were answered, or the one that wasn't? This is the Zeigarnik effect in action. The brain will endlessly perseverate over missing data points, or what some psychologists call unfinished business.

In fact, the brain hates missing information so much that it has a simple solution to fill in the gaps—just make it up! As previously explained, the brain is a puzzle-solving machine. The brain is designed to take a gazillion data points and quickly organize them into some semblance of a logical, coherent package, such as an idea or perception or memory. But sometimes the brain doesn't have all the information it needs to complete the picture, so it fabricates whatever data is missing and then proceeds to complete the picture anyway. This is a process called *confabulation*, and it is one reason why eyewitnesses of the same car accident will sometimes "remember" contradictory details (Kopelman 1987).

In short, instead of automatically defaulting to the Zeigarnik effect (in which you obsess about missing information) or confabulation (in which you just fabricate information), it is much better to intentionally and consciously identify the missing pieces.

Do you remember the negativity bias you learned about in chapter 2? Well, when you are not grounded in the facts, but instead default to conjecture, speculation, and even outright fabrication, that does not exactly help the negativity bias—which doesn't even need help in the first place. Once the negativity bias is activated, of course you will start to dread the worst-case scenario. That's kind of what the negativity bias is, by definition. It's okay; we all go there. Thankfully, when you name it, you tame it. In more scientific terms, when you describe your worst-case scenario with language, you are helping your brain connect the left and right hemispheres (Thinking Mind and Feeling Mind).

Here's another exercise to fortify the connection between the two hemispheres even more: on a scale of 0 to 10, quantify the probability of your worst-case scenario. The key to this step is not necessarily coming up with an absolutely accurate, scientifically precise probability—but simply to further engage the Thinking Mind. If you are already dreading a worst-case scenario, don't worry; you don't need to activate the Feeling Mind—it's already on! By describing the worst-case scenario with words and then going a step further to analyze it with numbers, you are well on your way to merging the two minds… which is one step closer to the Balanced Mind.

Here's another good question to ask yourself at this point: is your worst-case scenario a matter of life and death? Obviously, some situations really are a matter of life and death, such as terminal illness, a fatal accident, severe domestic violence, or a deployment to an active war zone. When a situation is truly life and death, ignorance is bliss for only so long—and then it really is better to face the facts as they are. But many worst-case scenarios that we portray for ourselves are not matters of life and death, and that is good to know as well.

Let's assume your worst-case scenario is not truly a matter of life and death. If that's the case, then do not try to convince yourself that your worst-case scenario is no big deal. Instead, simply ask yourself: what skills have I already learned to deal with this worst-case scenario? There is a time and place (usually after the fact) to refute, dispute, challenge, or correct an inaccurate, irrational, or illogical worst-case scenario. But that time and place is usually not when you are in the middle of an intense situation!

In fact, what happens when you dread something and someone else tells you, "Don't worry about that. You're overreacting. This doesn't even make sense"? When in the history of "don't worry" did anyone ever stop worrying...just like that? On the contrary, when we hear statements like this, we do not feel heard or understood—which causes us to worry even more! So instead of risking even more negative self-talk or self-invalidation, simply remind yourself that even if the worst-case scenario is true, you now have the tools to face it.

Clearly by now you know what your worst-case scenario is. So now it's to time to ask yourself, *What is the best-case scenario?* And then, once you have identified the two extremes (worst-case scenario on one end and best-case scenario on the other), you now have a wide-open field between those two end zones to ask yourself, *So what is the most likely scenario?* You certainly have the prerogative to divert all of your emotional energy into the extremes (either worst-case or best-case scenarios), but wouldn't it make the most sense to invest your energy into the most likely outcome? (By the way, did you just notice a reincarnation of TOM from chapter 2?) Now that your

Thinking Mind and Feeling Minds are back on speaking terms, and now that your dialectical juices are flowing, you are clearly in a much better position to make a Balanced Mind decision.

Check the soil in your garden of emotions. Are you grounded in the right information?

Weeding Your Garden

Here's another secret every gardener knows: even if you plant the right seeds in the correct soil, other plants will somehow magically sprout! Of course, we all know those plants to be weeds. The same applies to your emotions. In this case, weeds represent misguided notions we have about emotions themselves. We all have our personal theory of emotions. We get our ideas about emotions from our parents, our culture, and our experiences. Unfortunately, not all beliefs about emotions are completely accurate. Since trauma is an extreme situation that triggers extreme emotions, people who have experienced trauma are especially vulnerable to developing a skewed view of emotionality.

Take a look at the following very common "weeds." Do you recognize any of them? What would be healthier, more accurate statements to replace these unwanted plants? We rarely just come out and use these exact words, but often, what we say implies one or more of these assumptions. I will help you out with the first four, and then I will provide four more common misconceptions about emotions that you can practice weeding out on your own.

Weed #1: "I should not feel this way."

This belief assumes that there is a right and wrong way to feel. While there may be a right or wrong way to behave, emotions are simply messengers conveying information. Think of it this way: Is it possible to be both happy and sad at a funeral? Is it possible to be both happy and sad at a wedding? Which of these emotions are "correct"? Or are there valid reasons to have any of those emotions?

Let me give you a personal example. Several years ago, my mother-in-law unexpectedly died on the way to the hospital two weeks before the wedding of her youngest daughter. And to make this situation even more complex, she was the event planner for the wedding. Can you imagine the very mixed emotions we all experienced at both the funeral and the wedding? Was a part of us happy at the wedding? Of course. Was a part of us very sad at the wedding? Of course! Do you see how illogical it would have been for us to judge ourselves about our hodgepodge of emotions?

Weed # 2: "Only weak people talk about emotions."

Actually, it takes a lot of courage to be honest, vulnerable, transparent, authentic, and genuine about your emotions. If anything, we hide our emotions when we do not feel strong enough or safe enough to share them. While there may be a time and place to limit the full expression of emotions, talking about them is much more a sign of strength than weakness. For example, talking about emotions requires both the left and right hemispheres of the brain to be connected, not to mention both the prefrontal cortex and limbic system. Since when is using your entire brain a sign of weakness? On the contrary, research shows that we make our best decisions when we use our entire brain (Pham 2004).

Weed # 3: "Painful emotions are dangerous and destructive."

It is always good to distinguish between emotions and behaviors. Can behaviors be dangerous and destructive? Absolutely. But we need to always remember that emotions are simply the messengers, not the enemies. As you read in chapter 3, pain is a signal that something is wrong. In other words, the entire purpose of pain is to get your attention. Also recall from the beginning of this chapter that one of the purposes of emotions is to communicate. Now put both of those of together: the purpose of painful emotions is to communicate to you (and to others) that something is wrong and therefore, requires your attention. When you ignore your painful emotions, they only increase in volume. Why? Because that's their job! It is always much better to listen to your painful emotions when they whisper. And that way, maybe they won't have to yell so much.

Weed # 4: "Becoming emotional means losing control."

The main problem with each of these beliefs is that they are presented as absolutes. Is it possible to be emotional and lose control? Yes. Is it also possible to be emotional and *not* lose control? Yes. Is it also possible to not be emotional and not lose control? Yes. Is it even possible to not be emotional but lose control anyway? Also yes. Each of those scenarios is possible!

Probably the main reason we believe this assumption is because when we become emotional in front of other people, we start to feel self-conscious, and therefore we feel like we are losing control. I know that for me personally, when I become emotional by myself, I do not feel like I am losing control at all. But as soon as I become emotional in front of just one other person, I do.

Let's return to the wedding example I mentioned a few paragraphs ago. I was asked to offer a few words at my sister-in-law's wedding. As I shared a few thoughts, I briefly mentioned my mother-in-law. Of course I teared up and could not talk for about a minute. I became very self-conscious and felt like I was losing control. Here I was, in front of this large group of people at a wedding, and I am supposed to be saying something…and I can't talk! But think about it this way: is not being able to talk for a minute really losing control? Hardly. In fact, the world would be a *much* better place if we all randomly observed a minute of silence.

The real risk for losing control is not having *enough* emotions rather than the other way around. Consider this: Our jails are full of people with a mental health condition called antisocial personality disorder. People with this disorder have demonstrated behaviors that are so out of control (including homocide) that their best currently known prognosis is to be incarcerated for years on end—sometimes for decades, and sometimes for life. What causes these behaviors? Do these individuals lose control because they have too many emotions? No! The reason for these behaviors is because they *lack* basic emotions such as compassion, remorse, and empathy. So I tell my clients, "I'm not concerned that you have too many emotions. I would be much more worried if you did not have enough!"

Here are four more fairly common weeds that many of us find in our garden of emotions from time to time.

- "Emotions are stupid and pointless."

- "Negative emotions are caused by a bad attitude."

- "Other people know what I should be feeling better than I do."

- "The only way to deal with painful emotions is to ignore them."

Based on everything you have so learned so far in this book, reflect on the following questions: What about these assumptions is incorrect? What would be a healthier and more accurate belief about emotions?

Check your garden of emotions. Did you find any weeds? Do you need to do some weeding?

Controlling the Pests

Want to know another gardening secret? A garden does not just have internal threats (the weeds). There are also external threats... pests! In order to protect your garden, you must have a plan for pest control. The same concept applies to your emotions. Life is full of pesky problems. When we don't have a plan to deal with these problems, our emotions quickly become overwhelming. In this case, pest control refers to your ability to be an effective problem solver. Every single day, get in the habit of addressing each of your problems with this pest-control plan:

1. Define the problem.

2. Brainstorm possible solutions.

3. Eliminate solutions you are not yet willing to try.

4. Identify one solution you are willing to try.

5. Identify possible obstacles to your solution.

6. Come up with a plan to address each obstacle.

7. Try out the solution you selected.

8. Evaluate the outcome. Was it effective? What could be improved?

9. If necessary, ask someone else to help you with your solution.

10. If necessary, try another solution.

Let's explore each of these steps in a little more detail. First, remember the *one thing at a time* skill from the previous chapter? That applies here. Think of all the deadlines, commitments, issues, dilemmas, and challenges in your life right now, and pick just *one* to work on—not all five hundred! Next, find someone you trust (for example, a spouse, friend, parent, religious leader) and start to brainstorm possible solutions to this particular situation.

FYI...I like to abbreviate "brainstorm" as BS. (Like I tell clients, everything is fair game at this point, since it's just BS anyway.) After you and your accomplices are done brainstorming, the next step is for you (just you, not anyone else) to go through your list and start crossing off any BS that you do not want to try. That's right, you read that correctly. When we try to implement a solution that we are not ready for or we do not agree with, we tend to make excuses and end up not doing it anyway—so we might as well just save time and get it out of the way. But you still need to choose at least one of your BS's!

It would be great if we could just stop the process here. You've identified a solution to your situation. But if you are anything like me, life tends to get in the way of my solutions (even the best ones). That's why the very next step is to identify all the possible obstacles to your solution, and then the following step is create a plan for overcoming each of those obstacles. *Now* you are ready to give this solution a whirl. After you have implemented your solution, reflect on how it went. Was it effective? Why or why not? Is there anything that could be improved?

If your solution was effective, great! And if not, well, that is simply part of life. If your solution did not go as well as you had anticipated, it might mean that you just need to try it again. Or it could mean that maybe you need some extra help from other people to implement your solution. Or it might even mean that maybe you need to try one of those BS's that you crossed out in Step 3!

Were you able to find any pests in your garden of emotions? How did it go with pest control?

Fertilizing

Now that you've provided the right conditions for your garden (by planting the right seeds into the correct soil), and now that you have protected your garden from both internal and external threats (weeds and pests), there's one final step: fertilizing! In fact, you are going to fertilize your garden with a powerful compound: ABCD. In order to maintain healthy, balanced emotions, you will need to sprinkle your daily routine with the following chemicals:

Add positives. Do not just wait for something positive to happen or not happen. Make sure you have at least one positive experience every single day! Since trauma can result in more negative emotions, fewer positive emotions, and emotional numbness, it is especially important to fertilize your life with positive experiences.

Build mastery. Every single day, do something that helps you feel productive and constructive—in other words, anything that gives you a sense of satisfaction or accomplishment. Since trauma can cause feelings of powerlessness, or what psychologists call learned helplessness, or an *external* locus of control, it is especially important to fertilize your life with experiences that help you feel competent—what psychologists call a sense of self-efficacy or an *internal* locus of control.

Cope ahead. Don't just wait for the next crisis before you decide to cope. Cope now, whether you think you need it or not. Integrate your favorite coping skills from the previous chapter into your daily routine. Make coping your new normal—it's just how you do life, regardless of whether you feel triggered in the moment. The more you proactively cope as part of your new daily routine, the less triggered you will be in the first place, the less impact your triggers will have on you, and the quicker you will rebound when you are triggered. In other words, proactive coping builds resiliency. And if you know of a specific upcoming stressor, definitely start coping now. Instead of catastrophizing, which will only make your anxiety worse, why not practice, rehearse, and role-play your skills ahead of time? Even when it is not possible to use a specific coping strategy for whatever reason, at the very least visualize doing the coping skill anyway. Since trauma causes you to be reactive to triggers (when it's already too late), it is especially important to fertilize your life with proactive coping instead.

Do something meaningful. Every single day, do something that gives your life a sense of purpose, something that is consistent with your goals, values, priorities, dreams, plans, or aspirations. Let these things help you decide what to let into your life and what to focus on. Remember, the entire purpose of DBT is to build a life worth living. That is the whole point of everything you have already learned in this book, and will continue to learn.

Maria's Story

Maria is a twenty-five-year-old female from Honduras with a long history of trauma in both her home country and Mexico, including sex trafficking. She is currently in therapy to treat symptoms of trauma and anxiety. Though her therapy sessions, Maria has learned to plant the right SEEDS by taking care of her physical needs; has checked the soil by making sure she is grounded in the right information; has weeded out some faulty beliefs about her emotions; and has engaged in pest control by implementing more effective problem-solving. But she is not done working on her garden of emotions! She now needs to fertilize with ABCD. Here's how she did it.

Add positives. Despite the many challenges Maria is currently facing, she identified the following three positives she can always count on every single day: her morning coffee, talking to her friends, and taking a long hot shower before going to bed.

Build mastery. Despite everything in her life that is currently outside of her control, the following activities provide Maria a sense of accomplishment: practicing her English, gardening, and attending night school to become a hair stylist.

Cope ahead. The first time Maria presented in the clinic was for a panic attack. Maria met with a mental health professional and learned basic coping techniques to de-escalate and restabilize. After having another panic attack two weeks later—and missing a job interview as a result—Maria realized she could not afford to wait for the onset of another panic attack as her reminder to cope. Instead, she needed to cope now and daily. The same exercise she used to recover from her first panic attack (heart-focused breathing, self-soothing with the senses, and imagery) have become part of her new daily routine, whether she feels triggered or not. And if Maria knows ahead of time of a particular stressful event (such as another job interview), she does even more of her coping exercises. In short, coping has become her new normal—her new way of doing life.

Do something meaningful. Maria vividly remembers her first day in the US: confused, disoriented, and unable to communicate. Now that she has been attending English class for about a year, she is not only starting to learn the new language but also meeting other people from all around the world who have shared many of her experiences. Maria has found a tremendous sense of purpose in befriending her class-mates, providing them with a sense of community, and taking them under her wing as they also learn to navigate their new country.

So that's how Maria learned to fertilize her garden of emotions. What is your fertilizer?

Conclusion

So far, everything you have learned in this book has been about self-regulation. You learned about mindfulness as the middle path between overawareness and underawareness; dialectical thinking as the middle path between overthinking and underthinking; distress tolerance as the middle path between overreacting and underreacting; and emotion regulation as the middle path between overemoting and underemoting. That's a lot of ground to cover.

But hang on. This book is not over yet! We have one more extremely important area to cover: relationships. In every single inter-action with another human being, you represent (on average) roughly 50 percent of that relationship. And here's the tricky part: If you do not have the skills to self-regulate, your dysregulation will absolutely impact the relationship. And even if you have learned the skills to effectively self-regulate, you still cannot regulate someone else. So now what?

Chapter 7

Re-Engaging
with Others

By now, you already know the main message of this book: Trauma is an extreme experience that leads to extreme reactions that, over time, result in polarized responses to life that are either "too much" or "too little." That's why someone who has been traumatized ends up with an entire grocery list of contradictory symptoms, such as over-awareness *and* underawareness, overthinking *and* underthinking, overfeeling *and* underfeeling, overreacting *and* underreacting. DBT was developed as a therapeutic skill set to provide a middle path between the paradoxes (or dialectical dilemmas) of life. Trauma-focused DBT is a further fine-tuning of original DBT to address the polarities specifically caused by trauma.

Naturally, trying to go through life with both "too much" and "too little" causes a breakdown in the ability to self-regulate. Remember the driving analogy? If you are driving down the highway, and you randomly floor the accelerator or randomly slam the brakes or do both at the same time, it is not going to be a gentle ride. Your driving style is simply not safe—not for yourself, but also not for others!

You cannot possibly deal with other people effectively until you first find some level of balance in each of these areas. Think about it this way: How can you possibly be mindful of someone else if you are not even mindful of yourself? How can you handle someone else's thoughts, emotions, or reactions if you cannot even manage your own? So clearly you must apply everything you have learned so far in this book if you want to have the skills to deal with other people.

When you lack balance in the other areas addressed in this book, you will naturally have a lack of balance in your relationships as well: either too much or too little—or both at the same time. For example, you may be too aggressive in some areas of your life while too avoidant in other areas. In some aspects, you may be too dependent on others; in other aspects, you may be too independent. Once again, you will need to find another middle path.

So, how do we end up at the extremes again? Remember fight, flight, freeze from chapter 1? That's most of the answer right there. But there's actually a fourth trauma response briefly referenced in chapter 1, which deserves more attention here. As a reminder, a potentially traumatizing situation affects the nervous system in a very specific order:

1. Danger is sensed.

2. Social engagement goes offline (ventral PNS).

3. Danger persists.

4. Fight or flight is triggered (SNS).

5. Danger cannot be mitigated through fight or flight.

6. Freeze response activates (dorsal PNS).

As a review, both flight and flight result from an upsurge in the SNS (the accelerator), while the freeze response follows activation of the PNS (the brake). However, humans seem to have a unique fourth response to ongoing trauma caused by fellow humans: fawning. Fawning occurs when the social engagement system (which is part of the same branch of the nervous system that causes the freeze response) has been hijacked in an attempt to mitigate a human threat.

Instead of fighting the threat, fleeing the threat, or freezing to minimize the damage caused by an inevitable threat, fawning refers to attempts to befriend the threat. That's why fawning is sometimes called the please-and-appease response. Remember the old adage: "If you can't beat 'em, join 'em!"? That's the basic idea behind fawning behavior. You have most likely heard the phrase "people-pleasing tendencies." You may have also come across the term "codependency," in which you have an excessive, unhealthy need to be needed. Both people-pleasing and codependent traits can be signs of fawning. An extreme form of fawning behavior is a condition known as Stockholm syndrome, in which people develop strong fantasy bonds (sometimes including infatuation or seduction) with their abusers (de Fabrique et al. 2007).

Since the social engagement system is much more developed and nuanced in humans than in other animals, it should be no surprise that we see this behavior in humans. While many animals demonstrate submissive, fawning behavior toward superiors (such as the alpha male), this appeasement is more about social hierarchy than about predator versus prey dynamics. In other words, fawning does not seem to be a trauma response in animals, but it certainly can be in humans.

With all human relationships, we have four basic options: we can turn toward someone, turn away from someone, turn against someone, or turn within ourselves. All of these strategies can be appropriate, effective ways of dealing with relationships, depending on the situation. For example, sometimes it is healthy to be aggressive, sometimes it is healthy to be avoidant, sometimes it is healthy to be independent, and sometimes it is healthy to be dependent. And more often than not, it is healthy to be on the spectrum somewhere between those extremes. That's why resilient people know how to use each of these approaches, and also know when to switch from one approach to a different one.

But what if you use only one of these approaches for all situations in life? Or what if the approach you choose for any given situation is not the most effective way to deal with that situation? It is well known within psychology that we tend to project previous relationships onto current relationships. Therefore, an interaction within a present relationship may remind you (perhaps consciously, but most likely unconsciously) of an interaction from a previous relationship, which may in turn trigger a response that is not a good fit for the current situation. This process of transference makes the most complex dynamic in the universe—human relationships—even more complicated!

As a result of trauma, we tend to gravitate toward the extremes of too aggressive versus too passive or too independent versus too dependent, or both. For example, due to the fight responses, we may overlearn the turning-against approach, and therefore become too aggressive. Due to the flight response, we may overlearn the turning-away mode and become too avoidant. Due to the freeze response, we may overlearn the turning-inward strategy and become too independent. And due to the fawn response, we may overlearn the turning-toward style and become too dependent on others. Or you may overlearn all four and become too aggressive, too avoidant, too independent, and too dependent...all at once! Once you understand the fight, flight, freeze, and fawn responses in humans, you now understand why, once again, humans end up at the extremes of either too much or too little.

And so once again, we need another middle path. Regardless of your starting point, the middle path between these various extremes is called *interpersonal effectiveness*. Interpersonal effectiveness is a collection of skills designed to restore balance in relationships. Think of interpersonal effectiveness as basic people skills to better handle all of the drama that goes along with relationships (such as communication, conflict, and compromise)—but in a way that actually meets your needs without having to always resort to one of these extremes.

So why is interpersonal effectiveness so important? Why isn't it good enough for you to just learn to self-regulate, heal from your trauma, and never deal with anyone else for the rest of your life? Well, for starters, that's not very practical. But there is also a clinical reason.

The connection between trauma and relationships is extremely paradoxical. On one hand, so much of what generates trauma within the human race is caused by fellow humans. But on the other hand, we need fellow humans to heal from our traumas. Healing takes place within the context of relationships, not in isolation (which is simply a prolongation of the flight response). Do you see the dilemma? If you have been traumatized, then you need relationships in order to heal.

But because you have been traumatized, you are "allergic" to relationships—you have an adverse reaction to the very "medication" you need!

Of course, we can also be traumatized by nonhuman factors; for example, natural disasters (such as a tornado) or animal attacks (such as a shark bite) or an accident (such as falling off a ladder). However, it is a lot harder to take those sorts of traumas personally. Yes, they happened to *you*, but you probably did not have a deep, mutual psychological connection with the tornado, shark, or ladder. But when we are traumatized by fellow humans, the pain is even more painful. The pain is not just physical but also deeply psychological and spiritual. Whether we are abused by caregivers or assaulted by complete strangers, we are shocked that humans would treat fellow humans in this way. We do not have the same expectations for tornados, sharks, and ladders.

Since so much of trauma comes from fellow humans, and since we also need fellow humans to heal from trauma, we need to learn how to re-engage with other people. And this is not so easy! On one hand, we need to re-engage with other people without getting further re-traumatized in the process. But on the other hand, we also need to re-engage with other people without the defaults of fight, flight, freeze, and fawn. Tricky, right? And that's why we need to learn interpersonal effectiveness.

DEAR Adult

The main tool you are going to learn in this chapter is called DEAR Adult. This collection of skills will help you better navigate relationships by teaching you how to ask, assert, appreciate, and apologize, depending on the situation. Let's start with the DEAR acronym—Describe, Express, Assert, Reinforce—to show how all this works.

Describe. When you need to address a situation with someone, start off by describing the situation itself (and *not* the other person). Introduce the topic, and then stick to the facts of the situation: who, what, when, where. As you describe a situation, it is usually best to avoid the U-bomb as much as possible. The U-bomb refers to overuse of the word "you," which only causes other people to become defensive or to counterattack. As you describe, stay away from opinion or conjecture. Do not speculate, exaggerate, or embellish, which will only compromise your credibility. Instead, be truthful and honest, which will increase your effectiveness.

Express. Now that you have introduced the topic, express how you feel about the situation you just described. It is usually best to express how you feel with "I feel" statements. This shows you are taking ownership of your own emotions, without attempting to project or blame. Once again, try to avoid dropping the U-bomb. This is not about telling off the other person, but rather explaining how you feel about the situation.

Assert. Now that you have described a situation that needs to be addressed, and explained how you feel about the situation, you have provided two layers of context for your request. Before you even make the request, the person knows the situation you are talking about and how you feel about it. So even if they completely disagree with the request you make, at the very least they know what you are talking about and how you feel. This contextualization is critical for effective communication. When you make requests out of the blue, without introducing the topic first, people tend to feel confused, criticized, and attacked. And once again, try to avoid the toxic U-bomb.

Whereas the key phrase for express is "I feel," the key phrase for assert is "I need." The phrase "I need" has a completely opposite effect on people than "you need." "You need" sounds like an aggressive order, which only triggers people to become more defensive, defiant, or deflective. In contrast, "I need" implies a state of vulnerability, which has an endearing effect on people, and puts them in a much better position to hear you out.

Reinforce. In psychology, to reinforce something means to increase a favorable outcome. If you give me ice cream after I eat my vegetables, I may eat more vegetables. In that case, ice cream was the reinforcer. In the real world, to reinforce something means to strengthen it. If a fence is toppling over, it might be reinforced by adding an extra post. Both definitions apply to interpersonal effectiveness.

In particular, there are two things you want to reinforce: the request you just made and the relationship itself. After all, you need the relationship in order to meet your request. The best way to reinforce both your request and the relationship is to explain how what you are requesting is actually what is best for both of you, and therefore, best for the relationship itself. In other words, make sure you frame your request as a win-win proposition.

Here's the main reason that reinforcement is so important: if you skip this step, you run the risk of your entire spiel coming across as "me, me, me." Look at it like this, as if I'm the one practicing this skill: First, I describe the situation—from *my* perspective. Then I express how I feel—from *my* perspective. Then I tell you what I need—from *my* perspective. Even if you are using world-class tact and diplomacy, that's still a lot of me, me, me—which is neither endearing nor convincing. For this to work, that M needs to flip around and become a W...the "me" needs to turn into a "we"! When you frame your request as a win-win, you have just strengthened your request, you have strengthened the relationship, and you have increased the likelihood of a favorable outcome.

Each step in the DEAR sequence is critically important, and trying to dialogue with someone without one of the steps would be like flying a four-engine plane without one of the engines: it may be possible, but not recommended! So before we move onto the "Adult" part of this skill, let's talk a little more about why this specific sequence is so important.

Remember the Thinking Mind, Feeling Mind, and Balanced Mind from chapter 3? If you are really upset with a situation, chances are your Feeling Mind is already activated. Unless it is a life-and-death matter, it is generally not effective to dialogue with someone from your Feeling Mind alone. That's another reason to start off objectively, by describing the situation with just the facts. When you describe first, you are forced to activate the Thinking Mind—*not* because the Thinking Mind is more important, but simply because the Feeling Mind is already on! When you make sure to engage your Thinking Mind by describing the facts, that will also help bring your Feeling Mind down a decibel (or ten) before you express yourself subjectively.

Of course, both describing and expressing are equally important, which is why you do both before moving on to asserting. Remember from chapter 3 that we function the best as humans when both Thinking Mind *and* Feeling Mind are up and running and working together. In fact, that's precisely what we call the Balanced Mind. People are not convinced by the facts alone. People are also not persuaded by emotional reactions. That's why we need a balance. By describing and expressing, you are activating both the Thinking Mind *and* the Feeling Mind, and now you are in a much better position to make a Balanced Mind request as you assert. The reinforcement step also helps you maintain your balance between what you need and what the other person needs.

And speaking of balance, that's what the entire Adult component of this skill is all about. Whereas DEAR refers to the four-step sequence of how to organize your thoughts (what to say), Adult refers to your delivery (how you say it). The Adult Voice is the middle path between two extremes: Child Voice and Parent Voice. Think of the Parent Voice as a long, angry lecture and the Child Voice as a whiny, pouty temper tantrum. (Granted, neither parents nor children get a good rap from this classification scheme.) Using the Adult Voice, in contrast to the two extremes, means communicating in a calm, cool, and collected style. That's when people will actually listen to you, and maybe even take you seriously. Even though the Child Voice and Parent Voice seem like opposites, they are quite similar in that both are equally ineffective (Berne 1996).

It does not matter how perfectly you describe, express, assert, and reinforce; if you are not using an effective delivery, none of that will matter. Communication refers to what we say; metacommunication refers to how we say it. At the end of the day, people will hear and respond to your metacommunication much more than the communication itself.

Matt's Story

Matt is a thirty-eight-year-old veteran who served two tours overseas. He has struggled to reacclimate to some aspects of civilian life, especially his current employment at a small insurance firm. For example, Matt gets easily triggered when his supervisor asks him to take on extra commitments that he was not expecting. When serving abroad, surprise demands from his military superiors were sometimes tantamount to high-risk death missions. So when Matt's boss asks him to complete an unexpected task with an unexpected deadline, he notices his face start to flush and his fists start to clench. He is clearly poised for fight or flight, which was great for combat...but not so much for a cubicle!

Thankfully, Matt was willing to learn the DEAR Adult skill to help structure communication with his supervisor. The next time Matt's supervisor presented him with an unexpected request, here is how Matt applied this skill:

Describe. I have noticed that sometimes this job requires a sudden change of plans. I get it. That's exactly how it was in the military too.

Express. In fact, I think that's probably why I feel so stressed whenever there is an unexpected change. For me, unexpected changes used to be a matter of life or death!

Assert. So that's why it would be really helpful for me to have as much advanced notice as possible whenever there is a potential change in deadline, assignment, customer, or whatever it is.

Reinforce. Not only will that help bring down my stress levels, but I also think it would make me a better employee. I really appreciate working for this company, and so I really do want to be at my best.

Adult Voice. Throughout this exchange, Matt remembered to use his coping skills to stay mindful, grounded, and respectful. For example, he remembered take a few deep breaths while monitoring his tone of voice and body language.

Notice that in this particular example, Matt also used the *float-back technique*, which is especially useful for trauma survivors. For example, not only did Matt describe the current situation, but he also "floated back" and described a previous situation that was also triggering. Matt used the float-back technique again when he expressed why unexpected changes were so stressful for him. By helping both parties understand the connection between the current situation and a previous trauma, the float-back technique provides an extra layer of context for both the speaker and the listener.

Other Versions of DEAR Adult

Now that you have learned the basics of DEAR Adult to assert, it is easy to learn the other versions. Sometimes it may be appropriate to assert your requests, but at other times it may be more effective to ask. When that's the case, simply replace "assert" with "ask." Everything else stays the same (**D**escribe, **E**xpress, **A**sk, **R**einforce) and again, remember to use the Adult Voice!

Of course, relationships will not be very effective or balanced (certainly not very win-win) if you are always the one doing all the asserting and asking. That's why you need yet another version of this skill, one that considers the other person's perspective: **D**escribe, **E**mpathize, **A**ppreciate, **R**einforce.

In this case, *describe* the other person's perspective by summarizing or paraphrasing their key points. Ask the other person: "Did I get that right?" And if you didn't, keep trying until you do! Once you have adequately described the other person's perspective, move on to *empathize*. Instead of expressing how *you* feel (which is what you did in the first two iterations of DEAR Adult), you are going to validate the other person's emotions; for example, "I can understand why you would feel that way. That's how I would feel too!" (Later in this chapter, you will learn more about validation, so please stay tuned.)

Next, explain what you *appreciate* about the other person's perspective. The word "appreciate" has three basic meanings: to understand, to value, and to increase in value. If I appreciate your political opinion, that means I understand where you are coming from. If I appreciate you as a friend, that means I value you. But if my house has just appreciated, it does not have the same value as before—it now has even more! All three definitions apply to effective communication. When you appreciate someone's perspective, indicate that you understand where they are coming from, that you value their perspective, and if possible, try to *reinforce* by saying something that increases the value of their perspective even more. For example, see if you can articulate or even advocate for the other person's perspective even more than they are!

This may seem paradoxical. Why would you ever try to articulate or advocate for someone else's perspective just as much as, or even more than, they are? Here's why: When you do this, the other person feels heard, understood, and affirmed—in other words, safe. This has the effect of lowering their psychological defenses and quieting their limbic system (the reactive, emotional part of their brain). When someone is currently in fight-flight-freeze mode, they cannot hear anything you are saying. But when you show that you truly hear them, you help activate their social engagement system, which allows them to better hear *you* and see *your* perspective.

Since you are human, you will also occasionally make mistakes. You will sometimes do or say the wrong thing (or at the very least, not do or say the right thing). That's when you need another variation of DEAR Adult...this time to *apologize*!

First, *describe* the main points of what happened. Once again, just stick to the facts. Don't be defensive or overly dramatic. Then, as with the previous iteration, *empathize* by validating the other person's emotional response. Next, *apologize*, making certain that your apology is sincere. Even if you are not fully at fault, it is always possible to take at least partial responsibility for something you could have done or said differently. And finally, *reinforce*. In this case, reinforcing involves a behavioral follow-up; you actually need to *do* something to make amends and repair the damage. With DEAR Adult, to apologize, you can think of the reinforcement as restitution of the wrong and restoration of the relationship. As my grandmother (and perhaps yours too) used to say, "Actions speak louder than words!"

Of course, in real life, rarely will you only assert, only ask, only appreciate, and only apologize. A real-world conversation can and should have lots of back-and-forth. While it is helpful to practice and role-play each version separately, eventually you want to get to the point where you can blend each of these skills into a single conversation. Once you are proficient in using DEAR Adult to assert, to ask, to appreciate, and to apologize, you are now ready for DEAR Adult Advanced! This is what an effective, real-world conversation will often sound like: Describe; Express and Empathize; Ask and Assert and Apologize; and Reinforce. And remember to use the Adult Voice!

In some cases, it may be more appropriate or effective to write a DEAR Adult letter. Each component of the acronym can easily be a separate paragraph. For example, start off the letter by describing the situation. From there, move on to either express or empathize or both. Next, proceed to either ask, appreciate, assert, or apologize (or any combination thereof). Finally, conclude your letter by reinforcing the relationship with win-win thinking.

In some cases, you may want to write a DEAR Adult outline to help you organize your thoughts before talking with someone in real time. In other cases, you may want to send your letter as an email, and then offer to follow up later. For some situations, you may want to send your letter and just leave it at that. And for still other situations, you may want to write a letter for your own benefit—and *not* send it. You have options!

Think of the DEAR Adult skills as the foundation for interpersonal effectiveness. Once you are proficient at DEAR Adult Advanced (asking, asserting, appreciating, and apologizing), you now have the tools you need for most interactions. The rest of this chapter will focus on additional tips for fine-tuning the Adult Voice.

Using the Adult Voice to Validate

Clearly the Child Voice and Parent Voice are not terribly validating postures. The Adult Voice, however, is a master of validation! At its essence, to validate someone means to recognize their perspective or experience as legitimate. This means you acknowledge their thoughts, emotions, opinions, and perceptions. Now just to be crystal clear, validation does not mean you necessarily *agree* with someone—agreement and validation are two completely different beasts. It is very possible to validate someone whether you agree with them or not.

Validation has four basic levels. The first level is to be present and mindful. Maybe that seems too obvious, but this is the most important step. We all know it is possible to be physically present without being mentally or emotionally "there." We also know how dismissive it feels talking to someone when their mind might as well be on another galaxy. In contrast, the most validating thing we can do for someone is often to "simply" be a good listener. In many cases, that is the only level of validation we need to provide. In other occasions, being present and mindful is the foundation for additional levels of validation.

Once you are mindfully present with someone, the next level of validation is to *reflect back* what the other person is saying (both verbally and nonverbally). You can reflect back what a person communicates verbally by summarizing, paraphrasing, and asking clarifying questions. You can also reflect back what the other person communicates nonverbally by noticing their body language, facial expressions, and speech patterns (such as volume, speed, and vocabulary) and then mirroring some of these tendencies. For example, if the other person leans forward, that may be your cue to subtly lean forward. If the other person starts to talk louder or faster, maybe that is your cue to subtly increase your volume or speed.

The key here is subtlety—there is a world of difference between mirroring and mimicking. When you truly mirror someone's nonverbal communication, they do not notice it consciously, but it generates powerful feelings of connection, attunement, and empathy. Mirroring is a powerful force. Research has shown that when babies are not mirrored, this lack of reciprocity can have profound negative impacts on their subsequent psychological development (Tronick 2007). In contrast, research has also shown that even in the corporate world, basic mirroring achieves better business results than standard negotiation techniques alone (Peterson and Limbu 2009).

Once you are able to be present and mindful with someone, as well as reflect back both their verbal and nonverbal communication, the next level of validation is to *normalize* what they are saying (both the present and historical context). A great phrase to use when normalizing is to say, "It makes sense that..." For example: "It makes sense you are struggling with this breakup, especially considering the other breakups you've had." In one single sentence, you can normalize both the current situation as well as other prior experiences.

Finally, the highest level of validation is *radical genuineness*. This is when you are direct, open, and honest with the other person. Now of course, you would never want to be radically genuine with someone if you do not already have an established rapport characterized by all the preceding levels of validation. Think of radical genuineness as "speaking the truth in love." On one hand, radical genuineness requires all the previous levels of validation in order to work. But on the other hand, it is also the highest level of validation because you are communicating to the other person that you value their perspective and experience so much that you are willing to provide candid feedback. If a person trusts you enough to the point where it is emotionally safe to provide radical genuineness, then they will trust you even more after you have offered it. They will see you as the real deal (Linehan 2015).

Using the Adult Voice to Negotiate

Earlier in this book, you learned all about dialectics: the ability to see things from multiple perspectives, and even the ability to bring together opposites. That's what effective negotiation is all about. However, we cannot possibly negotiate using either the Child Voice or the Parent Voice. Clearly, effective negotiation will only be accomplished with the Adult Voice. Think of the Adult Voice as the spokesperson for the Balanced Mind.

The Adult Voice is mindful. In other words, the Adult Voice is both aware and accepting. For example, the Adult Voice is aware of volume, body language, facial expressions, triggers, timing, and proximity—in both yourself and the other person. In addition, the Adult Voice accepts the other person's wants and needs just as much as your wants and needs.

The Adult Voice also knows how to use distress tolerance skills to self-regulate. For example, the Adult Voice can self-soothe with the senses, engage in heart-focused breathing, and act opposite to ineffective word choices or body language. The Adult Voice additionally knows how to use emotion-regulation skills to stay grounded in the facts and engage in effective problem solving.

The Adult Voice knows how to use dialectical thinking. This voice can think in the middle, let go of the extremes, see things from multiple perspectives, and change its mind when presented with more accurate information. As such, the Adult Voice avoids power struggles and instead seeks a win-win consensus through negotiation and compromise.

The Adult Voice uses *connect talk* rather than *control talk*. Typical forms of control talk include commands, accusations, and blame. You know you are using control talk when you tell other people how they should think, feel, and act. The main problem with control talk is that it doesn't work! Control talk simply provokes the other person to become defensive, retaliate, escalate, or shut down. Ultimately, control talk undermines rather than reinforces the relationship.

Connect talk, in contrast, refers to using plural, collective, or inclusive words such as "we" and "us," as opposed to making "me" versus "you" distinctions. Connect talk values the relationship more than being right or winning the blame game. Research shows that connect words are more effective at persuading people than control words (Kehoe 2007).

The Adult Voice knows how to take personal responsibility. For example, the Adult Voice offers to be part of the solution, instead of just blaming the other person or demanding that the other person do all the changing. And finally, the Adult Voice knows how to appear confident without coming across as cocky.

Using the Adult Voice to Compromise

Even with the best of negotiation strategies, compromise can be elusive. Compromise is not always as easy as splitting the difference fifty-fifty. Remember, the whole point of the DEAR Adult skills is to reach a win-win in relationships, a resolution that is optimal for both parties, not to mention the relationship as a whole. That idea is very different from a simple fifty-fifty split. Furthermore, it is very possible for two reasonable people who both value their relationship and each other to still be gridlocked on different positions. Why does that happen, and how do you still move toward a compromise?

Have you ever had the same argument for years or decades, with no resolution? The reason two reasonable people often become gridlocked is because people have different values and priorities, and those values and priorities are often unspoken. Hence, the gridlock. What follows is a very simple yet effective tool for moving from gridlock to compromise (Gottman and Gottman 2015).

Using a separate sheet of paper for each of you, start by drawing two concentric circles., or download the template at http://www. newharbinger.com/55848. In the inner circle, write down your core values regarding the issue. These are the areas you are not willing to budge on, due to matters of principle or priority. In the outer circle, write down the details of the issue you are willing to be flexible with. Once both of you have completed both circles, take turns presenting your "donuts." As the presenter, your job is not to convince or persuade, but simply to explain which areas you can be flexible in and which you cannot. As the listener, your job is not to challenge the presenter, but simply to validate and ask clarifying questions to better understand their position.

In the course of doing this exercise, it is very common for both parties to realize there is enough overlap in the outer circles to work toward a consensus that also honors both inner circles. After respectfully sharing each other's circles, propose a tentative compromise that both of you are willing to attempt, at least on a provisional basis. This agreement is not a sacred binding compact written in blood—simply a trial run.

Congratulations...you have just moved from gridlock toward compromise!

Using the Adult Voice to Act Opposite

Obviously, we do not always use our Adult Voice. Especially when triggered, we all tend to default to either the Parent Voice (yell, scream, berate, lecture) or the Child Voice (whine, pout, sulk, complain). And when this happens, we are now at risk for what researchers have identified as the four most lethal relationship killers: criticism, contempt, defensiveness, and stonewalling (Gottman and Gottman 2015).

When you criticize, you attack a person rather than addressing the situation. Contempt is an extreme form of criticism. Not only do you criticize, but you literally add insult to injury with mockery or sarcasm. Defensiveness is when you make excuses for your actions or deflect the focus away from a critique. Stonewalling is an extreme form of defensiveness, in which your nervous system feels so assaulted that you experience what psychologists call diffuse physiological arousal, which triggers the freeze response. Your face may become blank and your eyes may start to glaze over (Gottman and Gottman 2015).

There are two major problems with criticism, contempt, defensiveness, and stonewalling. First, according to decades of research on married couples, they are literally the biggest predictors of divorce. And second, they all trigger a vicious cycle with ever-increasing intensity and toxicity. For example, criticism by Person A triggers defensiveness in Person B, which triggers even more criticism. Since Person A feels like Person B did not a hear a single thing they just said, they double down with even more rebuke—which, of course, triggers even more defensiveness, and the cycle continues (Gottman and Gottman 2015).

Even worse, once the criticism-defensiveness cycle becomes escalated enough, it morphs into the even more lethal cycle of contempt-stonewalling. Since contempt by Person A is a verbal assault in which Person B feels stuck (no fight-or-flight options), it triggers the freeze response in Person B. But the more Person B freezes up, the more Person A feels dismissed, and so now Person A ups the ante with even more contempt (Gottman and Gottman 2015).

So when you have lost your Balanced Mind, and your Adult Voice is out to lunch, how do you find a path back to sanity? Well, think back to the Acting Opposite skill from the previous chapter.

- Instead of criticizing (attacking the person and dropping the U-bomb), use at least one of your coping skills, and then proceed with a DEAR Adult to ask.

- Instead of defensiveness, use at least one of your coping skills, and then proceed with a DEAR Adult to apologize.

- Instead of contempt, do *lots* of coping (at the very least twenty minutes), and then proceed with a DEAR Adult to assert.

- Instead of stonewalling (and especially if you already have), do *lots* of coping (once again, at the very least twenty minutes) before re-engaging.

Contempt results from a hijacked SNS (the accelerator) while stonewalling results from a hijacked PNS (the brake). Either way, the powerful mind-altering chemicals of adrenaline and cortisol have already been released, and they will need at least twenty minutes to run their course (Gottman and Gottman 2015). Once both of you have calmed down, use your Balanced Minds to figure out which variation of DEAR Adult you need to resume a productive dialogue. And it may well be all of them!

Limits of Interpersonal Effectiveness

One huge caveat before we close out this chapter: There is a limit to what we can accomplish through the use of the various interpersonal effectiveness skills we just discussed. On one hand, there is no end to the core DBT skills (mindfulness, distress tolerance, emotion regulation, and dialectical thinking) you can use in any given situation, regardless of whether the situation involves other people or not. But on the other hand, you can only apply those skills to yourself—you can never force someone else to use their skills. Furthermore, there are some situations you can never change, no matter how many skills you use.

For sure, you are always better off using skills than not using them. And when you use your skills, you also model more effective approaches for other people. But you still cannot make other people learn skills or use their skills with you. This is especially true in abusive relationships. In fact, think of it this way: an abusive relationship is one in which you are still mistreated, no matter how you treat the other person. All the skills discussed in this chapter presume some level of equality in the relationship for the skills to work.

Therefore, it is really important to know that the ultimate goals of trauma-focused DBT are to help you heal from trauma and to build a life worth living. The goal is not to become a skills master for its own sake, and certainly not to set you up for more trauma. The skills taught in this chapter—and throughout the book—are simply the means to an end. Especially with relationships, you need to make a decision: to keep using skills to try to improve a relationship or to leave the relationship. It is beyond the scope of this book to make those decisions for you. But if that's a decision you are facing right now, please seek out clinical and spiritual consultation.

Chapter 8

Building a Life Worth Living

Even though the label PTSD is a modern term, the concept of trauma itself is ancient. For example, in Homer's epic saga *The Iliad*—written approximately 2,800 years ago—the Greek poet recounts the horrors of the Trojan War. And in his follow-up epic, *The Odyssey*, Homer narrates the homeward journey of Odysseus, one of the heroes of *The Iliad* who survived the war. But instead of surviving the war and simply moving on with the rest of his life, Odysseus faces one challenge after another. Each obstacle he encounters represents the ongoing effects of trauma—the war is long over, and yet life is still a battle (Shay 2003).

In modern warfare, many terms have been used to describe the aftereffects of surviving intense, ongoing trauma. For example, survivors of the Civil War were said to have "soldier's heart." The men fighting in World War I came home with "shell shock," while World War II veterans were diagnosed with "battle fatigue." When it was obvious that a large percentage of American soldiers returning from Vietnam were not the same people as before the war, researchers started to rigorously investigate the predictable symptoms and patterns that we now know as post-traumatic stress disorder (Chekroud et al. 2018).

The Hero's Journey

The modern concept of PTSD accurately encapsulates the negative effects of trauma that have been observed for millennia. However, poets, philosophers, and theologians alike have also documented another related yet distinct theme throughout recorded human history: people do not only *suffer* from trauma but also learn and grow from it. As a result, their lives are often deeper, richer, and more meaningful after a trauma than before. For example, Odysseus did not just suffer from the Trojan War, but he also became a stronger and wiser person as a result of it. In fact, the name "Odysseus" in Greek comes from a verb which means "to be angry, to hate, to be grieved"—speaking to his trauma symptoms. And yet, in the first line of *The Odyssey*, following the Trojan War, he is referred to as the "man of many turns." In other words, trauma was not the only turn taken in his life. Precisely as a result of the trauma, his life took many more turns—most of which demonstrated his increased strength and resiliency (Magers 2024).

The book of Job is widely regarded as one of the best literary masterpieces in history, and is still read and studied throughout the world thousands of years after it was written. In this book, a man loses everything—his family, property, and health—and yet, in the end, he lives a better life than he started with (Scheindlin 1999).

In fact, this theme is so universal throughout world literature that Joseph Campbell, one of the greatest literary thinkers of modern times, outlined the predictable steps experienced by heroes of literature from all times and cultures. He called this progression the "hero's journey." This journey invariably includes facing a life-altering trauma, accessing superhuman resiliency to survive, and ultimately emerging with a special gift that is then used to enrich the entire community. As a result of this transformation, not only does the hero benefit from the trauma, but so does everyone else (Campbell 2014).

In short, great thinkers throughout history have endlessly noted both the negative and positive effects of trauma—but historically, the emphasis tended to be much more on the ultimate redemptive and transformative role of trauma, rather than the adverse effects alone.

In modern psychology, this emphasis has shifted. Following the Vietnam War, there has been a deluge of interest and research on the negative effects of trauma—a zeitgeist that continues to this day, with no signs of abating anytime soon. The wealth of information we have learned about how trauma adversely impacts the brain and body has been a game changer—we now know exponentially much more about this topic than any previous generation. This paradigm shift has had incalculable influence on policy and treatment, and for the better.

But unfortunately, in our zeal to better understand the negative consequences of trauma, the field of psychology has mostly overlooked the positive upside (Rendon 2015).

Post-Traumatic Growth

Although modern psychology still focuses much more on the negative impact of trauma than the positive, this balance has started to shift in recent decades, as a small yet growing group of researchers have rigorously investigated a counterpart phenomenon now known as post-traumatic growth, often abbreviated as PTG. In stark contrast to our contemporary view of trauma, research originating in the 1980s has consistently demonstrated that half or more of trauma survivors report favorable outcomes as a result of their experiences. While trauma certainly causes intense suffering (by definition), it is capable of producing much more than misery alone. In fact, even though PTSD has been much more studied than PTG, the current research seems to indicate that the latter may be more common than the former (Tedeschi et al. 2018).

Consider this analogy: A brutal earthquake levels a city. Buildings are tumbled, highways are decimated, and major pipelines are burst. Although some parts of the city are more affected than others, the city overall is no longer functioning. What was once a busy and bustling city now lies in ruins and rubble. Now what? There are several basic outcomes:

- The city stays destroyed. It is never rebuilt.

- The city is mostly rebuilt, but there are clearly still signs of destruction. The city is able to function again, but not as well as it used to.

- The city is rebuilt exactly the same way it was originally built. The city is now functioning just as it used to (no better and no worse).

- The city is rebuilt better than it was before the earthquake. In fact, the city is now larger, stronger—and even more beautiful—than its original state.

You'll soon learn about a fifth possible outcome, but for now, let's use this analogy to better understand the concepts of post-traumatic stress and post-traumatic growth, and how these two phenomena relate to each other.

The earthquake represents any traumatizing event—and you are the city. As you learned in the first chapter, for something to be traumatizing, by definition, it must shake you to the core. In fact, trauma permanently resets your entire nervous system, including much of your brain circuitry. Trauma fundamentally challenges your most basic beliefs about yourself, about the world, and about life. In short, trauma significantly alters how you function moving forward. You simply cannot wake up the next day and move on like nothing happened. There is no going back.

Some people never survive a trauma, either physically or psychologically. That is the first possible outcome. The earthquake destroys the city, and the city stays destroyed. Some people are literally killed by a trauma. Other people are left in a comatose state for the rest of their biological life. And some people recover physically but have been so shattered by the trauma that they can no longer function as healthy, independent adults.

However, many people survive the trauma both physically and psychologically and are able to rebuild their lives to an extent, but life is different for them. Every single day, they still live with signs of the devastation (such as nightmares, flashbacks, intrusive memories, patterns of avoidance, or any of the other symptoms mentioned throughout this book). And because of these symptoms, they do not function as well as they used to pre-trauma. This is the second outcome, and represents PTSD.

The third outcome represents recovery from PTSD. The city is rebuilt exactly how it used to be before the earthquake, and eventually resumes its normal pre-earthquake functioning, as if nothing had happened. This seems to be either the implicit or explicit goal of most treatment models, including approaches that were specifically created to treat PTSD; treatment is a success when all the symptoms of trauma have been eliminated, and the person can now live their life as if the trauma had never occurred.

However, there are two major flaws with this treatment philosophy. First, as we learned in the chapter on dialectics, the universe is never the same two seconds in a row. Therefore, it is philosophically impossible to rebuild the same city as before the earthquake. In fact, this is exactly what people who have survived a trauma will tell you: your life will never be the same again—it is impossible to live life as if the trauma never occurred. And here's the second flaw with this treatment philosophy: why in the world would you settle for reconstructing the same exact city when you could build a far better one?

Let's turn to the fourth possible outcome. Let's assume the survivors of the earthquake rally together. They form committees and work teams. They pool their resources. They forge alliances from one end of the city to the other. They hire the best engineers, architects, and construction crews. They resolve to learn from the earthquake and rebuild an even stronger and more resilient city. That is precisely PTG.

All of the energy, coordination, perseverance, ingenuity, fortitude, and mobilization required to survive the earthquake and clear the debris are now precisely the same qualities that allow the citizens to rebuild an even better city. PTG starts off as an instinct to survive and eventually blossoms into an impulse to flourish (Rendon 2015).

So what is PTG exactly? How do we know if we have benefitted from the same trauma that caused us to suffer? The pioneers of the field have identified five key themes that consistently permeate study after study. PTG tends to be reflected in these changes (Tedeschi et al. 2018):

- Increased personal strength and resiliency

- Increased openness to new possibilities in life

- Increased ability to connect with other people

- Increased appreciation for life

- Increased sense of spirituality

What do each of these changes have in common? An increase! In other words, *growth*. While trauma certainly causes destruction and depletion, that does not have to be the final chapter of the saga. Taken together, each of these changes—individually, collectively, and synergistically—culminate in a transformative experience. As a result of PTG, people often become more resilient, more empathetic, more embracing, more connected, and more passionate. People who have experienced PTG are often wiser, more creative, and even more humorous. They have learned to take life seriously—but not too seriously. They often have a greater appreciation for both the fragility and finality of life, and therefore, live life to the fullest, cherishing every moment (Rendon 2015).

People who have experienced PTG also tend to be more dialectical. Whereas untreated PTSD causes a breakdown in dialectics, someone who has experienced PTG now has a fuller, deeper, wiser, and more nuanced view of life (Tedeschi et al. 2018). That person is now much more like the Chinese farmer you read about in chapter 2. Someone who has experienced trauma knows better than anyone that the world can be a dangerous, unpredictable place where bad things can happen for no apparent reason. But someone who has experienced PTG also knows that despite this reality—or perhaps even because of it—the universe also has an instinct for redemption and transformation. When we embrace life—both the good and the bad—life itself knows how to make lemonade out of lemons.

But remember, there a fifth possible outcome for the city leveled by an earthquake. Let's consider that now: The city is rebuilt even better and stronger than the original city (the fourth outcome)—and at the same time, there are still some remaining signs that there was indeed a severe natural disaster at some point in the history of this city (the second outcome). Do you see how the fifth option is a dialectical hybrid of the second and fourth outcomes?

For example, maybe a beautiful new worship center is built, but people still nostalgically reminisce about the quaint old chapel where they were married. And perhaps there are some areas of the city that could not be rebuilt at all. However, these are precisely the sectors that have been converted into parks, museums, and monuments. While there are still visual reminders of the destruction caused throughout the city, these reminders no longer trigger terror, but instead serve to remind the citizens of their strength, their resiliency, and their resolve to continue to make the city even better than before.

In other words, both PTSD and PTG can exist at the same time! This is a really important concept to keep in mind, especially as you review everything you have learned in this book. Do not think that PTG is synonymous with never again having a single symptom of PTSD. And do not think of having PTSD symptoms as a barrier to PTG. The more you apply the interventions you have learned so far in this book—plus one more that is coming soon—the more your symptoms of PTSD will decrease and the more you will continue your trajectory toward PTG. So if you continue to experience some symptoms of PTSD along the way, that's okay. In fact, those symptoms may be precisely what is inspiring you to continue your hero's journey of PTG (Rendon 2015).

While it is possible to have one without the other, PTSD and PTG are *not* opposites. In fact, they both flow from the same source: trauma. On one hand, if what happened to you is not severe enough to rock your world and shake you to the core, you will not be traumatized, since your current world remains intact (and therefore, no PTSD). And on the other hand, if what happened to you is not severe enough to rock your world and shake you to the core, you will also not experience PTG, for the exact same reason—your current world was not assaulted to the degree of needing to change. Just as trauma results in altered brain functioning, so does PTG. In fact, the brain alterations that result from trauma are precisely what prompts the brain to reorganize in new ways and patterns, which it would not have done without the trauma!

PTSD results because life can no longer be the same—for the worse. And PTG results because life can no longer be the same—for the better. Either way, there is no going back to a life before the trauma.

In the first chapter, you learned what causes post-traumatic stress. In this final chapter, you have learned what causes post-traumatic growth. Hopefully both perspectives have helped you better understand and appreciate the skills and concepts throughout this book. Each of the major themes expounded up to this point (mindfulness, radical acceptance, dialectical thinking, distress tolerance, emotion regulation, and interpersonal effectiveness) are not only the path to healing from trauma, they are also signs of growth—a richer and more fulfilling life.

In other words, each of these concepts is both the means and the end, both the journey and the destination. It takes each of these skills to clean up the rubble left by the earthquake of trauma. But now that you have cleared the debris, it turns out that the same skills are also what it takes to rebuild a better city than you started with. Without the trauma, you most likely would not have felt any need to master the skills that lead to a much more meaningful and vibrant life.

Hopefully the concept of radical acceptance in particular makes much more sense now. It is far easier to radically accept a trauma when you also understand the concept of PTG.

Telling Your Story

There's one more key ingredient—essential to both decreasing PTSD *and* increasing PTG—that needs to be addressed before we close out this book. And that is telling your story. There are endless ways to tell your story, not to mention countless models of trauma processing that will help you tell your story in the way that works best for you. It is not the role of trauma-focused DBT to tell you the best way to tell your own story, but rather to encourage you to tell it in a way that helps you feel understood, honored, and validated.

You can tell your story by writing it. You can tell your story by singing it. You can tell your story by acting it. You can tell your story through dance, canvas, or sculpture. You can tell your story using Word, Excel, or PowerPoint. You can tell your story on television, radio, or social media. You can write a book or blog. You can tell your story through massage, eye movements, and body scans. Your can tell your story through hypnosis, imagery, and guided visualizations. There are a myriad of options for telling your story, and there are many highly trained and competent trauma therapists who would welcome the privilege of guiding you through your hero's journey.

Many, if not most, ways of telling your story would benefit from the support of a professional trauma therapist. But there is one form of trauma processing you can get started with whenever you feel ready, either on your own, with a professional counselor, or a safe friend. And that is to *write* the story of your trauma.

As you write your story, if you feel triggered or overwhelmed at any point, just stop, take a break, engage your favorite coping strategies, and then resume whenever you feel ready.

Include as many of the following components as possible:

- Make sure your trauma story has a beginning, middle, and end.

- Recount the specific events that transpired in chronological order.

- What was happening before the trauma started?

- What happened while the trauma was occurring?

- Describe in detail what each of your five senses experienced during the trauma.

- Describe in detail what you felt physically during the trauma.

- Described in detail what you felt emotionally during the trauma.

- Describe in detail what you were thinking during the trauma.

- What happened after the trauma stopped?

- At what point after the trauma did you start to feel safe again—if ever?

Nobody else needs to read what you wrote if you do not feel comfortable sharing. However, one of the most powerful ways to heal from your trauma and shift into growth is having the opportunity to tell your story to a trusted individual who can listen compassionately, honor your story, provide authentic validation, and be able to absorb your story without getting triggered or overwhelmed themselves.

Now let's move on to the second part of this writing exercise. Think about everything you have learned throughout this book, and especially in this chapter about PTG. When you feel ready, reflect on the following prompts:

- How have your values or priorities changed?

- How have you become stronger or more confident?

- How has your life gained more of a focus or mission?

- How have you become a better problem solver?

- How have you become more accepting of life?

- How have you learned to appreciate the little things in life?

- How have you become more compassionate?

- How have your relationships become closer or deeper?

- How have you grown spiritually?

- What new interests or opportunities have you pursued?

For your ease in writing, you'll find both of these lists available for download at http://www.newharbinger.com/55848. Some of the prompts may not apply to you, and that's okay. If you can reflect on *any* of them, you are already showing signs of PTG!

Summing Up

As you recall from the first chapter, trauma is an extreme situation that forces people to the extremes. In particular, trauma causes a permanent reset to both the SNS (accelerator) and the PNS (brake), which in turn culminates in a series of responses that are either too much or too little, leading to a myriad of paradoxical PTSD symptoms, such as hypervigilance versus dissociation, rumination versus impulsivity, aggression versus passivity. The skills learned in this book are designed to provide a middle path between these extremes. In other words, each of these skills helps restore the nervous system to healthier and more stable patterns of accelerating and braking, as opposed to constantly pounding the two pedals—and often both at the same time. This restoration of the nervous system can greatly reduce the majority of PTSD symptoms, *but not all of them.*

Even once the nervous system has regained its balance, you may still experience the intrusive or recurring symptoms of trauma, such as nightmares, flashbacks, and spontaneous recollections of various details of the trauma. What is causing those symptoms, and what can be done about it?

As you may also recall from the first chapter, there's a tiny part of the brain called the thalamus whose main role is to integrate all the senses (except for smell) and transmit that information as a complete package to the other parts of the brain for further interpretation. However, during moments of danger or crisis, the thalamus goes offline, which means the brain does not get a chance to integrate the sensory information as single, coherent package. This is problematic, because the brain only knows how to file integrated memories into long-term storage. That explains why, following a trauma, you are left with fragments of what happened (something you saw, something you heard, something you smelled) which endlessly rattle around in your short-term memory—as if the trauma happened yesterday. These memory fragments quickly pop to the surface as vivid recollections. You may also experience even more intense reenactments of the trauma as nightmares (if you are asleep) or flashbacks (if you are awake). Either way, the brain is trying really hard to connect the dots and close the loop to get these memories into long-term memory—but it simply can't, no matter how hard it tries (Van der Kolk 2014).

And as you also recall from the first chapter, there is another tiny part of the brain called the amygdala, which is the alarm center in the brain. The amygdala is associated with both fear and anger. Fear tells us something bad *may* happen, while anger tells us something bad already *did* happen. Both emotions inform of us of risk or danger, whether perceived or real. But here's the deal with the amygdala: It's super good at remembering past threats, but it has no current sense of time. So anything occurring in the present that even remotely resembles something that happened in the past will trigger the amygdala to mobilize intense fear and anger—even if the trauma reminder is completely benign. You think you are reacting to a current situation (and you are, to an extent), but you are mostly reacting to a previous situation which the current situation reminded you of, probably at a deeply subconscious level (Van der Kolk 2014).

The science behind both the thalamus and the amygdala explains why telling your story is so critically important to healing from trauma and shifting into post-trauma growth, for several reasons. First, when you tell your story—and especially by including as many details as possible—you are helping your brain integrate everything that happened to you into one single, coherent narrative. Remember, this is what your thalamus failed to do. In other words, you are helping your brain put together the pieces of the puzzle, so that your brain can finally store the trauma in long-term memory. This will help your trauma memory become just like any other memory. It's still there if you really want to remember it—but not constantly present in the front of your mind (Tedeschi et al. 2018).

Second, when you tell your story—and especially when you sequence it in chronological order, with a clear beginning, middle, and end—this also helps your amygdala develop a better sense of time and context. So even though telling your story will most likely bring up many of the original emotions (which were probably frozen by the freeze response), your amygdala will start to learn that the circumstances that originally assaulted your world are no longer in play (Rendon 2015).

Third, when you tell your story, you are also making meaning out of what happened to you. You start to realize that the trauma you experienced both released and fostered incredible resiliency in you. You learn things about yourself and others that perhaps you could not have learned otherwise. Precisely because of the trauma, you have developed greater empathy, passion, openness, authenticity, appreciation, and wisdom. Your life may even have more direction and focus than it ever did. And finally, telling your story helps you realize that your trauma narrative is an important part of your overall life story—maybe even the most important part to you—but there is much more to your story than just the trauma. In fact, the final chapters of your story have not even been written yet!

In summary, original DBT was designed to teach skills to help restore your nervous system to a middle path of health and stability. This will help reduce many of your trauma symptoms—but not the symptoms related to memories of what happened. That's precisely why in trauma-focused DBT, telling your story is such a big deal. As you just learned in the preceding paragraphs, telling your story not only helps resolve your remaining trauma symptoms by providing integration for the thalamus and context for the amygdala, but telling your story is also high-octane fuel for post-trauma growth.

Final Thoughts

Throughout this book, you have been on quite the hero's journey. Along this journey, you have acquired a vast assortment of superpowers: dialectical skills, mindfulness skills, acceptance skills, coping skills, and people skills. Each of these skills is designed to restore balance to your life, to provide a middle path between the extremes caused by trauma. The power of these skills is inestimable. Because of these skills, you will not only be able rebuild the city ravaged by trauma but also build a much better and stronger city than you started with.

But even the best superpowers are useless unless wielded by a superhero. Along this journey, you have tapped into superhuman strength that you never knew was there—and developed even more resiliency than you started with. You have come to realize that the strength you have found truly is *super*human—above and beyond your own natural capacity. That's because the resiliency you have discovered and cultivated comes not only from your own untapped reserves but also from the strength of others, the strength of the universe, and the strength of your higher power.

When trauma strikes, we are leveled, reduced to ashes, knocked out, and brought to our knees. We hit our rock bottom. We meet our ground zero. In short, we do not start our journey feeling like a hero. But this journey is the only way that heroes are made.

Let's conclude this book with a simple mindfulness exercise from chapter 3 to honor the journey you have been on.

I am…

Here now…

Accepting…

Noticing…

Committing to…

What I care about…

The ultimate goal of trauma-focused DBT is not just to get out of hell or heal from PTSD. The ultimate goal is to build a life worth living. You've got this!

References

Baldwin, J. 1962. "As Much Truth As One Can Bear." *New York Times*, January 14.

Berne, E. 1996. *Games People Play: The Basic Handbook of Transactional Analysis.* New York: Ballantine Books.

Campbell, J. 2014. *The Hero's Journey: Joseph Campbell on His Life and Work.* Novato, CA: New World Library.

Chekroud, A. M., H. Loho, M. Paulus, and J. H. Krystal. 2018. "PTSD and the War of Words." *Chronic Stress 2.* doi:10.1177/2470547018767387.

Childre, D. L., H. Martin, and D. Beech. 2000. *The HeartMath Solution: The Institute of HeartMath's Revolutionary Program for Engaging the Power of the Heart's Intelligence.* San Francisco: HarperSanFrancisco.

de Fabrique, N., V. B. Van Hasselt, G. M. Vecchi, and S. J. Romano. 2007. "Common Variables Associated with the Development of Stockholm Syndrome: Some Case Examples." *Victims and Offenders* 2 (1): 91–98.

Dyer, W. W. 2007. *Change Your Thoughts—Change Your Life: Living the Wisdom of the Tao.* Carlsbad, CA: Hay House, Inc.

Farnsworth, W. 2021. *The Socratic Method: A Practitioner's Handbook.* Jaffrey, NH: Godine.

Firestone, R. W. 1987. *The Fantasy Bond: Structure of Psychological Defenses.* Santa Barbara, CA: Glendon Association.

Frankl, V. E. 1992. *Man's Search for Meaning: An Introduction to Logotherapy.* 4th ed. Boston: Beacon Press.

Gethin, R. 2011. "On Some Definitions of Mindfulness." *Contemporary Buddhism* 12 (1): 263–279.

Gottman, J. S., and J. M. Gottman. 2015. *10 Principles for Doing Effective Couples Therapy.* New York: W. W. Norton & Company.

Hafer, C. L., and R. Sutton. 2016. "Belief in a Just World." In *Handbook of Social Justice Theory and Research,* edited by Clara Sabbagh and Manfred Schmitt. New York: Springer.

Hayes, S. C., K. D. Strosahl, and K. G. Wilson. 2012. *Acceptance and Commitment Therapy: The Process and Practice of Mindful Change.* 2nd ed. New York: Guilford Press.

Heraclitus, and C. H. Kahn. 2008. *The Art and Thought of Heraclitus: An Edition of the Fragments with Translation and Commentary.* Cambridge, England: Cambridge University Press.

Jordan, J. R. 2016. *The Two Arrows of Suffering: A Mindfulness Approach to Suicidality.* New York: Guilford Press.

Kabat-Zinn, J. 2023. *Wherever You Go, There You Are: Mindfulness Meditation in Everyday Life..* 11th ed. New York: Balance.

Kehoe, D. 2007. *Communication in Everyday Life.* 2nd ed. London, England: Pearson Education.

Kershaw, C., and J. W. Wade. 2012. *Brain Change Therapy: Clinical Interventions for Self-Transformation.* New York: W. W. Norton & Company.

Kopelman, M. D. 1987. "Two Types of Confabulation." *Journal of Neurology, Neurosurgery & Psychiatry* 50 (11): 1482–1487.

Kübler-Ross, E. 1969. *On Death and Dying: What the Dying Have to Teach Doctors, Nurses, Clergy and Their Own Families.* New York: Macmillan Company.

Levine, P. A. 1997. *Waking the Tiger: Healing Trauma*. Berkeley, CA: North Atlantic Books.

———. 2010. *In an Unspoken Voice: How the Body Releases Trauma and Restores Goodness*. Berkeley, CA: North Atlantic Books.

Linehan, M. M. 1993. *Cognitive-Behavioral Treatment of Borderline Personality Disorder*. New York: Guilford Publications.

———. 2014. *DBT Skills Training Handouts and Worksheets*. 2nd ed. New York: Guilford Publications.

———. 2015. *DBT Skills Training Manual*. 2nd ed. New York: Guilford Press.

———. 2020. *Building a Life Worth Living: A Memoir*. 1st ed. New York: Random House.

MacLeod, C. M. 2020. "Zeigarnik and von Restorff: The Memory Effects and the Stories Behind Them." *Memory and Cognition* 48 (6): 1073–1088.

Magers, A. 2024. *Odysseus and the Oar: Healing After War and Military Service*. Flower Mound, TX: Dead Reckoning Collective.

McTaggart, J., and E. McTaggart. 2016. *Studies in the Hegelian Dialectic*. London, England: Forgotten Books.

Miller, W. R., and S. Rollnick. 2013. *Motivational Interviewing: Helping People Change*. 3rd ed. New York: Guilford Press.

Millman, D. 2006. *Way of the Peaceful Warrior: A Book That Changes Lives*. Emeryville, CA: H. J. Kramer, Inc.

Mullen, M. 2021. *The Dialectical Behavior Therapy Skills Workbook for Psychosis: Manage Your Emotions, Reduce Symptoms, and Get Back to Your Life*. Oakland, CA: New Harbinger Publications.

Peterson, R. T., and Y. Limbu. 2009. "The Convergence of Mirroring and Empathy: Communications Training in Business-to-Business Personal Selling Persuasion Efforts." *Journal of Business-to-Business Marketing* 16 (3): 193–219.

Pham, M. T. 2004. "The Logic of Feeling." *Journal of Consumer Psychology* 14 (4): 360–369.

Porges, S. W. 2011. *The Polyvagal Theory: Neurophysiological Foundations of Emotions, Attachment, Communication, and Self-Regulation.* New York: W. W. Norton & Company.

Porges, S. W., and S. Porges. 2023. *Our Polyvagal World: How Safety and Trauma Change Us.* New York: W. W. Norton & Company.

Rendon, J. 2015. *Upside: The New Science of Post-Traumatic Growth.* New York: Touchstone.

Reutter, K. 2019. *The Dialectical Behavior Therapy Skills Workbook for PTSD: Practical Exercises for Overcoming Trauma and Post-Traumatic Stress Disorder.* Oakland, CA: New Harbinger Publications.

Ritschel, L. A., N. E. Lim, and L. M. Stewart. 2015. "Transdiagnostic Applications of DBT for Adolescents and Adults." *American Journal of Psychotherapy* 69 (2): 111–128.

Scott, D. E. 2021. *The Interconnected Cosmos.* Stickmanonstone.

Shay, J. 2003. *Odysseus in America: Combat Trauma and the Trials of Homecoming.* New York: Scribner.

Scheindlin, R. P. 1999. *The Book of Job.* W. W. Norton & Company.

Shin, J. Y., S. W. Kim, S. G. Roh, N. H. Lee, and K. M. Yang. 2016. "Congenital Insensitivity to Pain and Anhidrosis." *Archives of Plastic Surgery* 43 (1): 95–97.

Spéer, A. M. 2023. "REST (Restricted Environmental Stimulation Therapy) and the Creative Process." FSU Digital Repository.

Stahl, S. M. 2021. *Stahl's Essential Psychopharmacology: Neuroscientific Basis and Practical Applications*. 5th ed. Cambridge, England: Cambridge University Press.

Tedeschi, R. G., J. Shakespeare-Finch, and K. Taku. 2018. *Posttraumatic Growth: Theory, Research, and Applications*. London, England: Routledge.

Tronick, E. 2007. *The Neurobehavioral and Social-Emotional Development of Infants and Children*. New York: W. W. Norton & Company.

Unthank, K. W. 2019. "How Self-Blame Empowers and Disempowers Survivors of Interpersonal Trauma: An Intuitive Inquiry." *Qualitative Psychology* 6 (3): 359–378.

Van der Kolk, B. 2014. *The Body Keeps the Score: Brain, Mind, and Body in the Healing of Trauma*. New York: Viking Press.

Van Dijk, S. 2009. *The Dialectical Behavior Therapy Skills Workbook for Bipolar Disorder: Using DBT to Regain Control of Your Emotions and Your Life*. Oakland, CA: New Harbinger Publications.

Yim, J. 2016. "Therapeutic Benefits of Laughter in Mental Health: A Theoretical Review." *The Tohoku Journal of Experimental Medicine* 239 (3): 243–249.

Kirby Reutter, PhD, is a bilingual clinical psychologist and trauma specialist who contracts with the United States Department of Homeland Security to provide mental health services to asylum seekers close to the Mexican border. Reutter has presented original research at MIT, delivered a TED Talk on the neurological effects of human trafficking, and provided over one hundred mental health trainings across the continent, including four trainings at military bases. He is author of *The Dialectical Behavior Therapy Skills Workbook for PTSD*.

"Who knew a book about treating trauma could be so enjoyable? This hope-filled and readable book with relatable examples and humor will be appreciated by clinicians, persons who experience trauma, and anyone who encounters life's difficulties. It is full of ways to reverse the neurobiological results of trauma and live a full life. I will be recommending this outstanding book to my colleagues and patients on a regular basis."

—**Lynette Pujol, PhD, MSCP**, clinical/prescribing psychologist, and deputy director of the MS in clinical psychopharmacology program at Fairleigh Dickinson University

"Kirby Reutter simplifies complex neuropsychological terms and theory so that anyone can understand. His reader-friendly voice uses relatable metaphors that empower learning and amplify healing. I highly recommend this book to anyone who wants to know how to regulate a dysregulated nervous system, especially given the overwhelm in today's world. Add this book to your self-help library. It's a necessity for practitioners and self-healers alike!"

—**Karen Possessky, LCSW**, private practitioner and health care ethicist

"*Healing with Trauma-Focused DBT* blends clinical wisdom with real-world practicality. Kirby Reutter offers relatable analogies, hands-on exercises, and personal examples that bring dialectical behavior therapy (DBT) skills to life. His authentic voice and deep expertise make this book both engaging and effective. Whether used alone or with a therapist, it's a powerful resource for trauma survivors and clinicians alike, offering tools to manage emotions and support lasting healing."

—**Sheela Raja, PhD**, clinical psychologist, professor at University of Illinois Chicago, and author of *The Resilient Teen* and *Overcoming Trauma and PTSD*

"*Healing with Trauma-Focused DBT* is a compassionate, evidence-based, and deeply accessible guide for trauma survivors and the professionals who support them. Kirby Reutter bridges cutting-edge neuroscience, polyvagal theory, and the core tenets of DBT with clarity, empathy, and practical guidance. Survivors learn to regulate overwhelming emotions, understand the physiological roots of their trauma, and rebuild a sense of safety and control. This is more than a book. It's a road map for reclaiming one's life after trauma—and a powerful reminder that healing is not only possible, but within reach."

—**Celia Williamson, PhD, LISW-S**, distinguished professor of social work at the University of Toledo, and executive director of the Human Trafficking and Social Justice Institute

"Kirby Reutter brings invaluable experience to this book, emphasizing core Hispanic values such as *familismo, comunidad*, and *resiliencia*. Combining trauma-focused DBT with mindfulness and radical acceptance, it supports healing deeply rooted in cultural strength. By highlighting connection, spirituality, and personal growth, the book offers practical tools that truly reflect our lived experiences. Ideal for those seeking hope and renewal after trauma, it helps readers honor their heritage while guiding them toward a balanced, meaningful life."

—**Maria Puentes, LMHC, BCBA, MCAP**, trauma and behavior specialist, expert in evidence-based clinical interventions, and program director at Mannaba Counseling Center and Training Institute

"Insightful and educational for clinicians and clients alike, this step-by-step guide is deeply compassionate and personable. Kirby Reutter nailed it with his concept of trauma-focused DBT, a natural and vital pairing that will stay with its readers and serve them for years to come."

—**Emma Lauer, LCSW**, psychotherapist, and author of *DBT Skills for Highly Sensitive People*

"Kirby Reutter masterfully walks us along perhaps the most sophisticated circuitry of our universe. He uses modern and century-old vignettes, grabbing our attention, gently teaching us, and holding out hope to tackle what seems impossible. Every day I see what Reutter describes as trauma manifesting as a 'medical disorder with mental health implications.' The book artfully provides clear and direct help to any who have experienced trauma. At the same time, it educates all healers on the journey so many are trying to navigate."

—**Adam Luginbuhl, MD, FACS**, professor of head and neck surgical oncology and microvascular reconstruction at Thomas Jefferson University, and director of Tumor Microenvironment at the Sidney Kimmel Comprehensive Cancer Center

"*Healing with Trauma-Focused DBT* is an outstanding prescription for learning and practicing DBT! This invaluable resource is full of pearls of wisdom. Kirby Reutter does a great job in reviewing theory in neuroanatomy, psychology, psychiatry, medicine, and self-help literature. DBT is an incredible tool for post-traumatic stress disorder (PTSD) and just about all matters in healthy living. It is a pleasure to read, with many useful acronyms and directions for practical application. Indeed, reading Reutter's book made me feel it was DBT Zen."

—**Fernando Guillermo Torres, MD**, child psychiatrist at South Texas Family Residential Center, aerospace medicine specialist, and psychiatrist in private practice

"Kirby Reutter excels at writing in an engaging and informative way, explaining abstract concepts in a manner that draws the reader in. Written with a down-to-earth yet professional voice, *Healing with Trauma-Focused DBT* is an excellent addition to bookshelves at home and in clinical offices."

—**Kristi Baran, LMHC, CADAC - IV**, supervising counselor at Gateway Woods Family Services

"*Healing with Trauma-Focused DBT* is a powerful, practical guide that integrates DBT, polyvagal theory, and trauma research into a clear, accessible, evidence-based approach. Kirby Reutter offers trauma therapists, DBT practitioners, and laypeople real, clinically grounded tools to support lasting healing. Thoughtful, clear, and deeply compassionate, this book advances the field and belongs in the hands of every clinician dedicated to effective, trauma-informed care."

—**Dennis Hannon, PsyD**, CEO of the Center for Psychological Growth and Resilience

"Kirby Reutter has crafted a very readable, thorough, and practical self-help book. He opens with a clear and concise introduction to some of the current thinking in the field of trauma work that helps the reader identify and understand the nature of problems related to trauma. From there, he escorts the reader through a series of skills and practices drawn from DBT that can help them bring a life thrown out of balance by trauma back into balance and then onward to growth, beyond the trauma."

—**Michael Maslar, PsyD**, director of the mindfulness and behavior therapies program at The Family Institute at Northwestern University

"*Healing Autistic Burnout* is a must-read. I especially like how Sharon Kaye O'Connor clearly explains the linkage between societal expectations and masking, which drains our energy and fuels burnout. As a neurodiverse clinician with decades in the field, I still learned a lot—including uplifting, practical strategies like 'dopamine dressing.' Insightful and refreshingly straightforward, *Healing Autistic Burnout* is an invaluable resource for autistic people, families, and professionals."

> **—Joshua D. Feder, MD**, editor in chief of *The Carlat Child Psychiatry Report*; executive medical director at Positive Development; associate professor at the University of California, San Diego; and forensic autism expert

"*Healing Autistic Burnout* is a wonderful, informative book, and a lifetime companion and social and emotional support for people on the autism spectrum. It provides a window into the experiences of neurodivergent individuals, and encourages them to better navigate the world and their lives. Sharon Kaye O'Connor's personal advice and experiences, interspersed with mindful awareness and practices, make the book a universal aid for autistic individuals and for those who are nonautistic."

> **—Tobi Zausner, PhD**, author of *When Walls Become Doorways* and *The Creative Trance*

"Sharon manages to be both understandable and informative with her observations and recommendations. I think neurodivergent and neurotypical readers alike will learn from this book to help bridge 'the language gap' that exists between neurotypes."

> **—Sean O'Brien, MSW, LCSW**, owner of Reset Counseling, and adult discoverer of his own neurodiversity

"We are increasingly aware of the causes and signs of autistic burnout, and the experiences and feelings that are endured. Fortunately, we are gradually developing strategies to end burnout, promote recovery, and reduce the likelihood of relapse. The author describes autistic burnout from her personal perspective, incorporating current research and practical guidance of value to autistic individuals and professionals. I enjoyed the explanations and advice on every page."

—**Tony Attwood, PhD**, clinical psychologist, adjunct professor at Griffith University, and author of numerous research papers and books on autism

"An important and helpful book, about a timely topic that isn't written about enough. Filled with sharp insights, informed by personal experience, and containing lots of practical applications, autistic readers will find this book extremely valuable."

—**Chris Bonnello**, autistic advocate (Autistic Not Weird), speaker, author, and former teacher

"Sharon Kaye O'Connor brings compassion, clarity, and lived experience to a topic many autistic adults know all too well. *Healing Autistic Burnout* helps readers make sense of exhaustion, offers practical tools, and will guide both autistic readers and the professionals who support them."

—**Julie Landry, PsyD, ABPP**, board-certified clinical psychologist, and cofounder of NeuroSpark Health

"Sharon combines expertise with heartfelt guidance, speaking honestly about the realities of autistic burnout while offering hope, practical tools, and a powerful reminder that neurodiversity is a strength. This isn't just a book—it's an invitation to create a future where authenticity and well-being belong to all."

—**Lindsey Cohen, MS, OTR/L**, neuroaffirming occupational therapist

"Sharon skillfully weaves practical information about autistic burnout with her own relatable experiences. She highlights the range and depth of individual experiences of autistic burnout, while offering perspective on universal themes that help decrease shame and isolation. Sharon's clear explanations and recommendations encourage self-acceptance and self-compassion, and gently ground the reader."

—**Elizabeth Donovan, PhD**, psychologist and founder of Psychology for Growth

I0112851

A Neuroaffirming Guide for

HEALING

Connecting with Your Authentic Self,

AUTISTIC

Restoring Your Energy &

BURNOUT

Advocating for Your Needs

SHARON KAYE O'CONNOR, LCSW

New Harbinger Publications, Inc.

Publisher's Note

NEW HARBINGER PUBLICATIONS is a registered
trademark of New Harbinger Publications, Inc.

New Harbinger Publications is an employee-owned company.

Copyright © 2026 by Sharon Kaye O'Connor
New Harbinger Publications, Inc.
5720 Shattuck Avenue
Oakland, CA 94609
www.newharbinger.com

Cover design by Amy Shoup

Acquired by Aicha Martine Thiam

Edited by M. C. Calvi

Library of Congress Cataloging-in-Publication Data on file

MIX
Paper | Supporting
responsible forestry
FSC
www.fsc.org
FSC® C008955

Printed in the United States of America

28   27   26

10   9   8   7   6   5   4   3   2   1   First Printing

Dear Reader,
This book
is for You.

Contents

Acknowledgments   vii

Foreword   ix

Introduction   1

Part I: Autistic Burnout: Hitting the Wall

1   Introduction to Autistic Burnout   5
"What Is Happening?"

2   Contributors to Autistic Burnout   17
"How Did This Happen?"

3   Connecting to Hope   27
Burnout Can Be Temporary

4   Turning Point   37
Radical Self-Acceptance

Part II: Uncovering Your Authentic, Autistic Needs

5   A Different Operating System   49
What Works for You

6   The Sensory Situation   55
Our Needs and Supports

7   Energy Is Everything   71
Pacing Yourself

8   Time to Expand   85
Restoring Your Energy

9   Slowing Down   97
Resting and Taking Care

Part III: Communication, Self-Advocacy, and the Path Forward

10   Autistic Communication Is Different Communication   111
      Communication Needs and Preferences

11   Self-Advocacy   119
      Getting What You Need

12   The Path Forward   135
      Finding Your People and Living Your Best Autistic Life

      References   143

Acknowledgments

Thank you to Aïcha Martine Thiam for dreaming up the idea for this book and for your support along the way. When we set out to create this book together, our shared vision was to write the book that we both might have needed at one point in our lives, and I believe so much that we have succeeded. To Beth Bolton, MC Calvi, Callie Brown, and the editorial team for their guidance. Amy Shoup and the art department for the beautiful cover. Daniella Sinder for the back cover image. Thank you to Lindsey Cohen for sharing your knowledge and neuroaffirming enthusiasm. Thank you to William Stillman for the beautiful foreword. And thank you to Analis Souza and the launch and PR teams at New Harbinger for bringing this book out into the world.

Thank you to N. and F. Moon, The Lad, Mom, Dad, Laura, and our families. To Allison. To dearest friends, both longtime and new-found. To every client I've had the great honor of working with. And to all the kind and patient mentors who showed me the way. In grateful memory of Joe McKenzie-Hamilton: We were all "better for the sight of you."

Foreword

Like the author of *Healing Autistic Burnout*, I, too, was a late realizer who only came to understand in adulthood that my neurodivergence had a name. Unlike the author, I grew up in the 1960s and '70s at a time when autism was known only among a select few in the psychiatric community as a rare anomaly. It wasn't until I was in my thirties that a confluence of synchronicities led to that *aha!* moment of clarity by which the truth was fully illuminated. Finally, I had answers and reasons and credible explanations for my way of being *that were not my fault*—and I was not alone in feeling so. It had a *name*! This was both intimidating and relieving.

So much of what I experienced then, I learned, is typical of those on the spectrum now. My recitation of lines of dialogue from favorite movies and TV shows, which I referred to as "movie talk," and which I used to appropriately replicate socially appropriate conversation or emotions, is nowadays called "scripting." What's known as "masking," I simply thought of as acting by attempting to "pass for normal." And instead of the term "stimming," I was merely trying to preserve my sanity and decompress by immersing myself in the comfort and familiarity of repetitious activities, such as replaying a certain passage of a favorite song because its harmony was so pleasing. Nor did I know anything of sensory sensitivities, only that I would come home from school drained and exhausted, overwhelmed from "doing people" all day long, coupled with enduring overhead florescent lighting and my polyester Brady Bunch bellbottom pants, which scratched me raw like sandpaper.

Now, in my sixties, it is liberating to know that I no longer need to "snap out of it," "toughen up," "get over it," and, in essence, be a less sensitive person because of societal norms and mores. By embracing those very sensitivities and educating others about them, I have created an entire career as a self-advocate and author

on these very topics. I take solace in knowing I'm exactly who I'm intended to be, doing what I'm supposed to be doing; I'm not in competition to keep pace with anyone else. Still, I wish I had had a compassionate mentor or, at the very least, a handbook to guide me in navigating life because, let's face it, the world *hurts*. Now those on the autism spectrum, and their friends and loved ones, have that handbook, thanks to Sharon Kaye O'Connor.

Inherent in this book's text are wisdoms and truths that can only come from someone who has walked the walk as an authentic experiencer. The desire to demystify and share this information is a form of altruism, and I especially welcomed the author's holistic summary recaps that permeate throughout, reminding us to calm, quell, and soothe ourselves in order to be mindful in our reflection. Even just the concept of pacing ourselves in order to conserve our energy is invaluable for those on the spectrum, in and of itself.

This author and other self-advocates have accepted the torch and are carrying it forward for a new generation of autists. Once I finished this book, I breathed a sigh of relief knowing that we, collectively, will be okay if we unite in the common understanding that we are all more alike than we are different. The next time I feel the need to explain, defend, or describe my experience, I will hand this book to those who are questioning my way of being, because it's all there, so beautifully encapsulated and accessible. In closing, I wish to express my gratitude for such an affirming and essential guide. Even though I've lived it, and worked in this field since 1987, it is still heartening to read.

—William Stillman
Award-winning autism author, consultant,
and self-advocate

Introduction

Most of what I've learned about autism, I've learned from other autistic people. I had never heard of autistic burnout or even knew much about autism itself at the beginning of my own major burnout in my thirties. Sure, there were autistic folks who I knew on a personal level in my life, but my years of graduate training and experience as a clinical social worker and psychotherapist hadn't prepared me for—or even put on my radar—this massive thing that was happening within my own nervous system. At that time, I didn't even know that I was autistic.

What started me on the journey of maybe realizing I had a few traits "in common" with autistic people was when my first child was in the process of being assessed by Early Intervention. He was almost two years old at the time and not speaking any words yet, and was in the kind of constant motion that suggested he was being propelled by some turbo jet pack. When the Early Intervention evaluators sporadically visited our tiny Manhattan apartment to conduct their assessments, they would point out small things that he did, like playing with toys differently or not responding to his name when called, and ask if he had been screened for autism. My own response was a mix of perplexion and incredulousness: "Why are they pathologizing these perfectly normal things? I do that as well, does that mean *I'm* autistic too?"

For my own official diagnosis that followed, it took years of piecing together small bits of seemingly unrelated information. In what I now look back on and understand as classic autistic fashion, my brain hyperfocused on the subject of autism, and it became my new official special interest. There hadn't been much written on autistic burnout at the time in the clinical sphere—an article here, a presentation there—and it certainly had never been a topic covered in my professional training. But in the informal discussions

among the autistic community I was becoming increasingly connected to, it was a subject that was discussed in almost a matter-
of-fact tone as if it was a common part of everyone's experience at
one point or another.

   Autistic folks in my life who had received their own diagnoses,
or discovered their own autistic identities long before I did, offered
their kind support and shared the info—the real stuff I needed to
know about autism—that helped me make it through this time. Just
having someone who truly understood, whom I could relate to,
made all the difference in the world. It was learning from and connecting to my community of fellow autistics that helped me find
my way through burnout, understand what I needed to know about
how my brain worked, and move forward with a renewed sense of
energy and life force. I am eternally grateful to the autistic folks in
my community who showed me the way. To you, friend and reader,
I hope that this book will offer a guiding beacon that will bring you
back to your own light.

Autistic Burnout: Hitting the Wall

Chapter 1

Introduction to Autistic Burnout
"What Is Happening?"

In the busy and often frantic pace of the world we live in today, the word "burnout" is used quite often. The term may bring to mind a person who has been overworked at a job or while caring for loved ones. Burnout is a great concern globally, as the pace we live and work at tends to move at an ever-increasing rate. Although general burnout can happen to anyone, autistic burnout is a whole different beast. It is a unique and intense category of burnout that occurs among autistic folks, requiring its own specific understanding, insight, and tools to recover from and move forward after.

Autistic burnout is the state of mental and physical exhaustion specifically experienced by autistic folks when our energetic resources have been depleted. During this time, you might lose abilities or skills that you had previously been able to access. You may find that you slowly enter burnout, in a such gradual way that you are not even aware it's happening—as if you've found yourself in a boat that's slowly drifting farther away from land, not noticing how far you've gone until you look up and can no longer see the shoreline. There is an unsettling disorientation that comes with being out in the vast ocean without a reference point—you may have no idea where you are; you might even wonder *who* you are.

You can also find yourself in autistic burnout suddenly, as if you've suddenly been plunged into deep water or someone switched off all the lights at once. Have you been headed into

burnout for a while, and you're just *noticing* now? As autistic folks, our sensory perception and experience of the world are different, so it may take us a bit longer to recognize and identify how we are feeling. It's been estimated that about 50 percent of the autistic population experiences alexithymia (Cuve et al. 2021), which is a difficulty in identifying emotions. Sometimes, you can be struggling and not even know it until someone else points it out to you. You may be used to rallying and holding it together—and you may have been doing so for so long that being in a state of burnout, or feeling "not quite right," becomes something that you're used to. And you may not catch the fact that you're not feeling well, or that burnout is even a consideration, until you're further down the line and closer to a state of crisis.

Because it may take longer for us to recognize when we aren't feeling okay, it can be difficult to implement the self-care practices or make the changes that are needed to shift course earlier on. Identifying how burnout shows up can be imperative, because if you understand what you're experiencing, you can take the cue to make changes or implement more practices of needed self-care.

So, what are the ways autistic burnout can present in our lives? Let's take a look at some of the symptoms that commonly occur in the burnout experience.

The Energy Is Gone

Exhaustion can be a primary and telltale sign of autistic burnout. Not the kind of typical fatigue experienced after a long day or after a night of little sleep, but a feeling of energy just being gone; it's run out. There is a particular variety of drained-ness that occurs with autistic burnout, and it is often very distinct from the kind of fatigue a few good nights of sleep can cure. When you find that your energy levels have become depleted to this degree, you may have things that you would like to do, but you may not have the energy to do them. Executive functioning can become a struggle during this time as well, because getting started on tasks or maintaining momentum can require energy that just isn't available.

During burnout, everyday tasks like cooking, cleaning, self-care, or getting through the work day can feel insurmountable. There can be a feeling of trying to run a marathon through a pool of water—every step is arduous and taxing, and yet you're not moving very far at all. Psychologist Andrew Solomon (2013) once said that "The opposite of depression is not happiness, but vitality." Autistic burnout is often misdiagnosed as depression due to this absence of vitality. It is also common for autistic people in burnout to experience despair or a feeling of hopelessness, fearing that we will never feel like ourselves again.

Everything Is Overwhelming

When you become so depleted, you may suddenly realize just how much energy is required to get through the day—from managing simple tasks of daily living to processing the sensory elements of your environments to navigating social interactions. Autistic burnout is particularly unique to the autistic community due to its relationship to autistic masking—the adjustments we make in our interactions to appear more neurotypical or less different. The more we mask, the more energy we use up, and this puts us at greater risk of burnout. All of these elements consume energy, and because we live in a world that wasn't created with autistic needs in mind, navigating daily life can drain our energetic resources faster than it drains those of our nonautistic neighbors.

When your energy levels fall off, you may find that you reach a point of overwhelm and overload much more quickly—that your tolerance for everyday sensory stimuli has diminished. During burnout, you may find that your sensory needs and discomforts become more pronounced. Sensory sensitivities may become heightened—small sounds that might not have bothered you before become suddenly painful or intolerable.

For me, one small warning sign that I'm headed for burnout is when the beeping sound from the microwave is suddenly painful, and I have come to recognize this as a cue to take inventory of my own energy and slow down. As your sensory needs become more

evident, you may find yourself opting for different clothing because the fabric in your usual jeans is too scratchy or suddenly the seams inside your socks are all you can notice.

With increased sensory needs can also come an increase in stimming, which is short for "self-stimulatory behaviors." Stims often take the form of repetitive movements and can look like rocking, flapping, spinning, repeating words or phrases, or listening to the same song on repeat. Stims are used to gain sensory input that helps keep our nervous systems comfortable and in equilibrium. Stimming is often employed to mitigate the sensory aspects of the environment when a person is feeling overstimulated, understimulated, or experiencing anxiety or another strong emotion. If you notice an increase in the need for movement or sensory input, it may be an indicator of increasing overwhelm—and that stimming may be a helpful tool. An increase in stimming can indicate that we're not feeling quite comfortable or that our energy levels may be dwindling.

When you no longer have the energy in reserves to manage the sensory stimuli of the environments you are in, this leaves you vulnerable to having more meltdowns. Meltdowns are events that happen when an autistic person's nervous system becomes completely overloaded. During a meltdown, a person may become tearful, yell, seek out sensory input, or show other signs of distress. These characteristics may appear outwardly if an individual's meltdowns tend to take the form of an "explosion." Meltdowns can also resemble internal "implosions," and the signs of the meltdown might not appear outwardly at all, even while the person is in severe distress. For folks who experience internalized meltdowns, they may not realize that they are actually having meltdowns, because the experience is so different from the explosion they expect.

Meltdowns that are internalized can often resemble, and be mislabeled as, panic attacks. The overload we experience during meltdown can easily feel like panic, or can even be panic inducing. But if we look a bit closer, we may actually see an accumulation of

a variety of sensory discomforts, communication frustrations, stressors, and masking that have brought our nervous system beyond its limit. Panic attacks also tend to come on more suddenly, while with meltdowns, there is often a sense of accumulating overload, or buildup, before they happen. This is referred to as the "rumble stage." Often, the panic we feel during a meltdown is secondary to the feeling of complete overwhelm or helplessness, or the need to escape to privacy to hide how much we're struggling.

Meltdowns are often confused with tantrums, especially in children, but it is important to remember that meltdowns are not a choice or an attempt to manipulate. They are the result of a nervous system that is absolutely beyond its limit, when the person can no longer manage. An individual having a meltdown is in an incredibly vulnerable state and requires care, understanding, and support.

More Emotion

In addition to heightened sensory needs, you may also find that you have more intense emotions during burnout, especially emotions that can be painful or uncomfortable. You may find that you experience emotion more intensely or that you become tearful or even angry more easily. You may also experience moods or emotions changing quickly, and they may be more difficult to identify. Alexithymia is a struggle during burnout because you may be feeling a lot of emotions simultaneously, so it might feel difficult to unravel the jumble of thoughts and emotions to tell what's what.

During burnout, you may notice that you are experiencing more anxiety, worry, or self-doubt. Because of the anxiety that can often surface, or become more intense, it is not uncommon to receive an anxiety diagnosis during this time. Of course, it is possible to both be autistic *and* have an anxiety disorder, but sometimes autistic folks seek therapy for what feels like anxiety, when what they are really experiencing is all the elements of autistic burnout converging together.

I Cannot "People" Right Now

When your energy levels are running low, you may notice that social interactions become increasingly difficult, and you may become unable to mask as much as you usually do. Masking can take the form of making or "faking" eye contact, even if it is uncomfortable or overwhelming. Some autistic folks have learned to fake eye contact by looking at the bridge of someone's nose, or at their eyelids, as a way of appearing to make eye contact without experiencing the discomfort or sensory overload that eye contact can often bring.

Masking can also include creating "expected" facial expressions or infusing inflection into one's voice. While masking, you may find yourself copying the speech patterns or gestures of the people you're talking to, or mirroring their emotional responses. Many autistics notice that they tend to pick up the accents of people they interact with, even if the conversation is brief. They may also pick up speech patterns, mannerisms, or traits from characters in movies, television, or books, and adopt those into their persona. Other elements of masking can include making small talk when it may not feel natural or refraining from talking about a special interest or favorite subject.

While masking, you may notice that you are suppressing stims, or the need for movement. You might also attempt to ignore aspects of the sensory environment that are painful for you. For example, if you're having a conversation with someone, and a firetruck drives by with its sirens blaring, you may avoid covering your ears in order to blend in, especially if the person you are talking to isn't covering their ears as well. Autistic masking is complex and can be done either consciously or unconsciously.

Masking can begin at such an early age that you may not even realize it is part of your experience until you no longer have the energy to do it anymore. During autistic burnout, you may wonder why you are suddenly so uncomfortable or "clumsy" in social interactions. You might question why you are unable to present yourself to the world in the way you once had. When it becomes difficult

to maintain interactions in the way you are used to, you might feel like a "shell" of your former self.

When you reach autistic burnout, all the tools and strategies of masking that you used to rely on might start to fall away, because the energy needed to maintain them is simply no longer there. It is during this time that you might actually start to seem "more autistic," with differences becoming more apparent, along with the inability to hide struggles or conceal distress when you're feeling overwhelmed or uncomfortable. In fact, much of the criteria used to identify autism has been based on observations of how autistic people appear while struggling or overwhelmed, and during autistic burnout, these traits become more prominent. This is a time when the differences in the way autistics naturally interact become clearer to ourselves and others.

When you say you can't "people" right now, it might mean that you can no longer interact with others in the way that you might have interacted before, to the degree that you would like, or in the way that might be expected of you. If you've managed to mask your differences up until this point, you may not currently have the energy to keep up the pace. And even though you may be running out of steam, the treadmill of life keeps moving. You may become self-conscious around others because you may not be able to mask in the ways that have previously been available to you. And even if you may ordinarily be happy to let your autistic quirks show through, you may be much more reluctant to let others see that you're struggling. This self-consciousness can lead some folks to want to isolate, so that their struggles aren't visible to those around them. You may not want others to see you while you're having a hard time.

The fatigue that comes with burnout may also bring increased cognitive difficulty or challenges with things like communication, translating thoughts into spoken speech (or whatever you use as your primary mode of communication), and word retrieval. These changes can feel foreign and scary, and can amplify the feeling of loss you may be experiencing. Because loss of skill is such a common feature of burnout, autistic burnout is often labeled as regression, especially in children.

Autistic Burnout Symptoms in Children

If you look back on your own childhood, did you ever experience autistic burnout then? Or if you are the caregiver of an autistic child now, is your loved one potentially running low on energy? Autistic burnout in kids can present as a loss of skill, a "backtracking," or an increase in overall struggle. Some kids, who may previously have had access to spoken speech, may stop speaking or start speaking less. They may experience new or increased difficulties with speech articulation. A child who previously had been using the bathroom independently might start having bathroom accidents. They may experience more challenges related to sleep. There might also be an increase in sensory sensitivity or sensory seeking in the form of movement and increased stimming. Burnout in kids can also bring about an increase in dysregulation, emotional distress, meltdowns, or aggression. It is important to remember that dysregulation is not a person choosing bad behaviors, but someone who is in discomfort and distress who needs understanding and support.

More Time in Our Inner Worlds

Because communication and being with people can feel more draining or taxing during this time, we may experience an increased need for solitude and going inward to conserve or restore energy. In autistic burnout, spending more time alone can be a form of needed self-care, but is often confused with the withdrawal and isolation of depression. It can be difficult for others, and even for ourselves at times, to distinguish whether we are pulling back from interaction due to feeling depressed or simply taking a much-needed respite in our own solitude. As autistic folks, sometimes solitude is where we are happiest, and we may need a great deal of alone time to spend with our special interests or in our own inner worlds. Often, it is in this space of solitude, away from being observed by others, that we may feel truly free and able to be our authentic selves, and we can begin to restore our energy and recharge.

Our internal worlds can be vast and vivid. We may possess imaginations that are not only visually detailed, but also able to create imaginative experiences and journeys involving all of our senses. Burnout can be a period in our lives when we feel a stronger pull toward spending more time in our inner worlds. If you feel an increasing need to go inward to rest and recharge, could it be a sign that you are tired, running low on energy, or in need of respite? If your autistic child or loved one seems to be going into their inner world more frequently, could this be a sign of fatigue, stress, or that they may need additional support?

Using Mindfulness to Tune In

Mindfulness is the practice of tuning in to awareness at any given moment, which allows us to connect to the subtle information within and around us. In relation to autistic burnout, mindfulness can help us answer the two most important questions: "How am I feeling?" and "What do I need?" We often think of mindfulness in the context of meditation, but mindfulness can be employed at any point in our daily lives. Whether we're taking a walk, washing the dishes, or having a conversation, we don't need to be sitting still in meditation to tune in to how we are feeling or what we may be experiencing. In fact, for many autistic and otherwise neurodivergent folks, being in motion can help us to think, feel, and observe more acutely.

Recovering from an episode of autistic burnout can start with learning to recognize the symptoms and signals that we are in one. Because we are all unique individuals, stress, fatigue, and burnout will manifest differently in each of our lives. If you can identify the feelings or symptoms that become present when you are under stress or starting to run low on energy, it can offer valuable information and awareness that you can use to plan your next steps forward. The practice of mindfulness can be a helpful tool that you can utilize to tune in to how you may be feeling and to identify what you are experiencing. Try the following mindfulness exercise, and consider the accompanying questions for reflection.

Mindfulness Moment

Incorporating the practice of mindfulness into our lives can bring us insight into our own experience. When we tune in to ourselves—body, mind, and emotion—mindfulness can help us identify when we may be experiencing symptoms of stress or fatigue, or conversely, when we may be feeling energized or experiencing feelings of joy. While tuning in to what is present for you in this moment, feel free to take on the role of the curious observer and just pay attention to anything you may be experiencing, without judgment. You may wish to write down any observations you would like to remember later.

Before you begin the mindfulness and reflection exercises in this book, take a moment to center yourself with a few slow, deep breaths, and get comfortable in whatever way feels right for you. When it comes to tuning in to how you are feeling and what you are experiencing, what would be most comfortable for you? Are you most comfortable sitting still in a quiet place? Or taking a walk in your neighborhood? Or making something creative with your hands? Some people do their best thinking while folding laundry or doing another task we consider mundane. Feel free to add movement like rocking or pacing as needed. How do you best tune in with your own thoughts and feelings?

When you are feeling comfortable and ready, observe how you may be feeling in the following areas:

Body

- How are you feeling in your body?
- What sensations do you notice?
- Do you feel energized? Fatigued?
- Do you feel heavy or light?

- Are you feeling warm or cold?

- Are you feeling any pain?

- Notice anywhere you may be holding tension (places where we often store tension include the jaw, neck, and shoulders).

Mind

- Are you able to identify any specific thoughts in your mind at this moment?

- Are there any worries or anxious thoughts?

- Are there any thoughts you are happy to greet?

- Any thoughts you would like to see drift away?

Emotions

- Are you able to identify an emotion you might be experiencing now?

- Are you experiencing more than one emotion right now? If so, what other emotions are you feeling?

- It's okay if you do not have any emotions that are immediately identifiable.

- If it's difficult to identify a specific emotion like joy, sadness, or fear, is there an image or a metaphor you might identify with? Perhaps it feels like you are attempting to run through water, pushing a boulder up a hill, or floating upward like a balloon, for example.

- Imagine trying to represent how you are feeling. Are there any song lyrics, movie lines, or pieces of visual art that resonate with this particular emotion?

Take a moment to stay with these observations until you feel like they have given you the information you need to know. When you are ready, bring your attention back to your breath. Focus on a deep inhale, then a slow exhale. With each inhale, you can imagine breathing in a silver-white light. With each exhale, you may imagine releasing stress or tension. Continue this pattern of deep breathing for as long as you like. When you are ready to conclude the exercise, I hope you will feel a sense of renewed energy and calm.

Note: You can do an abbreviated version of this check-in exercise at any point throughout the day by taking a moment to observe what you are experiencing related to your body, mind, and emotions, across different settings and situations. An even more simplified version of this exercise would be to think of one word, phrase, or image that describes how you are feeling in the moment. What you observe can help offer valuable insight into how you experience—and may be affected by—different environments and emotions.

Take a moment to reflect on what you've observed so far. If you find it helpful, feel free to note these observations in a journal, the Notes app on your phone, or simply carry them with you in your mind. Keeping notes can help you to observe patterns and themes over time, and develop deeper insight into yourself and needs.

Contributors to Autistic Burnout
"How Did This Happen?"

When you find yourself in autistic burnout, you may wonder how you ended up there. How have you found yourself so depleted in this way that others don't seem to experience or maybe even understand? When looking for the causes of your autistic burnout, you are looking for factors within your life that put any kind of stress on your system and deplete or consume your energy. The factors that lead to autistic burnout can be subtle and small stressors that accumulate over time or a big source of stress that occurs all at once.

Among the big stressors can be major changes or life events. These are the transitions universally recognized as life altering, like moving to a new place, going through a breakup or divorce, experiencing the loss of a loved one, beginning a new life with a partner, starting a new job, or having a child. These transitions often mark the end of one stage of your life and the beginning of another. Even changes that are very much wanted or looked forward to can tax your energetic resources.

When you experience major changes, these transitions can consume a large amount of mental, physical, and emotional energy to process. Big changes like moving to a new location can consume a large amount of physical energy—a great deal of time is spent packing, organizing, and physically transporting the contents of your life from one place to another. And although the physical

demands of moving can be quite visible and tangible, moving can also consume more invisible forms of energy, such as emotional and mental energetic resources.

As you leave one place and begin your life again in another, all of the feelings that come along with these changes can consume a massive amount of emotional energy. You might experience grief or sadness at letting go of a place where you used to live, where you may have many memories. Or you may be processing emotions surrounding what you wish had been different. There may be the feeling of relief at a fresh start or excitement about new possibilities. If the move was not something you wanted, you may experience a sense of loss. All of the emotions that come up during a transition like a move can require energetic resources to process and move through.

Following a move, you may now find you have to spend mental energy reworking some of the routines and ways of doing things that you have come to rely on. When the "moving" part is over and the boxes are unpacked, then comes the work of selecting a new grocery store and pharmacy, a new route to commute to school or work, and a new place to have something repaired. You begin the process of meeting new neighbors or people in the community, and start making new connections from scratch. When you go through the process of a major change, you often then realize just how many small changes are wrapped up in a major transition. A move isn't one transition—it's hundreds.

Parenthood

The transition into parenthood can be a time when many autistic folks find themselves experiencing major autistic burnout for the first time. When you suddenly become responsible for another person who is entirely helpless and relying on you for everything, it can be an experience that is physically, mentally, and emotionally exhausting. Early parenthood is also a period during which your time becomes much more limited and precious. You may no longer have the time or ability to take a walk by yourself, rest, or become absorbed in a book on a favorite subject to recharge when needed.

It may be during this period that you realize just how much you rely on time alone, or time with special interests, just to remain in equilibrium. You may not realize how many accommodations you have been making for yourself until your life no longer allows for you to make them. Entering a new stage of life that brings increased demands, responsibility, or a busier schedule can often highlight the accommodations needed most, without which you may begin to struggle.

Routine and Predictability

Many of us may find that we are most comfortable when we can live our lives with a degree of predictability or routine. Often, the routines that serve us best are the routines we can create and curate ourselves. When you are not able to have enough control or autonomy over your life or environment, the world you inhabit can become unpredictable, and the routines that you need for comfort and stability can become inaccessible. If you are living in an environment that feels outside of your control, processing all the variable elements of the unpredictable environment can demand more energy than you have to spare, and you may soon become depleted.

Autistic Masking

Our ability to feel safe and accepted within an environment can impact the degree to which we mask during our day. *Neuroception*, a term created by Dr. Stephen Porges and related to polyvagal theory (Polyvagal Institute, n.d.), is our brain and body's ability to sense whether a person or environment is safe for us. When you don't feel like you are entirely safe or comfortable being yourself, you might find yourself spending more energy to mask your differences and blend in. There may be a feeling of being observed by others or a fear that if you come across as different in some way, you might be judged, thought of as "weird," or misunderstood. Since masking is utilized for camouflage, it can also be viewed as a survival strategy. There are times when you may feel the need to

blend in or go unnoticed for your own physical or emotional safety. But when you are masking all the time, it can come at a great cost.

Some autistic folks will automatically mask when around other people, and may only relax and unmask when entirely alone in private. When you are trying to accomplish tasks at home or at work, you may benefit from having the space and privacy to focus, or to go about responsibilities without being perceived. If you are working at a job with an open floor plan office or in the service industry, you may be with and around people all day. These are environments that may prompt you to mask, heavily and constantly, all the time. The energetic cost of constant masking is massive and can be a direct contributor to burnout.

Mindfulness Moment

Because masking can either be conscious or unconscious, you may not even realize all of the ways in which you may be masking. Using mindfulness to consciously approach masking, consider these questions as they relate to your own experience. You might take some time to journal about these as you reflect.

- Do you know when you are masking? Or is it difficult to identify?

- What elements of masking do you utilize the most? (For example, making or "faking" eye contact even if it may not be comfortable, making or adjusting facial expressions, suppressing stims, copying others.)

- Are there any elements of masking that you feel serve you well?

- Are there any elements of masking that you feel may not be serving you well, or may consume too much energy to be a benefit to you?

- In what environments do you mask the most? (For example, school, work, or with friends or family.)

- Are there any situations or people in your life with whom you feel like you can let some of these elements of masking go?

- What about these people or environments feels safe and welcoming?

- What aspects of masking are you able to let go of, when safe to do so?

Managing Too Much for Too Long

Maybe you haven't had any major changes in your life, or big transitions, but perhaps you've been moving along at a pace that has been unsustainable, which is now catching up with you. Cumulative stress can lead to burnout when you have responsibilities that bring ongoing demand with fewer opportunities for rest and decompression. You may find yourself particularly apt to reach burnout in periods of your life like in school or college, when the pressure of time and the need to complete coursework by the semester's close can increase the weight on your shoulders. When there is the pressure of a looming deadline or final exam, you may push yourself a bit more than usual, and be more likely to ignore or push aside your brain and body's need for a break. During this time as a student, you may also be managing personal or professional responsibilities. Even though the semester is finite, life outside of school doesn't always allow for the breaks that are needed to rest and recharge before the new course load begins.

Although the work of school may be contained within the semester calendar, there may be other responsibilities in your life that bring indefinite demands over the long term. For folks in the role of a caregiver—whether to a child, a spouse, or an aging

parent—the caregiving responsibilities can be constant and leave little time for self-care or breathing space to decompress. While in the role of carer, it can be easy to put your own needs aside or on hold, and forge ahead and do the tasks that need to be done. When life circumstances require that you place your own needs on the back burner for any length of time, you may feel overextended but have no choice but to keep going. The cumulative stress and strain can lead easily toward a place of burnout, especially as our autistic systems may require more space or solitude than those of our neurotypical neighbors.

Trying to Keep Up

Even just regular "adulting" can include cumulative stressors that add up and deplete energy over time. Burnout becomes a real possibility when trying to keep up with our neurotypical counterparts. You may know people who can readily manage working forty-plus hour weeks, going to the gym, seeing friends, and also caring for a family and managing a home. However, this pace may not be attainable or sustainable for you. I have therapist colleagues who can schedule eight or nine sessions in a day, but I've had to recognize that such a pace would be unsustainable for me. To conserve my energy, I schedule fewer sessions in a day, with more breaks and downtime built in. It is important to recognize that having autonomy and control over one's work schedule is a privilege and a luxury that not everyone has. With that in mind, sometimes we are only able to make adjustments in the areas—which may be quite small—where we do have control, often outside of work or family responsibilities.

Minding the "Shoulds"

We often look to the closest people around us for guidance, or as a model of how we can structure and build our own lives. Your

nonautistic neighbor might think nothing of working a full day at an office surrounded by coworkers and lot of activity, and then meeting a group of friends at a crowded happy hour after work, whereas you may find yourself running on empty by the end of your work day and need to go home to quiet and solitude.

There can be a feeling of "If everyone around me is doing all of these things, is that what I should be doing too?" But not everyone's needs and capabilities are the same, and it is these "shoulds" that can lead to burnout because they ask you to override your own signals of stress and fatigue. This can bring you further out of touch with your own needs and what works best for you. Now I invite you to grab your journal and reflect on the following questions.

Mindfulness Moment

- What sources of stress are present in your life today? Where do they come from?

- What are the biggest sources of stress?

- What are the smaller sources of stress?

- Are there any new sources of stress, or have there been any changes or transitions recently? (For example, moving, the beginning or ending of a school year.)

- Are there any stressors or responsibilities you have been managing for a long time? This could be related to work, caregiving, school, or anything else.

- Are there any sources of stress, big or small, that you can put on hold temporarily right now?

- Are there any "shoulds" you've been holding onto that you can let go of?

Managing Illness or Injury

When it comes to the components of your life that can strain your energy, experiencing struggles related to your physical or mental health can be incredibly taxing. For folks who may experience an acute or chronic illness, a sudden injury, or an ongoing pain condition, you may find that your emotional and social energy becomes much more limited. Managing any pain or discomfort in the body can often be consuming and leave one exhausted. There may not be much energy left over for other things like work, caregiving, or social relationships, but there may still be life responsibilities that have to be attended to. And so, with diminishing energy, you may find that you are now spending energetic resources you don't have just to try and manage daily life, leading you to feel burned out and depleted.

Aging and Older Adulthood

When we were kids, our natural batteries might have had a greater capacity to store energy. As we move into adulthood and older adulthood, our overall energy levels can begin to drop off a bit. Our late teens and early twenties may be a time in our lives when we possess the energy for being busier or having a more active social life. When we reach our later twenties, thirties, forties, and beyond, we may not have as much energy as we did before. We may experience having a lower level of energy at our baseline. Imagine a smartphone that starts out with a battery that fully charges to 100 percent—over time, the battery capacity begins to diminish slightly, and a full charge may eventually only reach 80 or 90 percent. This, combined with many of the adult responsibilities that become pressing and nonnegotiable in parenthood or maintaining a livelihood, can create a perfect storm that leaves us running on empty. One relatively reliable recipe for autistic burnout

is an increase in demands plus a decreased amount of space and time for care for the self.

Burnout in Children

Although adults may have a greater degree of ongoing responsibility, this does not mean kids are immune to autistic burnout. We may associate the idea of stress with the demands of adulthood. However, children can experience various stressors that can increase the likelihood of autistic burnout as well. Many of the risk factors that can push children toward burnout mirror those experienced by adults. Being overscheduled without the downtime needed to decompress and recharge is as much a factor for children as it is for grown-ups.

For many autistic kids, just the school day itself can be long and overwhelming. There may be near-constant interaction in the classroom, as well as during free time, throughout which the child may feel pressure to mask or navigate social engagement. There may be sensory discomforts or not enough demand-free time for solitude or access to the inner world. With the ongoing buildup of stressors, it is not uncommon for kids to show signs of burnout toward the end of the school year.

For kids and adults alike, the accumulation of stressors contributes directly to autistic burnout, and it can be helpful to identify sources of stress, as well as the signs that we are experiencing stress, so we can respond with care. This awareness can help us recover from any current burnout we may be experiencing, and it can also help us prevent future burnouts by letting us recognize the early signs.

You can find an information sheet for loved ones and professionals supporting autistic folks at www.newharbinger.com/56715. This can be shared with anyone in your life who supports you and could benefit from learning more about your experience.

Mindfulness Moment

Take some time to answer the following questions in your journal or during a meditation to help you process what you've learned and understand your own experience.

- Are there any signs you can recognize that let you know when you may be struggling or experiencing stress or discomfort? Do you notice more stimming, more emotionality, or more need for more time in your inner world?

- Are there particular environments in which you notice these signs of stress the most? (For example, crowded places, loud spaces, school, other people's homes.)

- In what environments do you notice these signs of stress the least? This could be in nature, at home, or in another favorite location.

- When do you feel the happiest, most relaxed, and most yourself? What do you notice about yourself when you are in a relaxed state?

Keeping a record of your answers can provide you with helpful information to revisit later!

Chapter 3

Connecting to Hope
Burnout Can Be Temporary

When you find yourself in a place of autistic burnout, you may feel lost or disoriented. There may even be despair—and the worry that how you are feeling in this moment is the way that you will feel forever. In the midst of any given experience or emotional state, it can sometimes be difficult to imagine feeling any other way. You may struggle to imagine experiencing anything other than what is right in front of you, almost as if you are standing facing a large boulder, and the boulder is all you can see. What is present in the moment can feel like all that there is.

While this can be true for anyone, autistic or not, autistic people might experience this to a greater degree due to a tendency toward "black-and-white thinking"—perceiving things in a way that is all good or all bad, all or nothing. We can also experience the quality of "monotropism," a term coined by Dinah Murray (et al.) in 2005. Murray, an autistic researcher, described monotropism as the tendency toward focusing more intensely on fewer things, or only things that are inside our "attention tunnel." Monotropism can be experienced when you focus intensely on a special interest, your favorite subjects, or problems that are in the process of being solved. This can be applied to emotions, as well—it can begin to feel as if the current experience is all there is, and that it will go on forever.

Living in Our Intense World

When we feel things, we often feel them with great magnitude. The general heightened intensity of our experience led one team of researchers to create "The Intense World Theory" as a possible explanation of autism itself (Markram and Markram 2010). Our senses are often amplified, and it makes sense that our emotional experiences may be similarly intense as well.

We can find this to be true when we become absorbed in moments that are happy and peaceful, or when we are experiencing autistic joy. In these moments, we can almost forget the stressors in our lives or the items on our to-do lists. These may be moments where things we worry about feel a little bit further away or outside of our field of vision. Likewise, during times of struggle, it can be easy to feel like a difficult period is all-consuming.

Our experience can also be full of subtle nuances, hints of feelings or sensations that are difficult to name or describe. Analogies are often helpful in thinking about and describing particular experiences. In burnout, you may identify a feeling like you are carrying something really heavy all the time, or a feeling like a gray veil has come down between you and the rest of the world. There may be a feeling of constant and ubiquitous "drained-ness."

When I experienced my major autistic burnout in my midthirties—I'll call this the "Big Burnout"—I remember thinking that I felt like I was on an island, with everyone else far off in the distance. As another image, I sometimes liken autistic burnout to being within a dark cave. When in a place of darkness, it's hard to imagine that there's still light somewhere. It's important to remember that even if the light feels out of reach at the moment, it is still there, and it can be reached again. Finding that light again begins with gaining an understanding of what is happening. Having a language and context in which to identify and describe our experiences is critical for this beginning.

The Difficulty in the Not Knowing

One reason autistic burnout can be so disorienting is that in our first experiences of burnout, we may not yet have a reference point or the words to describe what is happening. It can be difficult to make sense of what we are experiencing for ourselves, and even more difficult to explain or convey to someone else. Because autistic burnout can often be the catalyst that leads to autism diagnosis, many folks experiencing burnout might not have ever even heard of the term "autistic burnout," and at the same time, might also have no idea that they are autistic. Without the words to contextualize our experience, it is easy to feel increasingly lost.

It has been incredibly difficult for those in our community to find good information about how our autistic brains work, to connect with neuroaffirming mental health care, and to gain access to the resources we need. Autistic burnout has not been part of the mental health lexicon for very long at all, even among professionals who have specialized in mental health or in the field of autism. It can be especially difficult to find answers during the times we need them most. It is encouraging that autistic burnout is slowly becoming more recognized within the mental health profession.

In fact, there are a few recent studies from the past few years that highlight and validate autistic burnout as being an observable phenomenon among the autistic community (Raymaker et al. 2020; Mantzalas et al. 2023). As awareness of autism and autistic life grows, thanks to the work in education and advocacy by autistic self-advocates, the field is slowly becoming more neuroaffirming and informed by the needs and concerns of autistic individuals. As a first step toward healing autistic burnout, being aware of our own autistic identity is especially important, but accessing proper diagnosis has been and remains a challenge for many in our community.

How Autism Has Been Underdiagnosed

While many autistic folks are diagnosed in childhood, many do not receive a diagnosis until much later, and others are yet undiagnosed well into adulthood. At the time of writing this book, the most recent Centers for Disease Control (CDC) data from 2022 measured the autism diagnosis rates at one in thirty-one among children (CDC 2025). This data has been published every two years since the year 2000, when the diagnostic rates were one in one hundred fifty. As our field has become more aware of the different and subtle ways in which autism can present, the diagnostic rates have been steadily increasing over the years. Although diagnosis rates are catching up, there are still folks falling through the cracks and flying under the radar, especially those who may not fit certain stereotypes.

Clinicians have long held social "deficits" and difficulties as a main hallmark of autism during the assessment process, along with "restricted, repetitive patterns of behavior" (like stimming or a need for specific routines). They may also look for a response to sensory stimuli that falls outside of the typical range, like hypersensitivity or *hypo*sensitivity—being *less* responsive to stimuli (APA 2013, 27–29). Because the diagnostic criteria are still framed from a perspective of deficits, folks who might have generally managed pretty well, who have found ways to cope with daily life in neurotypical society, might just be deemed *quirky* or *different*. Maybe they have always maintained friendships, but their friendships are with other *odd* or quirky people. Some autistic people are skilled communicators, but just communicate differently, with advanced or extensive vocabularies, or idiosyncratic speech. We may incorporate scripting (the repeating of words or phrases, often from a movie, TV show, or another source) into our speech, but blend it into conversations so seamlessly that others don't notice that we are speaking in movie quotes half the time.

Other people may have sensory differences but not realize it, because they have generally had their sensory needs met, or lived in environments that were inherently sensory friendly or already

well suited to their specific needs. Stimming that falls outside the stereotypical rocking or flapping can also easily go unnoticed—for folks whose stimming may look more like tapping their toes, rubbing their hands together, or twirling their hair, those sensory activities may not be immediately identified as stims.

When doctors are on the lookout for deficits, *differences* can easily go unnoticed. Add masking to the mix, and it can make an autism diagnosis especially elusive for some. When we find adaptations that help us blend in, on the one hand, it can make our lives go more smoothly, because we might not stand out as so obviously different. On the other hand, we may miss out on a diagnosis for a long time and, with that, a key piece to understanding ourselves.

Additionally, autism diagnosis has been historically based on outward characteristics, behaviors, and signs that clinicians are able to observe, instead of the internal and lived experience of the individual, and so those who may have a more internalized experience—who may not present with as many obvious, outward traits—are also likely to get missed. This is one of the reasons why self-diagnosis has become so widely accepted among the autistic community, since barriers to formal diagnosis continue to remain in place.

Diagnosis Gender Gap

We know that, also according to CDC data (2025), the ratio of boys to girls diagnosed as autistic is more than three to one. But that doesn't necessarily mean that autistic boys outnumber autistic girls by such a margin. The diagnostic criteria for autism have historically been based on how autism was observed to present in boys, and for a while, autism was considered to be a "boys' condition." It has even been theorized by some researchers to be "extreme male brain" (Baron-Cohen 2002). As autistic girls, women, and nonbinary folks often present differently, their autistic traits have often gone unnoticed until much later. For this reason, autism remains underdiagnosed in folks who are assigned female at birth (AFAB).

Because autistic girls and women can also be more socially oriented than clinicians may expect an autistic person to present, autistic AFAB folks are also commonly misdiagnosed with other conditions, such as anxiety, depression, borderline personality disorder, or bipolar disorder.

If an autistic woman appears to be socially connected and has friends, a partner, or children, her autistic traits may be dismissed or mislabeled as other things. Boys and men can also get misdiagnosed or miss being diagnosed altogether if they fall outside of conventional autistic stereotypes.

Missed Diagnosis Often Means Incorrect Supports

When we experience autistic burnout while still undiagnosed, the absence of a proper autism diagnosis can lead to treatment that is often unhelpful and even destructive. Many autistic folks have been hospitalized, given unhelpful medications, or undergone therapy where they did not feel understood. Imagine how different it could be if we could instead gain genuine guidance and insight into our own experience, find real self-understanding, and feel truly understood and supported by others.

Insight and Understanding Bring Hope

The glimmer of insight can bring such great hope. It's as if this knowledge of who we are and what we need can illuminate the path forward, even if the light seems faint at first. During the Big Burnout, I remember wondering if that was just the way it was going to be from then on—if I would feel that way forever. And I also remember the feeling when the lightbulb finally went on, and I finally, *maybe* had a word to describe who I was and what I was experiencing. I gained a framework to understand all of the difficulties I encountered, everything that made me different from other people, and even particular strengths that I had. And more

than that, the knowledge that there were other people out there who experienced the same things. To name what we are experiencing can help us finally feel a little less lost.

"How Long Will I Feel This Way?"

When you're going through a difficult period, it's very natural to wonder when you will feel more like yourself again. It can be difficult to predict how long a burnout will last, but in my experience, initial experiences of autistic burnout can often be the longest, because you might not know what's happening or aren't yet aware of the strategies that will bring you out of it. Have you ever visited a new place, and the journey there feels longer than the journey home, even though both trips are equidistant? Sometimes it also feels like time is moving more slowly when you are navigating new terrain, when everything feels different or new, and you don't yet know the way.

It can be difficult to pinpoint exactly when a burnout starts and when it ends, but for me, the Big Burnout stretched on for a couple years because I kept trying to push through. At that time, we had two young children at home, I was at the beginning of my time in private practice, and my responsibilities had increased exponentially. And although I was running out of energy, I continued trying to keep up with everything in the way that I always had—I had been an academic overachiever and in college, packing my schedule with far too many classes and credits, and inevitably collapsing into exhaustion at the end of every semester, but I had always made it through. This new era of parenting and professional life was different, however, and as I attempted to keep barreling through, I just kept feeling worse.

I couldn't ignore my own needs anymore, and it was only once I began to gain a greater understanding of my autistic self and authentic needs that I started to turn the corner. Finally making sense of my experience allowed me to use this new self-knowledge to make necessary adjustments and implement the self-care practices I needed to recover from burnout. And quite encouragingly, it

has been my experience that once we gain a better sense of our needs, even though we may still encounter burnout from time to time, burnouts can become fewer and further between, less severe, and shorter in duration. This is because we now know how to best care for ourselves. It is my hope for you, friend and reader, that your growing self-knowledge will provide you with a similar road map to guide you through this time, as well as the future, and that your insights will always keep you connected to the light that will carry you through.

Autistic burnout can be a time when we experience difficult emotions, which tend to improve as we recover from burnout and our energy restores. However, if you feel you may be currently at risk of or are having thoughts of suicide, call or text 988 (US), or visit 988lifeline.org. Outside of the US, visit findahelpline.com to find resources for your country.

Mindfulness Moment

When you are experiencing a difficult time, mindfulness is a helpful tool for not only identifying how you are feeling, but also reminding yourself that how you are feeling is a temporary state, which can pass.

Maybe you've already been here before, and then your experience changed and became lighter and gentler again. When we're struggling, it can be helpful to hold on to this reminder: some days feel like this, and some days do not.

In a way, every experience and emotion that you have is transient and passing. There may be times when you are feeling positive and hopeful, and other moments where those sentiments feel inaccessible and far away—and that's totally okay.

Some days are just meant to be gotten through—meaning that if all you do with the day is survive, and you do nothing

else, that is enough. You don't have to have everything figured out right now. Feelings and experiences can be compared to the weather—sometimes you are just waiting for the storm to pass. It's important to remember that it will.

Feel free to join in this exercise by taking a moment to tune in:

- How are you feeling in this moment?
- Can you identify how you are feeling in your body, mind, and emotions?
- Can you characterize how you are feeling by comparing it to the weather?
- Are you experiencing a feeling of calm, like a clear day? Maybe the restlessness that happens before a thunderstorm? Or does it feel like you're existing within a tornado?

Take a moment and just sit with these observations.

Now imagine that however you're feeling is just weather moving through.

The weather is always fluid and changing.

Whether it's a misty rainfall, turbulent hurricane, or clouds drifting to reveal nearby sunlight.

If you feel that the weather of the place where you are is sunny and calm, take a minute to stay there and enjoy the beauty, warmth, and peace.

If you are in a place where the weather feels less welcoming, imagine the weather just outside of where you are— outside the perimeter of the rain or the storm. Imagine the sunlight and the warmth beyond the edge of the clouds. If

you choose, you may imagine this beautiful weather getting closer, moving in your direction. If this beautiful weather still feels far away right now, inaccessible, that's okay. Sit for a moment knowing that it is out there, and that it will one day return.

Feel free to write about your experience, reflections, and thoughts in a journal, or simply make a mental note to keep with you, before you take a deep breath and continue with your day.

Chapter 4

Turning Point
Radical Self-Acceptance

Autistic burnout has a way of bringing us face-to-face with our limitations, which can then bring up all sorts of feelings and questions we may ask ourselves—"Who am I now vs. who I thought I should be?" On a physical and practical level, we may find that we need much more rest, that we may not be able to engage in paid work to the extent that we could before. Maybe we have to cut our hours, take a disability leave of absence, or if those aren't options, find a way to somehow make it through the day to come home and basically collapse.

Burnout is a time when many face the realization that they can no longer do the jobs that they have been doing—that the roles are too demanding, too chaotic, or simply the wrong fit. We may feel adrift, and feel our identity shifting when we no longer feel strongly tethered to a career or vocation. Sometimes burnout calls for us to take a break from school and working toward our educational goals, or putting certain dreams on hold. It can mean that we find ourselves having to ask others for help with tasks or responsibilities.

We may struggle to be the person we want to be in our relationships with family, friends, and acquaintances. Maybe you wish you had the energy to catch up with a friend you haven't seen in a while, or make a phone call to a relative to let them know you're thinking of them. But you simply may not have the energy to reach out. Maybe the thought of managing a conversation feels

overwhelming, and the thought of meeting up with a friend feels entirely out of reach.

For parents in burnout, there may be a feeling of regret that you spend most days in survival mode, managing the essentials, and may not have the energy to play with your children as much as you would like. You may find it takes all the energy you have just to complete basic tasks of daily living, and there isn't much energy left over. Maybe you would like to connect with other parents at the park, on playdates, or within the school community, but the thought of making small talk and the pressure of masking feels like too much. There can be a feeling of loneliness or isolation, if we want to connect with people but don't have the energy.

Just the "Emergency Lights"

Burnout can be such a time of living in survival mode—to conserve our energy, only the most essential functions are operating. It's like when there is a power failure and the emergency generators kick in—the generators have a finite amount of fuel and energy in reserves, so they aren't spending energy powering every light, appliance, and device in the building. They're fueling only the essentials—medical equipment, refrigerators, essential heating and cooling sources, and select sources of lighting. On an airplane, the emergency lights are designed to remain functional even in the event of a power failure. When our energy levels are so depleted, we may only have enough energy to power the "emergency lights," or essential functions within our system. This can inevitably mean there is less energy available for masking or engaging with others. We may notice feeling more self-conscious, or even feelings of shame, if we aren't able to be the person we want to be or the person others have always perceived us to be.

As burnout can bring heightened sensory discomfort, it can also generate more meltdowns or shutdowns, and we may feel self-conscious if we experience these struggles in the presence of others. Many autistic folks are experts at hiding their discomfort and distress, especially when around other people, but then fall

apart into a meltdown as soon as they get home or are finally in a space of privacy. During burnout, we may not have the energy in our systems to keep the meltdowns at bay until we are alone. We may find we simply don't have the option to delay and deny our needs anymore.

The Messages Received

One major barrier to self-acceptance can be some of the messages we have received around autism and autistic traits in general. These are messages given to us by others, whether consciously or unconsciously. Just listening to some of the language that has historically been used—and is still used—around autism can be disheartening for sure—the search for a "cure," the myths that we can't feel empathy, emotion, or love because we may perceive and express these things differently, or the idea that the goal of therapy for autistic kids is to make them appear less autistic and more neurotypical.

Autistic traits and characteristics have long been viewed as dysfunctional instead of different. While autism is widely accepted as a disability, many autistic folks, including myself, do not believe that autism is inherently a disorder. Still, many within our community have had the experience of others attempting to change or "correct" their autistic traits from a young age. Even if well-meaning, the messages akin to "You should be different from who you are" can chip away at our sense of worthiness and belonging, and these are messages that can stay with us for a long time. The messages we receive suggest we are still not as understood or accepted as we would like to be. When we experience ableism from the outside world, it is easy for that ableism to become internalized.

We may have also had experiences of feeling different or "other" from the time we were very young. For some, it was simply a matter-of-fact knowing that we were different from peers, in a way that was neither good nor bad. It just *was*. As a child, I wondered if I was an alien, since it felt that my peers and I were from different worlds. We spoke different *languages,* were interested in

completely different things, and I felt the constant pull to return to my own inner world, which others didn't seem to experience. It's not uncommon for autistic kids to find little in common with peers around their own ages, so you may remember having a preference for interacting with kids much younger, almost in the role of a teacher or caregiver, or gravitating toward adults.

Some autistic folks have had the experience of being bullied or ridiculed, and some have even experienced abuse or violence due to caregivers or others who have not understood or accepted their differences. But even if the criticism or response from others may not have been quite so overt, there still may have been a palpable sense that others were noticing our differences. As many autistic folks are sensitive to the thoughts, moods, and perceptions of those we interact with, we can be acutely aware when the person we're talking with is noticing that we are different. We may feel awkward or uncomfortable in interactions sometimes because we may feel like we are operating in our nonnative language and outside of our native culture. It may feel as if we are constantly and quickly trying to translate every bit of information that comes our way, and we may overthink our communication with others to avoid being misunderstood. As these experiences accumulate over time, they can contribute to a sense of feeling the need to hide who we are.

We may mask until we can't anymore, but when burnout occurs, our autistic traits often become more noticeable. When that happens, we may be experiencing ourselves without masking for the first time that we can remember. Maybe ironically, autistic burnout can become a doorway to greater self-understanding and self-acceptance.

Mindfulness Moment

In your journey toward self-acceptance, part of your work can be letting go of any messages you have received that aren't serving you.

- Can you think of any old messages you received in your earlier life that you have been carrying with you?

- Can you remember how you felt when you received these messages?

- Can you let go of them, or even just put them aside for now?

Imagine yourself gathering up all these messages and putting them into a box. Once they are all safely in the box, imagine closing the lid and locking it with a key.

Then imagine throwing the box, along with the key, away. You could imagine throwing into a fire or tossing it out into the ocean. Imagine watching the box sink, float away, or be consumed by a beautiful bonfire, transmuted into beautiful clouds of smoke that float up to the sky.

To replace the old messages, are there any *new* messages that you can create for yourself, that you would like to carry with you as you grow in your self-understanding and self-love?

Imagine yourself opening a beautiful new box filled with the new messages you would like to create for yourself and hold on to. Imagine these new messages glowing and sparkling as you take them out and learn them one by one.

What beautiful messages of love and care will you find there?

Feel free to write them down in your journal to refer back to whenever you may need a reminder of these beautiful messages.

Two Choices

When I experienced the Big Burnout, I had recently started my psychotherapy practice, I was in the process of my minister training, and was in the thick of early parenthood. So I went through a period when I was around people all the time. I spent years masking 24/7—until I couldn't anymore. After putting the pieces together and coming to the realization that autistic burnout explained what I was experiencing, I suddenly realized there were only two choices available: I could hide away at home forever, so that nobody would notice my differences, *or* I could be an openly autistic person and let most people know up front, or soon into our interactions, about my neurotype. I found that opting for the latter took a massive amount of pressure off and allowed me to venture out into the world again. The previous worry about seeming different or odd started to give way to the knowing that I simply needed to do things differently.

Part of gaining the ability to feel more comfortable doing things differently was looking to other autistic people as role models—listening to autistic musicians, reading books by autistic authors, and connecting to the autistic community. Seeing others who were different in the same way helped me realize just how much we have in common—and how we are so connected.

As we find comfort, inspiration, and a sense of kinship from autistic role models, it is also helpful to remember to avoid comparing ourselves or our accomplishments with other autistic folks. As this point, it may seem obvious to avoid comparing ourselves with our neurotypical neighbors, but as we can more easily relate to the folks within our community, comparing ourselves with other autistic people can be an easy trap to fall into. Even though we share so many common characteristics, we all have our own unique strengths, needs, energy levels, and paths. And your path is uniquely your own.

"...As Any Autistic Person Would"

After spending a good part of our lives living within neurotypical society, and following neurotypical rules, it can be a great relief to let go of some of the pressures of masking. In their 2019 TEDx talk, Dr. Jac den Houting explained the newfound self-acceptance that was brought by their own autism diagnosis. They realized, "I wasn't a failed neurotypical person. I was a perfectly good autistic person" (2019). I found this to be true as well. In burnout, when I suddenly found myself with reduced ability to mask, social interactions became much more stressful, and I began to measure my "success" in these interactions by how well I thought I had "passed." Afterward, I would painstakingly review even brief interactions in my mind and wonder—Did I make enough eye contact? Did I move around too much? I had been judging myself against neurotypical standards. Through understanding my experience in burnout and shifting to view myself through an autistic lens, I learned to let that judgment go.

When we no longer view ourselves through a neurotypical lens, but an autistic one, it brings our differences into a different focus, with a new and more positive light. Now when I find myself in an interaction, wondering if I may seem noticeably different, I think: "I'm doing as well as any autistic person would." If there's something I find difficult, or I need an accommodation to do something in a different way, my mantra has become "As any autistic person would."

When we look at the things that make us different and radically accept them as vital parts of who we are, we may feel less of an urge to run and hide. During burnout, I found that accepting these differences was the only way forward. And once I acknowledged the struggles and allowed them to settle into their right-sized place, I newly noticed some strengths peeking out of the cracks as well. You may find that as you mindfully acknowledge your own

challenges, you may become more aware of your strengths too. Strengths and unique, wondrous traits that might have previously been overshadowed by shame or the instinct to hide. Radical acceptance can mean making peace with your limitations, but it can also allow you to truly see your gifts and the wonderful qualities that are unique to you (Linehan 2020; Brach 2021).

Decatastrophizing and Radical Self-Acceptance

In moments of struggle, we may experience the tendency to catastrophize—especially if we make a mistake, miss a cue, have our intentions misunderstood, or feel like we have fumbled within a social interaction. In these moments, it can be easy to spiral into shame or self-judgment. While in burnout, we're more likely to experience negative feelings about ourselves, and those feelings tend to *stick* to us a little more easily while we're in an energetic dip. Catastrophizing can bring us the feeling that because one thing has gone wrong, *everything* will go wrong.

To help decatastrophize, it can be helpful to look at each event within the greater picture. Each occurrence is *one* event out of a lifetime of many things. Sometimes we get it right, and sometimes we fumble, despite the best of intentions. That's us, and that's also everyone. Forgive yourself for mistakes as you would a dear friend who might have made the same fumble. Notice the feelings that are there, and let them go. If it's helpful, think of another time when you might have felt the same feelings of catastrophizing but then everything actually worked out okay. Sometimes we need to hold onto those reminders that imperfection is a normal part of being a person (Brach 2021), and that even when we're not perfect, we can still be okay (Linehan 2021).

Part of radical acceptance can begin with acknowledging what is there, as if from the viewpoint of a neutral and curious observer. Marsha Linehan (2021), creator of dialectical behavior therapy, encourages beginning with acceptance of whatever is there in the

present moment. Allowing ourselves to see what's there, without judgment, can help us to look at the challenges we are facing. And when we can see the challenges or strengths clearly, it can help us to then find a way forward.

Removing judgment can help to take away the emotional charge that sometimes comes with difficulty. We don't need to judge ourselves for struggling, as the judgment just compounds the struggle. Just setting the intention to let go of judgment can help us along in this process. See if you can catch yourself in moments that you may be experiencing a judgmental thought toward yourself. Notice that the thought is there, but don't engage with it, and let it go. Practicing nonjudgment can be so instrumental on the road to self-acceptance, and this includes both nonjudgment of self and nonjudgment of others. When we can extend empathy and nonjudgment to others, it creates a gentler world, but it can also be great practice for extending empathy and nonjudgment to ourselves. Sometimes it can be easier to extend care and empathy to others than to ourselves, so if it is helpful in times of struggle, think of yourself as you would a dear friend. What kindness, warmth, empathy, and acceptance would you give to this friend? Now extend that same warmth and care to yourself.

Mindfulness Moment

Take a moment to reflect on the following questions as a curious observer, without judgment, by just observing what *is*.

- What makes you uniquely you, and what kind of love and magic do you bring to this world? What words feel best to describe yourself?

- Is there anything you can identify that feels like a struggle for you right now?

- Can you look at these struggles with acceptance, peace, and nonjudgment?

- What are the things that you need to do differently, in your own unique way?

- Can you look at these differences with acceptance, peace, and nonjudgment?

- What are the things about yourself that you like most?

- What aspects of yourself are you most proud of?

- What are the things that are different about you that you really love?

Feel free to write in your journal about these reminders of celebration and acceptance of your whole self to carry with you.

The practice of radical self-acceptance is just that—a practice. You will find that there are days when self-acceptance feels a bit easier and others when it feels a bit more difficult. This is totally normal, like the movement of the waves. Sometimes the tide is heading outward, toward the ocean, and other times it is flowing back toward the shoreline, bringing abundance. Try to stay present—and connected with yourself—during these natural ebbs and flows.

Uncovering Your Authentic, Autistic Needs

Chapter 5

A Different Operating System
What Works for You

Through a neuroaffirming lens, being autistic is sometimes compared with having a different operating system. Similar to computers or smartphones, which can run on varying operating systems like iOS, Windows, or Linux, "neurotypes" are different types of brains that exist among the population. Like an operating system, each neurotype has its own unique features, challenges, and strengths. If you've ever switched from an Android phone to an iPhone, or from a Mac to a PC, you'll notice there are many things about each operating system that stand out as being different from the other—like layout, appearance, and functionality. But neither type of system is necessarily "better" than the other.

Even within just the autistic neurotype, we can see different profiles of individuals. Some autistic folks don't communicate through vocal speech at all or are mostly nonspeaking, utilizing other forms of communication. Others rapidly develop spoken speech at an early age. Some in our community are gifted in math, engineering, and science while others excel in the areas of art, music, and writing. Some autistic folks thrive in professions where they can work alone, while others enter caring professions where they spend their days supporting and interacting with people.

Within the autistic community, there are also varying ways of experiencing thoughts and ideas. In Temple Grandin's book *Thinking in Pictures*, she described her own thinking as visual, sometimes in

the form of "full-color movies" (2006, 3). Others experience an ongoing inner monologue of words in full sentences. Some people experience thoughts consisting of imagery or "impressions" of feelings and emotions which need to be decoded into a language to communicate to others. There are many ways to experience our thoughts, impressions, and inner worlds, which can offer great benefits and a richness of experience and ideas. Different ways of thinking can bring new ways of looking at challenges, finding solutions, and creating art and innovations.

Mindfulness Moment

- How do you experience your own thoughts and ideas—through images, words, impressions, senses, or a combination of these things?
- What is the most comfortable medium for you to convey your thoughts and ideas? Words, visual art, sculpture, music, movement, something else?
- Have you found any challenges related to your particular way of thinking?
- Are there any supports that would be helpful in working with these challenges?
- Can you think of a time when your unique way of thinking was helpful in solving a problem or finding a solution to a challenge?
- What do you like about your particular way of thinking?

The Importance of Neurodiversity

In the late Steve Silberman's book *Neurotribes*, he explored the idea that different neurotypes bring with them their own positive and

beneficial attributes. As opposed to the viewpoint that differences like autism were primarily "checklists of deficits and dysfunctions," he believed that different neurotypes were natural variations that each brought something to the table in contributing to our communities—and to society as a whole (2015, p. 16). Neurodiversity is as natural and important to life and civilization as biodiversity (Silberman 2015; den Houting 2019).

This neuroaffirming approach is useful in explaining the autistic way of being because it helps move us away from a medical model, which pathologizes our differences, toward a more balanced and equitable view of autistic traits. As we step away from the medical model of disability, which suggests that there is a deficit inherent within the individual that needs to be corrected (Olkin 2022), we can move toward frameworks like the social model of disability, which espouses the idea that there are barriers within the environment or society that are at odds with the disabled individual's needs. If we can identify and remove those barriers, the individual will have access to the conditions needed to thrive (den Houting 2019).

The "Curb-Cut Effect"

One classic example to highlight the social model of disability is the use of curb cuts on sidewalk corners for wheelchair accessibility. Without these ramps built into the sidewalks, many areas would be inaccessible to wheelchair users, and it would make for more difficult and dangerous street crossings for those with mobility issues in general. The ramps accommodate the need of wheelchair users by removing a barrier to accessibility, creating a more equitable environment. Interestingly, when disability accommodations such as curb cuts are implemented, their benefits often reach far beyond the group they were originally intended to help (Glover Blackwell 2017).

Curb cuts and ramps are also highly useful for non–wheelchair users, including parents with strollers, kids on scooters or bikes, or other folks with mobility issues. "The Curb-Cut Effect" suggests

that when accommodations are made for groups who are vulnerable or disabled, they often benefit society as a whole (Glover Blackwell 2017; Karp 2011; Greve 2007). When disabled individuals are accommodated and have their needs met, this has a way benefiting the greater society. Individualized accommodations for autistic folks could also carry the same benefit—the option to work individually versus in a group setting, having a quiet space at work or school to avoid overwhelm or distraction. Even nonautistic folks could benefit from having access to these adjustments.

For autistic folks, accommodations within the environment and within our lives tend to be key, as we are often quite sensitive to the environments in which we inhabit. If we consider autism not as inherently a disorder but as a difference, we can view it as an equally valid way of being. We are then more likely to see and accept autistic needs as just as legitimate and important as nonautistic needs. If we can approach our differences with the mindset that autistic traits are not wrong—and therefore not meant to be fixed or changed, but rather supported and accommodated—we are more likely to be able to access and utilize our unique skills and attributes.

Doing Things Differently

It can sometimes take a while to realize that the neurotypical way of doing things isn't feasible. When we try to do things the neurotypical way, we can run into difficulty, as if we were trying to run a Mac application on a Windows computer—it just doesn't work. As autistic folks living among a nonautistic majority, it also means that we may be unlikely to be able to look to the people around us for clues or examples of how to go about our lives. We may be occasionally fortunate to have autistic role models or community members we can glean insight from, but otherwise we may find ourselves traversing our paths and finding our own ways through much trial and error.

This forging of our own paths makes it all the more important to listen to our own inner guidance from our bodies, minds, and

emotions. As we increasingly connect to our authentic selves and honor our individual neurotypes, our experiences—whether challenging or affirming—can all contribute to learning what works best for us.

In everything we do as autistic folks, we need to find our way of doing things that works specifically for us. You may find that your way of doing things may be vastly different from the practices of those around you. You may also experience that your way is not always understood by others. But doing things in a way that works for you can lead to greater success—and is often far more sustainable for you and your unique operating system. In the upcoming chapters, we will explore a few important areas where you can tap into your own experience, insights, and inner wisdom to identify the supports and accommodations that will be most beneficial to you.

Mindfulness Moment

- Can you identify an area of your life in which you have found it helpful to complete a task, solve a problem, or go about an aspect of your life in a way that is different from what might be considered the "norm"?

- How did you arrive at this inventive solution?

- Can you think of any other areas of your life that may benefit from similar creative or unique solutions?

- What solutions might you be able to incorporate or implement?

Next up, we'll take a look at all things sensory, and how we can best understand and accommodate our important sensory needs.

Chapter 6

The Sensory Situation
Our Needs and Supports

Our sensory systems impact how we perceive and experience everything in world—and within ourselves. Learning about sensory needs and sensory supports to utilize when necessary is a vital part of supporting our overall well-being. Having a strong sensory foundation helps us better understand ourselves, our experiences, and how we can feel most comfortable as we go about our lives.

The sensory systems are traditionally the wheelhouse of occupational therapists (OTs), who are trained to assess the different sensory needs and profiles of each individual and to recommend the supports and accommodations that would be most beneficial. "An OT can then guide each individual's exploration of their sensory needs and development of sensory supports to optimize participation in daily life" (Cohen 2024).

Because it can often be difficult to locate or connect with an occupational therapist due to geography, insurance issues, financial barriers, or other various challenges, you can also learn about your own sensory profile through observing your own experience and preferences. For this chapter, I consulted with a dear friend and neuroaffirming occupational therapist in New York City, Lindsey Cohen, for her sensory knowledge and wisdom.

Sensory Differences and the Core of Autism

Our sensory experiences tend to be different from those of nonautistic, or "allistic," folks. Even so, every person, whether autistic or nonautistic, has their own profile of sensory needs. Although autism has historically been identified through observing differences in behavior and social interaction, and even considered by some to be a condition primarily of social or behavioral differences, at the core of autism is a difference in how we experience and process our environments. Within the autistic community, each person has their own sensory profile which impacts how they experience both their internal and external worlds.

Sensory Sensitive

Sensory sensitive folks tend to have systems that are *overre*sponsive to stimuli. If you are more sensory sensitive, you may find many aspects of the world to be intense, overwhelming, or *too much*. Sensory sensitive folks tend to be the ones who find noises to be too loud, food to be too spicy, or lights to be too bright. You may find that you become anxious or distressed in crowded places, or you may feel that you are at times being bombarded with sensory information. A sensory sensitive person might actively avoid experiences with lots of sensory input, like loud concerts, or may find it difficult to go to things like the dentist or medical appointments because there may be a heightened experience of pain or discomfort. Sensory sensitive folks may also be particularly overwhelmed by social interactions and need extra time in solitude to avoid overload.

Sensory Seeking

Sensory seeking folks tend to have systems that are *under*responsive to sensory input, so it takes more input for them to feel

comfortable. If you're sensory seeking, you may seek out spicy and flavorful foods or enjoy sports or activities with lots of fast motion and high impact. You may prefer to listen to loud music or love having lots of bright colors and lights around you. Some folks seek out sensory input in the form of socialization or interaction with others. If you are a sensory seeker, the sensory information from the environment will frequently feel like it's not enough, so you may find that you create your own additional sensory input.

Stimming to Create Equilibrium

Seeking out sensory input doesn't always mean that we are sensory seekers. We might, at times, create our own sensory input through stimming—like rocking, flapping, fidgeting, or pacing—to mitigate sensory discomfort or overload that we may be experiencing. It may seem counterintuitive to seek sensory input to reduce sensory overwhelm, but specific types of sensory input can be soothing for our systems, and sometimes creating a particular sensory experience to focus on, like deep pressure or listening to music, can help to block out, or balance out, the input from other stimuli that has become too much.

Combined Sensory Profile

While you may lean solidly toward a sensory seeking or sensory sensitive profile, it is also common to find sensory seeking *and* sensory sensitive traits within the same person. Someone might love spicy food and seek out lots of intense flavor but find things like bright colors or lots of visual input to be overwhelming. Another person might love loud music but find strong scents nauseating. Some of our senses can be turned up really high, and others can be turned down really low. To visualize the dynamics across all of our different senses, autistic self-advocate Lyric Rivera (2024) offers the image of a musician's mixing board—each control is set to a

different level. Every autistic person has their own variation of the sensory mixing board.

The Five Senses—And Three More!

To determine your own individual sensory profile, think about your own sensory experiences and preferences. Let's first talk a little bit about each of the senses. We all know about the main five senses (seeing, hearing, tasting, touching, and smelling). But did you know that there are three additional physical senses that impact our day-to-day experience?

The first one is proprioception, which gives us a sense of where our bodies are in space. Lindsey Cohen says we take in proprioceptive information through the sensors in our muscles, skin, and joints, and the proprioceptive sense helps us to feel grounded, oriented, and safe in the world (Cohen 2024). The vestibular sense helps us to sense movement and orientation, and we perceive vestibular information through our inner ears (Cohen 2024). Last but not least, interoception is the sense that helps us to be aware of what is happening in our bodies. It is the sense that alerts us to when we're hungry, thirsty, or may need to use the bathroom. It can also help us determine what emotions we are feeling, and so it makes sense that the common autistic experience of alexithymia is closely tied in with challenges with interoceptive awareness (Brewer et al. 2016).

Observing Your Senses

As you consider each of your own senses and sensory experiences, think about what feels most comfortable and right for you. You may want to write down your observations of your sensory experiences, as well as what types of sensory supports and accommodations you feel would be most helpful for each sense, creating a handy sensory reference for your specific needs. Let's go through them all!

Visual

What kinds of visual environments do you prefer? Do you feel most comfortable in uncluttered spaces with neutral colors, or do you prefer lots of visual information and bolder colors? Someone sensitive to visual input might become overwhelmed or distressed by bright lights or many objects within an environment, while someone who is a visual sensory seeker might enjoy looking at bright colors, lights, or sparkly things. Do you prefer bright lighting or soft, dim lighting? Some folks find that they are bothered by fluorescent lighting or LED lights but feel comfortable in natural sunlight or indoors with incandescent bulbs. What type of lighting do you prefer? Do you find that you are more comfortable while wearing sunglasses, or are you especially sensitive to glare on cloudy days? Your preferences can help you understand what kind of visual environment feels most comfortable for you.

Sound

Auditory sensory seekers may prefer listening to loud music or being in environments with lots of auditory stimuli, like concerts, loud movies, or busy places. Someone who is more sensitive to sound might find loud sounds painful or overwhelming. Volume of sound is one factor, but pitch, timbre of sound, and the number of sounds happening at once also play an important role. What kind of sounds, volumes, and pitches do you prefer?

If you play an instrument, or have a favorite instrument, what kind of pitch range do you gravitate toward? Do you prefer natural sounds, like birds and ocean waves? Or do you prefer the sounds of traffic and human-made activity? Imagine an auditory environment that feels most ideal for you. What do you come up with? If you find that you are sensitive to sound, there are lots of wonderful earplugs, over-the-ear headphones, and ear defenders on the market today. Many are made with the sensory needs of the neurodivergent adult in mind. Some find noise-canceling headphones to be helpful, while others find that the sound doesn't feel quite

natural, so trial and error can help you find what's best for you. If you find that you are more sensory seeking in the form of sound, can you access headphones that allow you to turn up the bass or adjust the sound profile of what you are listening to for an optimum sensory experience?

Smell

The sense of smell can be quite sensitive for some autistic folks, and many may find strong scents overwhelming and even sickening. Someone with sensitivity in the area of smell might find smells like coffee, garlic, or other strong scents nauseating or over-powering. Others may note less sensitivity to natural smells but are much more bothered by "chemical" smells like perfume, air freshener, or even deodorant. For people who experience sensory seeking related to the sense of smell, they may not notice subtle smells and may often seek out strong scents in the form of spices, perfumes, candles, or incense. Some sensory seekers even report enjoying "odd" smells like gasoline or the smell of skunk. If you are sensitive to smells, avoiding foods or places with strong scents can be most comfortable. For those who seek out strong scents, you may find it helpful to keep a rollerball of essential oil or fragrance with you to sniff whenever helpful. You may also enjoy adding scented candles or incense to your home, or visiting restaurants with bold spices.

Taste

The senses of smell and taste are so closely linked together that our sensory preference for smell is often similar to our prefer-ence for taste. So, if you find that you are sensitive to smells, are you sensitive to flavors as well? If you seek out bold scents, do you also prefer food with lots of flavor? Some autistic folks prefer foods that are often referred to as "beige" or "bland," and may find too much flavor to be overwhelming. If you are sensitive to food flavor

and texture, you may find that you have a list of "safe foods" that you can reliably consume comfortably. Some autistic folks enjoy a "samefood," literally eating the same food repeatedly for a period of time. Sometimes we may find that we have a samefood for a while and then suddenly can't stand it anymore, and we must find a different preferred food to eat. It is also helpful to note that some autistic folks struggle with avoidant/restrictive food intake disorder (ARFID), which is not to be confused with picky eating, and requires the help of a professional.

For those of us who are sensory seekers when it comes to flavor, we may seek out foods with bold or complex flavor profiles. We may enjoy trying new foods and seek out variety, finding flavors to become boring or unpalatable quickly. We might also struggle to eat food that is bland and may be more likely to perceive our food as lacking flavor, adding additional spices and seasonings to amp up the taste. What kinds of flavors and foods do you prefer? Do you prefer foods with strong flavors or food that is more mild? What about food texture—are there any textures or consistencies you prefer versus textures you avoid? What do you notice about your own patterns and preferences?

Tactile/Touch

Our sense of touch very often starts with the clothing we wear. Our clothing preferences can give us excellent clues to our tactile sensory preferences. What kinds of fabrics do you prefer to wear? Do you prefer natural fabrics like cotton or synthetic fabrics like acrylic? Do you notice you find certain fabrics scratchy, "sweaty," or uncomfortable? The fabric of jeans can feel notoriously scratchy or stiff, so some folks who wear jeans may prefer to purchase a larger size for a more relaxed fit.

Do you prefer clothing that is looser or more fitted? Some prefer clothing that is loose and flowy, while others prefer clothing that fits a bit more snugly. With looser fitting clothing, the fabric moves around more and touches the skin much more intermittently and unpredictably. Clothing that fits more snugly offers

constant predictability of tactile input. The fit of clothing can also be tied into the proprioceptive sense, which we'll explore in a moment!

And there's also socks—some love them, some hate them. A lot of autistic folks find that the seams of their socks bother them, so they find it helpful to wear their socks inside out, so that the seams of their socks are facing the outside, not touching their feet. There are also more brands of seamless and sensory-friendly socks on the market today. Some autistic folks find that their feet are extra sensitive, so they prefer to have their feet covered with socks or footwear much of the time to limit sensory input to the feet. Well-fitting socks can also provide consistent, uniform, and predictable sensory input to the feet. Do you prefer to wear socks? What do you like or dislike about them? What types of socks and footwear do you find most comfortable and why?

Folks who tend to prefer walking barefoot are often seeking sensory input to the bottoms of their feet. Or they may be particularly bothered by the feeling of their feet being confined or feeling "claustrophobic" in shoes. Many with heightened sensitivity may experience discomfort when their bare feet touch the floor or ground. This is one reason why some autistic folks walk on their toes—to avoid sensory input to the bottoms of their feet.

Someone with tactile sensitivity might also be uncomfortable with physical touch or affection and may be "tactile defensive." Some may find lighter touch to be painful or distressing but are happy with firmer touch like hugs. Some folks may not mind physical touch but may find unexpected touch to be uncomfortable or disorienting, so they might prefer that others ask before touching them.

One way of seeking out tactile sensory input is by touching objects in the environment. Some may prefer to touch soft objects like blankets or stuffed animals, or do tactile projects like knitting, sewing, or sculpture with clay. Walking barefoot on different surfaces can also provide varying types of input. What are your own tactile preferences? Do you seek out different textures of fabric in clothing or blankets? Do you have a preference for wearing shoes or going barefoot? You can also observe what kinds of tactile

experiences you prefer by trying out different fidget tools to see which ones feel best—there are a variety of sensory fidget tools on the market today, including ones that are squishy, spiky, stretchy, or spinning. Through trying out different stim tools, we can learn which ones are most beneficial for us.

Proprioception

Proprioception tells us "where we are in space." Lindsey Cohen says: "This is the input from our skin, muscles, and joints that is constantly being sent to our brain" (2024). And with this input, we often get a sense of grounding. Cohen says this input helps us to feel safer and more comfortable in our bodies and within our environments, and that some individuals need more proprioceptive input to access that feeling of grounding. Proprioception is also instrumental for self-regulation—when we feel safer and more grounded, we are much more able to feel calm and regulated.

Proprioceptive sensory seekers often seek out input via impact, motion, compression, or pressure. As our clothing can give us insight into our tactile preferences, it can also shine a light on our proprioceptive needs. For folks who are underresponsive in the proprioceptive sense, they may feel that they are either lost in space or not quite in their bodies. They may seek out clothing with some weight or compression. Weighted blankets are so popular because they can give a comforting sense of grounding and compression. A smaller and more portable version of the weighted blanket is a weighted lap pad. Input can also be provided by a weighted or compression vest. Some folks seek out proprioceptive input by squeezing into tiny spaces or leaning against a wall. Temple Grandin's famous "squeeze machine" was designed to provide comforting compression, offering grounding proprioceptive input (Grandin n.d.).

Proprioceptive sensory input can be obtained through seeking out high-impact activities like crashing into a crash pad. "Heavy work" in the form of "strong pushing and pulling exercises…can really be integrated into a daily routine at any age" (Cohen 2024)

and across different environments, such as at school or work, even in day-to-day environments such as the grocery store. Daily activities such as cleaning and mopping can be a way of integrating proprioceptive input into your routine (Cohen 2024).

For helpful forms of exercise, lifting weights, pedaling a bicycle or exercise bike with high resistance, wall pushups, floor pushups, and planking can also provide input to the proprioceptive receptors in our joints. Folks who struggle with proprioception may find that they easily bump into things or struggle with posture because their sense of being upright in space can be affected. For those sensitive to proprioceptive input, they may be more likely to feel "stuck or claustrophobic. Their sensory system is *over*reactive to the proprioceptive input" (Cohen 2024).

If you think about your own proprioceptive needs, what feels best for you? Are you more likely to feel lost in space, out of body, or that "stuck" or claustrophobic feeling? For proprioceptive input to the joints, fidget tools with some resistance for squeezing can be helpful supports. These are usually made from foam or gel, and are highly portable, so you can carry them with you. Other helpful tools can include trampolines and stretchy bands. Chewing gum, chewy tools, and eating foods like crunchy chips can also provide soothing proprioceptive input through the receptors in the joints in our jaws. What kinds of proprioceptive supports would be most helpful for you?

Vestibular

The vestibular sense is "how our inner ear detects positional changes and the responses from our motor and visual systems to maintain a sense of balance," Cohen says (2024). Folks who seek out vestibular input might rock or sway, or enjoy input through swings, riding a bike, running, or other types of motion through space. A seeker of vestibular input might love spinning or being upside down. Folks with vestibular issues may struggle with balance "because their vestibular system is not quite as fine-tuned" (Cohen 2024). For folks with sensitive vestibular systems, their movement

may be more cautious or limited. They may also experience motion sickness more easily. If you have a sensitive vestibular system, you may find the movement of swings to be overwhelming or nauseating, or may be especially prone to feeling carsick. Cohen says one way to minimize vestibular discomfort is by limiting movement, but especially by "limiting how much your head is moving." For those prone to motion sickness, for example related to car travel, looking out the front window in the car, as if driving, can help minimize discomfort. Also helpful can be keeping a focal point, known as "'gaze stabilization,' to limit visual feedback that could interfere with equilibrium" (Cohen 2024).

Interoception

Interoception is the sense that tells us what is going on inside our bodies. It can alert us to when we may be hungry, thirsty, or need to use the bathroom. For someone with sensitive interception, they may sense any pain or discomfort within the body, such as a stomach ache, as intense and consuming. While the discomfort is present, "they can't think about anything else" (Cohen 2024). Some folks with underresponsive interception might not have as much awareness if they are sick or have an injury and may have a high tolerance for things others would find painful.

Our interoceptive sense can vary, so one aspect of our interoception can be especially sensitive, while another aspect may have difficulty detecting a need within our bodies. For example, an individual may be especially sensitive to cues of hunger but not experience the feeling of thirst when they need to drink water, meaning they become dehydrated before becoming thirsty.

Interoception can give us a sense of temperature, as well as cues about our comfort within an environment. If we struggle with interoception, we may have difficulty recognizing whether the room we are in is too hot or too cold. What do you notice about your own interoceptive awareness? Are you able to identify when you are hungry or thirsty? What about when you are tired or too hot or too cold? Do you find that you are sensitive to pain and

discomfort, or that you don't even notice things that others may find uncomfortable? These interoceptive clues can offer valuable insights into your awareness of your body and environment.

Empathy and Emotion

Although not officially considered one of the senses, empathy—the ability to sense emotions, thoughts, and general "vibes" from others—is very much like a sense. We know that some autistic folks are particularly attuned to the emotions, thoughts, and energy of others. Some autistic folks report experiencing *hyper*empathy, experiencing the emotions of others as if they are their own, and may become easily overwhelmed by the emotions of other people. They might also be quick to sense when there is a subtle change of energy within a group or environment, or the emotional state of the person with whom they are interacting.

Others may struggle to connect with or perceive the emotions of others, almost as if those emotions are far away. Our sense of empathy can also vary depending on the person, situation, or environment we are encountering. In a busy, crowded, or overwhelming environment, it may be difficult to sense the emotions or energy of another person because the stimuli of the environment may be overpowering our subtle perceptions.

Psychologist and autism researcher Dr. Tony Attwood has referred to this phenomenon as empathic attunement, or a "sixth sense sensitivity," where the autistic individual "is able to pick up emotions in other people using channels that neurotypicals aren't aware of, that are accurate...but can be overpowering" (2019). Attwood also explains that we can be more sensitive to picking up on and absorbing the negative or difficult emotions of others, which can be distressing or overwhelming—something that can contribute to autistic folks withdrawing from social interaction (Attwood 2019).

Autistic author William Stillman has written books about how autistic individuals can be particularly sensitive to picking up the emotions and thoughts of others (2006). Due to this heightened

sensitivity, many autistic people are drawn toward spirituality and the helping and caring professions, where their heightened sense of empathy is an extraordinarily useful gift. Do you find you sense the emotions and "vibes" of people and places? Do you ever struggle with identifying the emotions of others, or do you find that you often know how others are feeling before they themselves are aware? Do you experience environments like crowds as overwhelming or energizing? These clues can offer great insights into your own experience with perceiving the energy around you.

Sensory Needs Change

You may find your sensory needs changing at various points throughout your life. For example, as a child, I never liked being barefoot and much preferred wearing socks and shoes. I would even wear water shoes while swimming because the sensory input to the bottoms of my feet bothered me so much. As an adult, I find that I prefer to be barefoot much of the time when I am indoors, where the surface of the floor is smooth and predictable, but I still like to wear footwear outside, even at the beach. If you look back over the course of your own life, do you notice that any of your sensory needs or preferences have changed over time?

Our sensory needs also tend to change under stress or fatigue, and this is often when they become more pronounced. When our systems are under increased stress, sensory sensitive folks will generally find certain stimuli more painful or distressing. For sensory seekers, they may notice an increased need for sensory input. We know that one of the signals of autistic burnout is an increase in sensory discomfort.

Additionally, folks who experience menstruation often find that their sensory discomforts are heightened in the week before menstruation begins, when the body can often experience reduced tolerance to pain (Hellström and Anderberg 2003). You might also experience more sensory discomfort during illness or when you're generally not feeling well. Knowing how to make adjustments to keep our sensory systems more comfortable and in equilibrium is

important for maintaining overall well-being and instrumental in healing autistic burnout and preventing future burnouts.

Sensory Supports Across Environments

Understanding your sensory profile and how different needs may present across different environments can help you create a list of your own most helpful sensory tools and supports. What sensory tools are most beneficial for you at home? At school? In the workplace? Can you think of any sensory tools that would be useful to carry with you as you go about your day, almost like a sensory tool kit or first aid kit? Choosing a selection of sensory-friendly clothing, small and portable fidgets, and headphones or earplugs for your sensory toolbox can help you stay more comfortable and regulated wherever you go. When entering particularly intense or challenging sensory environments, it can also be helpful to have a plan of exit in case you become overwhelmed or a system of taking breaks as needed.

Anxiety or Sensory Discomfort?

Sensory discomfort can frequently masquerade as anxiety. In fact, many autistic folks, especially women and AFAB folks, are diagnosed with anxiety disorders before they discover that they are actually autistic. Sensory discomfort can feel a lot like anxiety because it can be so unsettling and disorienting. When we think of sensory discomfort, we may think of the more classic physical pain like we might experience when going to the dentist or if we drop something heavy on our toe. Sensory pain can feel different—for example, if someone is bothered by a sound, they might not necessarily feel pain in their ears but might feel a discomfort within their nervous system. When we experience odd or overwhelming sensations within our nervous systems, it can be easy to interpret these signals as anxiety.

Sensory discomfort can also *cause* anxiety, so there can sometimes be a bit of a chicken-or-the-egg question of which one was present first.

If you find yourself in a situation or environment where you reliably feel anxious, you may find it helpful to ask yourself, "Am I anxious? Or am I overwhelmed? Is there some kind of sensory discomfort that I may be experiencing here, which could be leading to anxiety?" Take a look around the environment and take note of the sensory elements that you observe. Is there anything that might be bothering you? And remember that sensory pain does not always feel like pain in the "classic" sense. We can experience sensory pain in the form of disorientation, a "sick" feeling, or what I call "vague, nebulous discomfort"—a sense that something is bothering us, although we may not immediately be able to discern or describe what it is. Some people experience sensory discomfort or overwhelm in the form of anger or another emotional response that can seem to appear out of nowhere. There may be just a subtle feeling, difficult to pinpoint, that there is something in the environment that doesn't agree with your system.

We can also become so accustomed to sensory discomfort that we spend much of our lives in a low-grade state of unease or overwhelm because we almost become used to it. Like a person who lives with chronic pain, going about their lives with some degree of discomfort humming in the background all or most of the time. Many autistic folks can go for years living in a subtle and persistent state of sensory discomfort, which can be one of the most taxing experiences for our nervous systems and a powerful and primary contributor to autistic burnout. If we can gain a deeper insight into our sensory systems—and the elements within our lives or environments that may be contributing to sensory discomfort—we can then begin to implement the changes we need to alleviate as much of this discomfort as possible. The more we know about our sensory systems, the more we can create the gentle conditions necessary to support our well-being.

Up next, we'll talk about all things energy, as well as how to mindfully stay in tune with and preserve your energy levels!

Chapter 7

Energy Is Everything
Pacing Yourself

In my experience, energy is the foundation and currency of autistic life. Energy is required to self-regulate, to process the many sensory aspects of the environments we inhabit, and to translate our inner thoughts and impressions into language and communication. We utilize energy to interact with others, often in ways that may not be our natural way of interacting. If we are masking or communicating in ways that don't feel natural for us, the energetic cost can be substantial.

How well an autistic person will be able to do in any given situation depends on how much energy they have in their reserves. When we start to run out of energy, we may begin to notice the sensory aspects of our environment becoming overwhelming or painful. Or we may seek out additional sensory input to help keep our systems in balance. When our energy levels start to become depleted, we may have less emotional resilience or tolerance for stressful stimuli, or we may have more difficulty communicating our thoughts to others. In your own experience, how do you know when your energy levels may be starting to run low? Are there any signs or signals that you can observe?

Our diminishing energy levels can lead us into autistic burnout, and if we continue to expend energy we can't spare, that can keep us in burnout for a longer period of time. Staying mindful of our energy levels—being aware of the aspects of our lives that drain our energy and the elements which we find helpful and restorative—can help us to recover from any autistic burnout we may be

experiencing, and can also help keep us healthy, preventing future burnouts.

Energy Accounting

The concept of "energy accounting" was coined by autistic psychologist and author Maja Toudal, in collaboration with psychologist Tony Attwood (2025). In their book *Energy Accounting*, Toudal and Attwood suggest that within our daily lives, there are some aspects that drain our energy and others that give us energy—each component of our lives is basically an energetic "credit" or "debit." Energy accounting is a way of mindfully keeping track of what drains your energetic batteries versus what you find restorative. For example, if you find interactions like small talk draining, that would be considered an energetic credit, as it is withdrawing and depleting energy from your "account." A debit would be something that brings you energy, or deposits energy into your account, and could be something like spending time with a special interest.

To visualize the energetic debits and credits in your daily life, you can create a chart with two columns—one for items that deplete your energy (credit/withdrawal) and another for those that restore your energy (debit/deposit). If you want to get even more specific, you can assign a value of points to each item you include in your chart. For example, if you find making a phone call to be draining but not devastatingly so, you might specify that phone calls cost you twenty points of energy. Something that costs more energy, like going to a dentist appointment, might get assigned a value of one hundred points. It's the same with activities that bring you energy—maybe reading an article about a favorite subject would bring you fifteen points worth of energy, while spending a whole day in solitude would offer one hundred fifty points. As you keep track of the debits and credits in each column, it can help you to gain a more detailed sense of the input and output of your

overall energy. This is just one way of conceptualizing the flow of our energy, bringing it from something that can feel somewhat intangible and difficult to keep track of to something we can more easily visualize (Toudal and Attwood 2025).

Store and Restore

Whether you are formally utilizing the concept of energy accounting or simply staying mindful of what brings you energy versus what costs you energy, this awareness can make it more possible to plan or anticipate the events, tasks, and responsibilities in your life with higher-energy demands. Whenever I'm approaching an event which might require a high energy cost, I find it helpful to employ a practice I call "store and restore."

Ahead of a task or event that brings a high energy cost, it can help to spend some time before the event increasing downtime or reducing demands to store up some extra energy in our reserves. Maybe you have a big trip or an important meeting planned. Planning for a lighter schedule with reduced energy demands in the hours, days, or weeks leading up to this event can help you to increase your stored energy, which can then serve to power you through the energy-demanding event. When scheduling tasks or events, it can be helpful to not only consider whether you have time for the event itself, but whether you also have the time and space to store and restore surrounding the event.

If you have a commitment on your schedule from 1 to 2 p.m. in the afternoon, would it be helpful to block out the time between 10 a.m. and 1 p.m. to store up some needed energy, and then from 2 p.m. to 4 p.m. to restore and recover? If you have time only for the event itself, but not for the store and restore time surrounding it, is this commitment still feasible for you? Or would it potentially cost you more energy than you have to spare right now?

Mindfulness Moment

Think of an event or commitment that you have on your schedule in the near future. This could be related to work, family, socializing, or attending something like a doctor's appointment. Take a moment to think about the demands this commitment may place on your energy and how you may want to store and restore your energy surrounding the event.

In a journal, take a moment to answer each of these questions:

- What is the day of the week and time of this appointment?

- How much time do you need to block out of your schedule to store up some of your energy before this event?

- It is feasible with your schedule to block out as much time as you need? If not, how much time does your schedule allow for downtime before this event?

- How would it be most helpful to spend this down-time? (Reading, listening to music, learning about a special interest, drawing, resting?) What feels most right? If there's any feeling of pressure to be productive during this time, let that feeling drift away. Try and make store and restore times as pressure-free as possible.

- Now look ahead to the restore time after the event. How much time do you feel that you need to recover?

- Does your schedule allow for the full and needed recovery time? If not, how much time is available to you for recovery?

- During this recovery time, what feels best for you? (Resting, listening to music, watching a favorite show, taking a walk?)

- If enough restore time isn't available to you immediately following the event, could you take some time later that day, the next day, or some-time later in the week to catch up on needed restore time?

Feel free to keep these notes with you to draw from when-ever you may have energetically demanding events on your schedule that might call for store and restore!

I recognize that we don't always have the degree of control that we would like over our schedules and responsibilities, and so some-times our lives may only allow for smaller changes to be made, or we may need to incorporate some flexibility with when we take our store and restore times, sometimes necessarily deferring needed downtime until later in the day, or another day entirely. If you find that you have to delay this restore time, it may help to hold on to the knowledge that the restore time is on the way and that you will be able to rest soon.

It can also be helpful to utilize a visual representation. When planning for store and restore, you can formally block out time in your schedule, before and after the event, which can serve as a tangible representation of the commitment to yourself, and refer back to it if you need a reminder that downtime is approaching soon. Remember that time you have planned for solitude or rest still constitutes as having a *plan*. If someone asks you to make a commitment during a time you have already planned out for soli-tude or downtime, it's entirely valid to say that you already have plans, because you do!

Longer-Term Restore

Some energy-demanding tasks or events require extended rest or recovery time. For example, after attending an important meeting or big family gathering, you may need a day or two to decompress, having a few days with little to nothing on your schedule. You may find that during this decompression time, you might be able to complete smaller and easier tasks, but prefer to minimize interaction with others as much as possible. This may be a time when you want to engage in activities that require a smaller energetic output, like resting, listening to your favorite music, or watching a favorite show. You may find you have the energy to prepare simple, familiar foods for yourself, but not the energy to look up new recipes, track down new ingredients, or cook something more complicated. Maybe you can manage responding to a quick email about schedule logistics, but need to wait until you have more energy to respond to messages that require more thought or nuance.

Sometimes, after events that are particularly demanding of our energy, our need for rest and recovery can extend for longer periods of time than we might have expected. We may not necessarily be able to bounce back after a day or two, but might actually need to take it easy for several days, or even a week or more, for our energy to restore to the levels that are more comfortable for us. This is normal for many autistic folks, so if you find that it's taking a while for your energy to restore after a higher-energy-cost event, listen to yourself, and rest and reduce demands as much as you can until you feel like your energy has returned.

Avoid Jumping Back in Too Quickly

You may notice that after some self-care practices, your energy starts to come back a little bit. When this happens, it can be easy to feel like you want or need to jump right back into your routine and responsibilities at full speed. But jumping back in too soon can quickly place your energy levels back in the negative again. If at all possible, continue to take it easier for a while, even once you feel

your energy begin to restore, until your energy more fully recharges, so you don't end up depleted again.

Have you noticed that some smartphones, when charging, will remain in an energy-conservation mode until the phone has charged to a higher percentage, around 80 percent? Think of your own energetic batteries in the same way—try and continue in energy-conservation mode until you have a greater amount of energy in your reserves. If you were to think of your energy as a percentage, like a smartphone, how much energy feels best to have recharged before resuming your more normal routine—is it 50 percent? Maybe 80 percent? Spend some additional time restoring your batteries in the ways that feel right for you, until your energy batteries are more fully restored. Switching into energy-conservation mode when you sense a stressful or overwhelming time can also help to prevent future burnouts or at least help to reduce the severity and duration of new burnouts you may experience.

The Different Types of Energy

Interestingly, you may find that certain activities can both bring you energy and drain your energetic batteries. For example, if you attend a party with a lot of people, you might find it enjoyable and energizing with respect to mental stimulation or the joy of connection, but you may also experience that after the party you are exhausted, or "peopled out," and in need of additional rest, solitude, or recovery time. So, it can also be helpful to pay attention to how much of each *type* of energy you have.

Our energy doesn't necessarily fit into one global category, as we possess different types of energy—physical, mental, emotional, and social. Can you think of any more types of energies that you experience? We can be running low on one kind of energy, while still having a good amount of another. For example, at the end of a long day of work, you may have the physical energy to go to the gym or ride your bicycle, but may not have the social or mental energy to have a five-minute conversation with a neighbor. You

may find that you have the mental energy to read a book, but find that physically, your body is in need of rest and stillness. You may also experience times when you have the mental energy to listen to music but don't have the emotional energy to listen to songs that are "heavy" or emotionally demanding.

Minding the Different Types of Energy Levels

When you think of the different types of energy, what do you find most demanding versus restorative? Restoring physical energy can often come in the form of nutrition, exercise, and quality sleep. For mental energy, time and space to decompress without having to tackle any mentally intensive tasks can be beneficial. This could include time spent watching a favorite movie or show, such as one you've already seen several times and know almost by heart. This way, there is less pressure to pay close attention and follow the story or suspense in wanting to find out what happens. Watching a movie you already know, or a video which doesn't demand super close attention, can be a mentally low-pressure activity that can give you the space to allow your thoughts to drift away and return.

When it comes to conserving or restoring your emotional energy, what do you find most helpful? It could be listening to a favorite song or listening to a lighthearted podcast. It could be watching a comedy or doing something tangible you can focus on, like gardening, playing a musical instrument, or working on a craft. Does minding your emotional energy include talking to a friend or loved one, or processing your own emotional landscape in solitude and space? Having conversations ties into our social energy as well—what kinds of interactions do you find most helpful and restorative? Do you love to talk at length with a friend about deep subjects or shared interests? Do you like to socialize in small groups, larger groups, or one-on-one? What about larger events like concerts or events out in the community where you can connect with

neighbors? How do your own energy levels respond to each of these things?

Related to social energy, do you find that you need lots of solitude or prefer to be connected to others most of the time? If you were to think about your time in percentages, out of 100 percent, how much of your time would you prefer to spend in solitude versus with other people? What value do you place on solitude versus connection, and what is the most comfortable balance of both? This information can be helpful to reflect on and keep in a journal, along with a list of restorative activities you find helpful based on your energy levels. Try keeping a list of low-energy, medium-energy, and higher-energy activities that you can engage with whenever you need some restorative time.

Mindfulness Moment

Now take moment to consider how much of each type of energy you have in your own reserves at this moment. If feels more natural to create an image as opposed to describing your energy levels in words, feel free to create a drawing, chart, or graph to depict the level of each type of energy you have right now. Feel free to write or draw your observations in your journal.

Physical Energy

- How are your physical energy levels at the moment?
- Are you feeling fatigued or energetic?
- Would you benefit from rest, tasks that require physical activity, or some movement or exercise?

Mental Energy

- How are your mental energy levels?

- Are you feeling able to take on tasks that are mentally demanding, such as filling out a form, planning out next week's schedule, or doing a crossword puzzle?

- Would you benefit from doing an activity that is less mentally taxing, like watching a favorite show or doing an activity like knitting, which is repetitive and doesn't require intense attention?

Emotional Energy

- How is your emotional energy at the moment?

- Are you experiencing, or have you experienced, any intense emotions or emotional events recently that may require some recovery time?

- Do you feel up for engaging in emotionally demanding activities, such as having deep conversations to support a friend, or would it be helpful to have some emotional downtime, listening to a lighthearted podcast or your favorite music?

Social Energy

- How is your social battery at the moment?

- Have you experienced any demanding or refreshing social interactions today?

- In this moment, do you find that you are seeking connection and interaction, or solitude and alone time?

Being able to check in with our energy levels at any given time can help us to know when we are starting to become depleted—and

when to take action to conserve our energy. Maintaining awareness of our different types of energy can also help us become conscious of the signals that our energy is beginning to return.

Observing Our Energy Patterns

Through mindfully observing our energy levels at various points throughout our days and our lives, we can learn how our energy often responds to stimuli. We may also notice that regardless of what is on our schedule, we may naturally have more or less energy at different times during the day. Similar to being a morning person or a night owl, you may find that your energy levels are highest or lowest at similar times every day.

Think about the patterns of energy that you experience daily— what time of day do you feel most energetic and alert? It can be beneficial to go with your natural rhythms instead of fighting them. Coordinating higher-energy-cost activities like work projects, social-izing, or doctor's appointments for times when you naturally have more energy can help optimize the energy you have available to you. It can also be helpful to schedule periods of rest or downtime for when your energy levels are naturally lower. For example, I find that my energy levels are highest in the morning, drop a bit in the afternoon, and then start to come back a bit more toward the early evening. For this reason, I tend to schedule mornings as my busiest times, when my energy is at its peak.

To get a sense of your own energy's peaks and valleys, can you make a drawing that shows the arc of your natural energy levels throughout the day or week? Some folks find that they start out the week with lots of energy, and then that energy tapers off toward the end of the week. Others may find that they feel they are dragging on Mondays but become more energized as the work-week goes on and the weekend approaches. How can you work with your own natural energy flow?

Budgeting Your Energy

Understanding your natural energy patterns can help you to budget your energy by finding a pace that is right for you. You may have heard the classic expression "Slow and steady wins the race." I have also found that *slow and steady* is often what makes the race *possible*. Similar to the way a runner needs to find a comfortable pace to make their energy last for the duration of the race ahead, finding a pace that works for you can make it more possible to sustain your energy so that you can more comfortably attend to the routine and responsibilities ahead of you, in both the short term and the long term.

Pacing ourselves can be especially vital for the folks in our community, and we may find that our unique ways of making our energy last can look quite different from what works for those around us. One option is the *slow and steady* approach, to spend small amounts of energy slowly and gradually over a longer period of time, similar to the way that a long-distance runner would. Others may prefer to spend more intense energy in short bursts, alternating with periods of rest or downtime to recharge, similar to a sprinter. You may even find that you draw from each style at different times or for different tasks. It might sometimes feel like each day is a sprint that exists within a larger marathon, and that balancing the short-term and long-term needs calls for a blending of strategies.

It can help to pay extra attention to how much energy we may be spending at the *beginning* of things. Sometimes, we may approach a new task or interaction with great excitement, enthusiasm, motivation, or even anxiety, which may naturally cause us to burst out of the starting gate, using up a ton of our energy right at the beginning, setting us up to run out of steam. Similarly, if we have too much on our schedule, we may be barreling through, trying to get everything accomplished, and running on adrenaline without even realizing it. In these situations, it is very easy to be moving along quickly, unconsciously spending all of our energy, and then suddenly crash or hit the wall. We can avoid this crash by frequently checking in with ourselves, especially when we are busy.

Ask yourself how much energy you are spending at the present moment and whether you are moving at a comfortable and sustainable pace. If not, can you pull back on your energy expenditure and slow down, even if just a little bit, to avoid the crash?

"Spoon Theory"

Another way to conceptualize the usage of our energy can be with the "spoon theory," an idea coined by Christine Miserandino in 2003. Miserandino originally created the spoon theory to explain to a friend what it was like to live with a chronic illness. According to the spoon theory, we wake up each morning with a finite number of "spoons," which are units of capacity or energy. Everything we do and each task we complete consumes some of those spoons. If we do too much and spend too much energy, then we run out of spoons for the day. This is why you may sometimes hear folks with disabilities or illnesses say, "I ran out of spoons." In the autistic community, this can be a way of saying that we have run out of energy and can't take on anything more at the moment. This is why planning out our days, minimizing the number of tasks we have to do in a day, and prioritizing rest can be so important.

"Fork Theory"

In response to the spoon theory, the fork theory was also created (Jenrose 2018). The fork theory is based on the colloquialism, "Stick a fork in me, I'm done." The idea behind the fork theory is that each of us has a limit to the demands or stressors we can manage. If we compare each stressor or discomfort that we experience to being stuck with a fork, we might be able to sustain being occasionally stuck once or twice—but when fork sticks add up, at some point we hit our limit of what we can sustain. There are times when our energy is so depleted, and we may find ourselves so overwhelmed, that we feel like we are at our limit and we can't manage even one more thing.

The Washing Machine Theory—Just One More Thing

When I think of autistic burnout, and even the meltdowns or general overwhelm we often experience, I compare our systems to a washing machine that has been overloaded and is now shaking off balance. Sometimes, there may be a question of "What triggered that meltdown?" Or "What caused this autistic burnout?" Just like the way the last dish towel added to the laundry load is probably not the sole cause of the washing machine becoming overloaded, there is probably not a single cause of the meltdown or burnout. There is typically no *one* item in the washing machine that singlehandedly caused the overload—it's the combination and accumulation of *all* the things. What we may identify as a "trigger" may just be the last thing we can see or identify in a long list of energy withdrawals, fork sticks, and stressors. Similar to using energy accounting to determine what taxes and restores our energy, we can also take a look at the things that add to and reduce our overall overload. If you notice the presence of extra stressors or elements that put a drain on your energy, even if you may not be feeling signs of burnout at the moment, it can be a great time to implement additional self-care.

Next up, we'll continue talking about how our energy is impacted by our environments and the demands we experience, as well as some ways to care for ourselves and bring our energy back.

Chapter 8

Time to Expand
Restoring Your Energy

In burnout, it's almost as if our own personal energy, or life force, has diminished a little bit. Like our own inner light is slightly dimmer. When I talk about energy in this chapter, I am using the word in two different ways. One would be referring to the energy we have in our systems, which powers us through the day, like fuel in a gas tank. The other meaning of energy has to do with our own personal life force energy. Practices like energy healing and Reiki, meaning "universal life energy," suggest that each of us has our own personal energy field, which can affect, and be affected by, the environment around us.

Some people are able to visually see this energy, while others, like myself, are able to feel the energy of others. Our personal energy, in addition to our physical senses, also brings us information about the world around us. As mentioned by William Stillman (2006) and Tony Attwood (2019), autistic folks seem to be particularly sensitive and adept at perceiving the energy and emotional states of other people, as well as subtle shifts within the environment. In my experience, we often process other people's emotions through our own personal energy and might even absorb others' energy into our systems, especially if people are in close physical proximity to us. Because of this heightened sensitivity, we may frequently feel bombarded by environmental stimuli.

I believe this is why some of us need extra personal space—because our energy is so sensitive to the energy of other people that it can very easily feel like others are "too close." Do you notice

how on the side mirrors of cars it usually says, "Objects in mirror are closer than they appear"? This means that when you look in the mirror, what you see will look farther away than it actually is—in reality, it is much closer. I have found that many autistic folks have the opposite experience. We may perceive others as being "too close," even if they are physically farther away, because they are being perceived by our personal energy. If they are occupying a space within our own energy field, even from halfway across the room, it can be perceived as overwhelming or intrusive.

You may be perceptive of when energy shifts or changes occur before there are any outward signs, like when the person you're talking to might have a change in mood or might suddenly become enthusiastic about a new idea. You may have a sense of this before they verbally express it. What do you notice about the energy you perceive from other people and how your own energy feels in response to others' emotions or shifts in emotional states?

For some autistic folks, we may be likely to pick up on when someone else is upset, but because we don't know why, there can be a tendency to assume it's because of something we did, when that may not be the case at all. Some autistic folks will find that they spend a great deal of energy being hypervigilant, anticipating the needs of those around them to try and keep everyone happy, perhaps as an unconscious way of avoiding negative emotions from others and potentially absorbing those emotions into their systems.

Our sensitivity to the emotions of others can sometimes create a feeling of responsibility to take care of those around us if they are experiencing difficult emotions. This is why we may feel a particular affinity for social justice or a drive to be helpful. When we lessen the pain of others, it can also reduce the pain or distress we are experiencing as our energy meets theirs. Being in caregiver mode too much over an extended period of time can drain our energetic batteries, leaving us with little energy to care for ourselves. At times, it can be helpful to step away from emotionally caring for others to fortify our own energy for a while.

Tension as Protection

One way we may naturally respond to outside stressors is by tensing or contracting our own energy, similar to the way muscles tense under stress. Due to our sensitivities, we may frequently carry extra tension in our bodies, almost as if we use our physical bodies as a shield to brace against uncomfortable sensory elements or block out energy from other people or environments that feel chaotic, intrusive, or overwhelming. This tension can often be carried in the abdominal muscles, which actually resemble the shape of a shield that we might hold in front of us. We might also notice that we are carrying extra tension in our arms, neck, or jaw.

I call this "protective tension," and in a way, it is a brilliant adaptation we have adopted for managing and protecting our sensitive energy and sensory systems in an overwhelming world. But remaining in this tense state all the time can wear us down. When we are overwhelmed and depleted, it can also feel like we have become smaller, like we have condensed, or like our own energy or inner light has become dimmer and more constrained. We may notice that our posture is less upright, as if we have been carrying something unduly heavy on our shoulders for a long time. We can notice these physical signs in our bodies that we are depleted.

We may also find that while masking, or if there are other people around, we are consciously or unconsciously suppressing our own personal energy, or laboriously holding it in. This can be through the tension created by masking, suppressing needed stims or the movement we need to feel comfortable, and refraining from doing things that bring us joy, like singing or existing in our natural flow state. In a sense, the adjustments we often make around others can also diminish our light or make us smaller.

But what if you could expand? What if you were no longer suppressing your energy into a tiny, contained space, but rather allowing your aura to radiate outward by spending some time free to be yourself, without demands and without the pressure of masking?

"I Do Not Wish to Be Perceived"— Time to Be Free

There was a ubiquitous meme going around the internet a few years back featuring variations on the phrase "I do not wish to be perceived," which was widely embraced by autistic and other neurodivergent folks, and even printed on t-shirts and other merch. It seemed like everyone agreed on one thing—the need for the privacy to just be ourselves. Spending time in privacy can be so imperative for many autistics because it can often feel like the only time we can truly relax and be our full selves is when we are alone. This can be due to not wanting to be observed by others or being aware or self-conscious of things we may naturally do that are different, which others might not understand. There may be occasions when you've stopped what you were doing upon realizing that someone was looking in your direction. Some of us may not feel fully at ease to unmask until we are completely alone.

For many autistic people, just having someone else at home— even if they are in a different room—prevents us from feeling like we have the privacy and space to just be. When there is someone else around, even if we're not interacting, we can still experience this as a drain on our energy. It's almost as if the presence of others keeps us in "standby mode." Similar to the way that appliances continue to pull energy from electrical outlets even when they're not in use, the presence of others—and the awareness that we might be perceived or interrupted at any moment—can prevent us from fully disconnecting to recharge. What are your own privacy needs, and what do you notice about your own ability to relax around other people versus when you are completely alone? Are there aspects of your unmasked self which you reserve for only when there is no possibility of being perceived?

I compare the autistic need for privacy to the magical and mystical characters from books which spring to life and become active when there is no one around. This time and space and privacy can often be what we need to lift the tension we are carrying in our bodies and allow our energy to fully and freely expand, like a bright ball of glowing light. Sometimes we best experience magic and

wonder when we have the space to freely stim, move about, and access our own inner worlds.

The Inner World Calls

Actor Daryl Hannah—who was diagnosed with Asperger's syndrome, which would now be a diagnosis of autism under present-day DSM-V (APA 2013)—expressed in an interview with Dan Rather, "I wouldn't say I was introverted; I was more out there somewhere. I was off in the dreamworld all the time" (2014). She described a period of time when she remained out of school and was allowed to "sort of exist in my imaginary world for a good year or so and sort of slowly reintegrated...back into the 'normal' world." The inner or imaginary world can be such a vital and important place for autistic folks, and the pull toward our inner worlds can be powerful.

These can be spaces of great wonder and adventure, often more vibrant and interesting than the world outside of us. For many autistic folks, the worlds within us can be deep and expansive, and filled with multisensory imagery and experiences. Some autistic folks also experience hyperphantasia, or the ability to create vivid and realistic imagery in our minds. We can experience going inside ourselves as restorative and necessary, and especially so when we are experiencing burnout or becoming fatigued. We may notice that when we are tired, the pull toward our inner world is the strongest—and in fact, that may be one of the first signs that our energy is dwindling.

Visiting our inner worlds can feel like a peaceful pulling back from the outside environment, or we may feel as if our energy is floating slightly upward. In these moments, we may feel a peaceful respite, or even a sense of euphoria. It's like taking a little vacation. Sometimes, I find that I can exist in both worlds—the inner world and the outer world—simultaneously and concurrently, almost as if in split-screen. I also find that if I need to access the inner world to recharge my energy but can't due to frequent interruption, I begin to run out of energy more quickly.

When we are constantly and intermittently being pulled out of our inner worlds, we may not be able to fully recharge, and are more likely to continue running on fumes, headed for burnout. This is why I'm a big advocate for affording autistic children and adults time and space to just *be*, free from demands, to occupy and enjoy their inner worlds. This time to restore and recharge is so important. Take a moment to reflect on your own inner world and what it is like for you. Do you find it similarly restorative? Feel free to note some observations in your journal.

Mediation and Visualization: Expansion

Similar to accessing the inner world, meditation can be an excellent way of taking some time for stillness away from the busyness of life, slowing down, and expanding our energy. Meditation can help remind us that even when we're feeling depleted and our light feels dimmer, there is still a persistent light within us that remains—a little bit like a pilot light on a stove. Even when the burners are inactive, the pilot light is still quietly and steadfastly glowing.

Here's a quick meditation exercise that you can try:

1. Take a moment to get comfortable in whatever way feels best for you.

2. Give yourself a moment to take a few slow, deep breaths.

3. Now visualize a bright ball of glowing light in the center of your chest, near your heart.

4. With each inhale, imagine this light slowly growing a little bit stronger and brighter.

5. Watch as this light continues to expand until it extends beyond your physical body, outward into the space around you.

6. Feel the calm and the sense of lightness and expansion that occurs as your light grows and glows brighter.

7. Take a moment to sit within this bright light, and enjoy the warmth, safety, and feeling of peace. Observe any thoughts or feelings that may come up for you during this time and let them drift away.

8. When you are ready to come back, bring with you this feeling of peace, expansion, and self-love.

9. Carry with you into your day this brighter and restored light that is your own energy.

Feel free to note down any reflections in your journal to keep with you to look back on.

Special Interests Are the Stuff of Life

The autistic tendency toward intense focus on a few subjects can bring us great joy, learning, and growth. Sometimes referred to as having "restricted interests" (APA 2013, 28) or the more neuroaffirming "monotropism" (Murray et al. 2005), our minds can have a way of intensely committing to thinking about topics that interest us. For some folks, that may be music or animals, trains or bird-watching. Discovering a new special interest can bring an excitement and magic akin to falling in love. There are some special interests that we may only discover and engage with for a brief period of time, while others, we may carry with us for decades or throughout our lifetimes.

Spending time with our special interests can also help us expand and feel more fully ourselves. Do you have a special interest right now? Is there any subject you could talk all day about and never run out of things to say, never tire of the topic? What knowledge do you have that brings you great joy to share with others? Special interests can be a way of connecting to ourselves, as well as other like-minded people.

I consider time with special interests to be almost like sacred time, as it is time where you can connect with what is most joyful for you. This time can bring a feeling of lightness, expansion, or being in "the zone" of focus. Connecting with special interests is a way of honoring and celebrating your authentic self. Sometimes we may want to talk about our special interests with others, or we might feel they are so special to us that we want to keep them private or only share selectively with those whom we especially trust.

Do you engage with your special interests as much as you would like, or would you like more time to connect with these favorite subjects? As it can be helpful to schedule rest and downtime, sometimes it can also be helpful to schedule time with special interests on your calendar. Would you like to block out an hour or two, or whatever amount of time feels attainable, to engage with the subjects or activities you love most?

Nature

Connecting with nature can bring us a sense of peace and restoration. Whether walking by a river and listening to the waves, wandering in a forest, stepping outside to get some fresh air, or simply looking out the window to see the sky, nature has a way of helping calm our senses and refresh our energy. What are the elements of nature that you enjoy most? Is it the sound of rain? The way the light dances off the leaves in the summer? Or the intense and electric energy of a thunderstorm? Think about some of the aspects of nature in which you find the most comfort and delight. Is there a way to connect more to these aspects of nature? What about a

favorite natural location? If you're not able to get to your favorite nature spot at the moment, or even get outside, are there ways of drawing from nature which can offer a moment of calm—looking at a photo of a beach or a field of flowers, or listening to recorded sounds of the ocean or a rainfall? Some autistic folks also enjoy connecting with animal friends. Do you have any pets or a favorite animal with whom you can share some refreshing time and companionship?

Exercise

One of the most helpful tools I have found in healing autistic burnout—and avoiding future burnouts—is exercise. It seems almost paradoxical that spending energy exercising would actually increase our energy levels, but my energy levels are always highest when I incorporate exercise into my day. Depending on your own profile of needs and abilities, is there a form of exercise or movement you can incorporate into your own routine? It can be a walk, a run, or even some simple stretching. Forms of exercise like yoga and tai chi can benefit the body *and* help to reduce stress (Chawla 2023; Abbott and Lavretsky 2013). Committing to exercise can seem daunting, like one more thing to have to do, but I have found that even five minutes of exercise is better than *no* minutes. Is there a form of exercise you like, in a time frame that feels comfortable and attainable for you? What time of day feels best for exercising? For some, starting out the day with exercise provides energy for the rest of the day. For others, exercising in the evening helps to shed the day's stressors. Others may prefer a midday walk or a trip to the gym to lift weights. What feels most comfortable and right for you?

Minding Your Physical Health

As difficult as it can be during burnout, staying on top of our physical health is so important in maintaining our overall wellness. This

can include things like regular checkups, dental cleanings, and bringing any new symptoms or concerns to your healthcare team. If you find that making a call to schedule an appointment consumes a large amount of your energy, can you opt for online scheduling or call at a time of day when your energy levels are naturally higher? If at all possible, try to schedule your appointments during times when you have a bit more energy in reserve, and bring with you any sensory tools or supports you may find helpful.

Neuroaffirming Therapy and Coaching

During burnout, we may or may not find talking to be that helpful, as we can sometimes experience communication as taxing. But if you might find talking beneficial, is it helpful to consider therapy or coaching with an autistic, neurodivergent, or neuroaffirming provider? An autistic provider can be especially helpful at understanding, reflecting, and helping us to make sense of our experiences. Fortunately, an ever-increasing number of openly autistic therapists and coaches are now present in the field, and with the advent of telehealth, location has become less of a barrier to connecting with support that feels like a better fit.

Energy Work and Acupuncture

Sometimes we may not feel that talking is the most supportive therapeutic modality. As alternatives, energy work and acupuncture have been instrumental tools in helping to keep my energy moving. Modalities like Reiki have been shown to reduce stress, pain, and anxiety, and are even becoming more present in Western medical settings such as hospitals (Richeson et al. 2010). The key is to reduce stress on the nervous system however possible. I have also found acupuncture to be invaluable for keeping my system in balance, reducing stress, and improving overall health. Acupuncture,

which comes from traditional Chinese medicine, helps to facilitate the balanced movement of energy, called "chi" or "qi," for optimal wellness (Mayo Clinic 2024). After an acupuncture session, I notice my energy feels much stronger, more vibrant, and healthier. Acupuncture also has a growing presence in medical settings and is even covered by many health insurance plans. As autistic folks, we may experience that we feel generally less integrated with or connected to our physical bodies than nonautistic people. Taking care of our health and wellness helps us to work in partnership with our physical bodies so all aspects of our beings can thrive.

Now that you have some ideas for preserving and restoring your energy, in the next chapter, we'll continue talking about additional ways of caring for yourself.

Chapter 9

Slowing Down
Resting and Taking Care

The messages we receive from society often suggest that we must be productive all the time. Very often, we can find that our sense of worth or worthiness is tied in with our productivity. In a world where everything is moving quickly, and productivity and hustle hold such a high value, we may find it difficult to keep up, which can lead to feelings of internalized ableism or self-judgment. In the current hustle culture, there can be financial and social pressures to be endlessly *doing*, seemingly with a demand to be productive all the time. Resting and slowing down might even receive the unfortunate and misguided label of "lazy."

If you find yourself internalizing these messages, which are difficult to get away from, try thinking of it this way: Sometimes rest can be one of the most important and productive things we can do in a day. Rest helps us to manage and restore our energy levels, rejuvenating our bodies and minds, and allows us to return to our daily activities with new energy and sharper focus and acuity. Rest can look like taking a nap, meditation, listening to music, or even going for a walk or run.

I also encourage you to give yourself permission to not have everything you do be "productive" every moment. If you need a reminder, rest is a basic need, and you are inherently worthy of rest, just by being a person. You don't have to do anything to *earn* rest. Many autistic folks naturally need more rest and downtime than our nonautistic counterparts, and so you may find that you function best if you take a short break or nap in the middle of the

day, if at all possible. Or you may find it restful to decompress by engaging in a favorite activity or taking a walk. Sometimes, when feeling fatigued, we may feel that we should push ourselves to continue getting things done, even to our detriment. But sometimes it's better to rest and then come back to our responsibilities later with fresh energy. Rest is ultimately an investment in having more energy later. So, one question you may want to ask yourself when feeling tired could be: "Is it possible that resting could actually be the best use of this time?"

Slowing Down

If you find that your schedule does not allow for a break, is it possible to just slow down for a bit? If you find yourself feeling overwhelmed, is there anything on your current to-do list that you can save for later or a different day? Take a look at your schedule or to-do list for today—what is essential and absolutely *must* be done today versus what can wait until tomorrow or another time? There may be essential tasks that absolutely have to be done today, especially if you are a parent or caregiver, but you may be able to identify tasks that can wait. You may find it helpful to create a list of things that must get done today, along with a larger, *rolling* to-do list of things that are on the agenda to be done soon but aren't urgent. If you find that your mind is occupied with trying to remember everything you have to do, writing it down in a list can be especially helpful. That way, you can write down everything you may need to remember for later and walk away from it with that mind space now free to think about other things.

Find the Life Hacks

For things that must be done, are there any easier or more efficient ways of doing them?

What creative life hacks can you employ? For example, staying hydrated and eating enough food is something we must continue

to do to keep our physical bodies going. But we may find ourselves without the energy to cook or even to assemble a sandwich for ourselves. For these times, instead of making a sandwich, is it possible to just grab a handful of each component of the sandwich— some bread, some lettuce, some protein like cheese or turkey, and maybe a tomato—to eat from a few food groups without spending the energy to put a sandwich together? Or, if cooking is possible but cooking every day consumes too much energy, look for ways to consolidate cooking and meal prep so that you can have a few days a week with food ready to eat.

On staying hydrated, is there a favorite cup, mug, or water bottle you enjoy drinking out of? Sometimes drinking from a favorite cup can help make the experience of drinking water or another healthy beverage more enjoyable, which can give us some motivation to keep us staying hydrated. Carrying a water bottle that you can fill up a couple of times a day can help you keep track of how much water you're drinking to make sure you have the right amount for you.

Cozy Clothing and Dopamine Dressing

When our energy is low, wearing comfortable clothing of preferred fabrics, weights, and textures can support us in getting through the day by not introducing sensory aspects that bother us or pull at our attention, like a shirt that doesn't fall quite right or pants that get bunched up. What kind of clothing would be most comfortable for your day ahead?

We may also find that choosing our clothing for the day requires energy in the form of making decisions, and so we may find that wearing the same type of outfit, like a uniform, can save energy on decision making. Whether it's jeans and a sweater, or a dress with leggings, having an outfit formula can be an efficient way of getting dressed each day.

Another aspect of choosing clothing is "dopamine dressing," referring to the neurotransmitter of dopamine, which can make us feel happy and motivated (Cleveland Clinic 2022). Dopamine dressing is basically dressing in clothing that makes us happy. Whether that means bright patterns, favorite colors, or a cool vintage vibe, creating an outfit we enjoy wearing can be a reflection of our personalities and who we are. Dopamine dressing can require a little more energy to plan and curate outfits, but the energy gained from the joy of wearing fun clothes can give us a boost of energy and joy.

Celebrating Small Accomplishments

In low-energy mode, when we are just trying to get through the day, it can be easy to slip into the mindset that we're not accomplishing much or we haven't really gotten anything done today. But if you look at all the small things you do on a regular day and add them up, you would have quite a list. I would like to remind you that you don't need to accomplish anything big today. In addition to keeping a to-do list, it can also be helpful to acknowledge the things you've already done, no matter how small the tasks may seem.

Try making a list of all the small things you've accomplished today. Getting out of bed is one thing. Taking a shower or making yourself a cup of coffee also count. Did you text a friend or wash a dish? All of these are things that consume energy, and so when your energy is running low, it can be helpful to recognize and honor the things you are accomplishing, no matter how small they might seem.

It can also be helpful to acknowledge the bright spots and things that bring you meaning, like petting a dog, greeting a stranger, looking at the trees, or listening to the water. Doing so can help light your path through burnout by honoring the small things that bring big significance.

Now May Not Be the Time to Push Yourself

There are times when we may need to push ourselves to finish a task, complete a to-do list, leave the house, or go to an event. Sometimes, we may find that once we've pushed ourselves to leave the house, we're happy we did, and end up either accomplishing what we set out to do or enjoying our time. In burnout, we may find that pushing ourselves often doesn't help and can often make things worse. If you're not sure about taking on a task or going to a social event, take a minute to reflect—is this a time when I just need a little push, and later I'll be happy I did the thing? Or am I likely to feel exhausted, overwhelmed, or even resentful the whole time if I say yes? Sometimes just asking ourselves this question can offer us great clarity in what decision is best for us.

Mindful Use of Screens

We may gravitate toward our devices with screens for many reasons. Screens can, at times, be useful for self-regulation, letting us watch a favorite video or read about a favorite subject. Screens can also offer mental stimulation from doing things such as visiting an online forum or looking up an interesting question. As neurodivergent folks, we might find screens helpful as a way of connecting with other like-minded people or those who share a similar interest, whom we would not meet otherwise. Or we may use screens as a way of accessing social connection when we might not have the energy to make a phone call or meet people in person. If we're feeling lonely or isolated, going on social media or joining a forum can feel like dropping into the town square, where people can gather and share thoughts and ideas. In that regard, screens can be a vehicle for connecting with others.

Another reason we may reach for screens is that we may be attempting to self-soothe by finding an escape from the overwhelm of the environment around us by focusing on something else, almost as if we are carving out a mental space for respite that feels

all our own. The input we gain from the screen can also be a form of stimming, and we might seek out this input as a way of mitigating the sensory overload from the environment around us.

One challenge we may find with screens is that we may reach for them in attempt to reduce overwhelm but they may end up actually *adding* to our overload. When information comes at us at a rapid pace, such as on social media or when we are bombarded by ads, using screens can sometimes be the opposite of soothing. So how can we utilize our devices in ways that work for us?

Mindfulness Moment

If you find yourself frequently reaching for your phone or tablet but want to reduce how often you use it, try checking in with yourself in those moments by asking some of these questions:

- Why am I reaching for the phone right now?

- What am I hoping to gain? Am I overwhelmed and looking for escape? Soothing? Sensory input? Intellectual stimulation? Connection?

- Am I reaching for my phone out of habit? And is it possible it may not be helpful or useful for me in this moment?

- Is there anything else that would feel better to do right now?

It can also help to have a list of a few analog alternatives, like coloring or fidget tools, to reach for in place of screens.

Feel free to note all of this in your journal so you can refer back to it later.

As you explore why you reach for the screen, you may decide you want to try other options to meet the needs you're identifying. If you're seeking a form of sensory input, are there any analog solutions you can reach for? Some options include tangible activities like knitting, drawing on textured paper, or playing an instrument. Are there small fidget tools you can carry with you, or fidget jewelry you can wear, as a potential screen alternative?

If you're seeking an escape, can you listen to a favorite song or podcast, or look at a book or magazine? Are you able to drop into your internal world for a bit to enjoy a beautiful scene of your own creation? What about looking at the sky or out the window? Reducing use of screens can help us slow down and bring us to a calmer and more peaceful place. As you reduce your speed and calm your mind and energy, you may experience the ability to notice beauty and small details within your environment, and even find that you have a sharper memory. As an alternative to pulling out your phone, you could try carrying a small notebook to write down your observations, create drawings, make fun lists, or write down topics to look up later.

Also, think about *how* you may be using your phone—if stepping away from technology may be not be possible, what about changing the way in which you use it? For example, if your phone is the only distraction item you have available to you at the moment, what would make it most useful for you? Instead of doomscrolling through social media, can you download a library book on a reading app? Or play a hidden picture or puzzle game? You may find it helpful to delete social media apps or hide apps on your home screen so that the pull toward engaging with the phone is lessened. Additionally, could it be useful to create time limits for apps on your phone, set your phone screen to greyscale, or keep your phone in a location that is just out of immediate reach but still accessible if you need it?

Notice any observations when stepping away from technology or social media. Do you feel your mind slow down to a more

comfortable pace? Or notice new details from your environment that you hadn't observed before? Try to note any benefits of adjusting your screen usage, as recognizing them can also help inspire you to continue new, more helpful habits.

A Cue for Change

Autistic burnout is not a failure, but it can be a cue that some things in our lives may not be working for us and that we could benefit from some changes. Maybe you realize your work schedule is unsustainable, and you want to consider how you might possibly reduce your hours or find a role with an easier commute. Maybe you find yourself overscheduled, and so you set some guidelines for how many non-work/extracurricular events you can have each week. For example, you may find that you want to socialize no more than once per week, no more than two weeks per month. Or you might decide to turn your phone on silent after 9 p.m. so that you can read and disconnect without interruption. What changes would you like to consider implementing for yourself over the longer term?

Now May Not Be the Time for Big Decisions

Although burnout can be a time that highlights our needs and can help us see what areas of our lives we'd like to change, it can also be a time to approach any big decisions with caution and care. Sometimes when we are overwhelmed, our emotions may start to spiral and everything may seem impossible. We may feel the need to upend our lives and move to the middle of nowhere or a tiny island where we can escape from our stressors. Big, life-changing decisions tend to be best made when we're in a state that is calmer and more balanced, where we can take a wider and more long-term perspective.

For example, burnout can be a time to reflect on whether a work situation is too intense, too overwhelming, or requires a schedule that is unmanageable, but it may *not* be the time to quit on the spot. You may realize you don't feel emotionally supported enough in your relationship, but it may not be the time to initiate a breakup. In burnout, our perceptions can often skew negative, so even if there are things that need to be changed, when we're wearing "burnout goggles," it can easily seem like everything is terrible, and it's easy to lose sight of positive things we may also have going for us. When we feel this way, we can often benefit from giving ourselves a little time and space to breathe, continue making mindful observations, and form a balanced and complete picture. Then, once we allow for some rest and self-care, our energy starts to return, the clouds start to clear a little, and we can make decisions from a more balanced state.

"I'm in a State"—Knowing When to Pause

Part of knowing that it may not be the best time to make big decisions is recognizing that we may be in a place of overwhelm, difficult emotions, or an escalated nervous system. If it's difficult to pinpoint the emotions we're feeling, it can be enough to just recognize that we are in a state of being unsettled. Sometimes, this can be all the information we need to act in a way that is mindful and caring to ourselves. You can always dig deeper later if you would like to explore or get to the root of a specific feeling.

One super simple way of checking in with how you feel is just creating two categories—one if you're feeling happy and well, the other if you're experiencing overwhelm, fatigue, or difficult emotion. You could label these categories anything you want—"Clear" or "Cloudy," "Happy" or "Heavy," whatever resonates for you. Just identifying which category your current state falls into can provide helpful information on what you need to do next. If you're feeling

"Clear," continue going about your day. If you're feeling "Cloudy," what do you need right now to support you?

Comfort Items

Do you have any items that bring you comfort or that make you happy to just have with you? This could be a favorite soft blanket, a beloved stuffed animal, a cool rock, or just an item that you enjoy looking at or holding. It could also be a photo of a friend or loved one, or a piece of art. Can you invite and incorporate things that bring you comfort into your space? Maybe a plant that reminds you of resilience and vitality? What about a favorite type of tea that you find cozy or soothing? You may find that just holding a warm cup of tea and experiencing the warmth in your hands can bring a sense of calm and comfort. What are some comforting items you'd like to keep with you, or have in your environment, to bring you peace and calm?

Music and Art

We can also find such great comfort in music and art, whether we are actively creating or simply listening or observing. For those who find music helpful, songs have a way of expressing thoughts and feelings beyond what words alone can capture. Or you may find that drawing or painting your experience offers you a way of conceptualizing and communicating your inner world. Connecting to yourself and making sense of your experiences through music, art, poetry, and other mediums can offer a way to process experiences that may feel abstract, move that energy through, and facilitate healing.

Just for Today

When you are focused on just getting through the day, sometimes "Just for today" can become a helpful mantra. As a practitioner of Reiki, I have found that one aspect that has always resonated with me is the saying "Just for today" (Usui n.d.). This phrase appears at the beginning of each of the five Reiki principles, with the purpose of setting an intention for the immediate day ahead of us. I love this approach because sometimes, when we're experiencing overwhelm or burnout, it is helpful to just focus on what we can do to manage today. So just for the day ahead, see if you can care yourself in some small and attainable ways. If "today" feels like too much, just look ahead to the next few hours, or even the next few moments. A good place to start is right here in the present moment.

As you move ahead with new clarity and insight into what works for you, it's time to talk about communication and advocating for your needs.

PART III

Communication, Self-Advocacy, and the Path Forward

Chapter 10

Autistic Communication Is Different Communication

Communication Needs and Preferences

When I teach nonautistic folks about autism, I am effectively teaching another language, but sometimes, I have to first help them understand that the autistic way is another valid language to be learned. Since we experience the world differently from our nonautistic neighbors, it makes sense that our communication would look different as well. Although these differences have often been pathologized, Dr. Damien Milton (2012) took a revolutionary look at autistic communication in a way that moved beyond viewing autistic communication as deficient.

Dr. Milton (2012) coined the term "double-empathy problem" to explain why autistic communication is so often misunderstood by nonautistic folks—because autistic and nonautistic people are effectively speaking different languages. Each perfectly valid, but different. Among other autistic people, our communication can be quite effective and well-understood. The challenge arises when we approach communication across different neurotypes, causing information to become misunderstood or lost in translation (Milton 2012; den Houting 2019).

Speaking Differently

For autistic folks who communicate through spoken speech, we may notice that our use of language is different. We may employ large words or words that are not commonly used in our region, such as an American using the word "lift" for elevator, or words that were more common in a different era, making for an "old timey" way of speaking. We may take on the accents, prosody, or speech patterns of others who we spend time with or characters from movies or television that blend together in our speech. We may have accents entirely unique to ourselves, creating our own "idiolect" that is noticeably different from those around us.

Spoken speech can also feel difficult or effortful for many autistic folks because it may feel, even if just at times, like speech is not our natural language. For some, such as autistic folks with apraxia, coordinating the subtle movements required to form words can require an incredible amount of energy. For others, who may think in images, feelings, or multisensory impressions, translating our communication into words, or as I like to call it, "making sentences," also requires a great deal of energy that is sometimes beyond our reach.

When we are tired, this translation into words can become extra difficult. Sentences can become much more jumbled, and language might be assembled out of order. We may also find that we have a vast amount of information in our minds that needs to not only be translated into words, but also distilled into a single, simpler stream of language that would allow the information to be conveyed to the listener. This creates almost a bottlenecking of information, where *everything* gets stuck and then no words come out.

Because of all the effort, energy, and planning it can require to utilize spoken language, we may often need extra time to formulate our thoughts, translate them into speech, and then convey them to someone else. This is why many find writing to be a more effective way of communicating. For nonspeakers who communicate via a letter board or typing, it is especially imperative that they have the time and space to communicate in the way that feels right

for them, and for their communication to be valued just as much as vocal speech.

Unspoken Communication

Our unspoken, or nonverbal, communication is also frequently misinterpreted by nonautistic folks. We may have difficulty with eye contact, or our facial expressions don't match what others expect them to be. Some autistic folks may have faces that are extremely expressive, while others have more minimal expression. And for many, the degree of expression we have in our faces can fluctuate, depending on how much energy we have in our systems. This may be true, at least in some part, due to masking, and when we no longer have the energy for masking, our facial expressions may disappear as well.

When our outward facial expression doesn't reflect our internal state to an outside observer, this is known as "incongruent affect." This can be a real area of struggle and frustration because sometimes our faces are doing the "wrong thing," and others can misperceive our feelings and our intentions. Nonautistic folks tend to interpret our body language through their own lens and assign meaning to our facial expressions based on what *they* would mean if they were making the same expression. But our language is different.

Some autistic folks may experience laughing during times of stress, overwhelm, or anxiety, which can easily be misinterpreted by others. Some may show minimal facial expressions during a time when someone else is sharing a struggle and may mistakenly be perceived as uncaring, even if we are overwhelmed with care and empathy. The disconnect between how we are feeling in our internal state and how our outward facial expressions are interpreted can pose a real source of struggle and challenge for those in our community. Our empathy may be overlooked or dismissed because it doesn't present in the same way as neurotypical empathy, even though our empathy can be deep and profound,

and even painful. When others experience pain or emotion, we often experience it too, almost as if it is our own.

When our natural communication is misunderstood, it can create further pressure to mask and make adjustments to our faces to create expressions that match with what others expect from us. This may be especially true for autistic women and AFAB folks, who face even greater societal pressure to "smile." We may find that when we are resting in a neutral expression, others may immediately ask us "What's wrong?" even though we might be absolutely fine.

On the other side of the same coin, our persistent neutral or calm expression may cause others to believe that we're doing fine when we aren't. Something that is even more difficult is that we might express that we are struggling but not be believed because our faces outwardly don't resemble what a struggling person "should" look like. This can lead our struggles to be dismissed or invalidated, and we may become hesitant to share in the future.

In keeping with Dr. Milton's description of the double-empathy problem (2012), I have found that autistic people are much more likely to pick up on the emotional states of other autistic people, regardless of how our facial expressions may outwardly appear, and that sometimes, it takes an autistic person to recognize the struggle of another. This may have a lot to do with how we take in information, as we may find that we are less likely to rely on reading the facial expressions of others (Attwood 2019). Instead, we might sense what others are feeling through energy. In my experience, energy can be a natural autistic language and a means of communication in itself.

As we tune in to the subtle energy of others, doing so can provide us with an insight into their experience or emotions. We may find this process more challenging in overwhelming environments or when our systems are overtaxed, as if the sensory bombardment or stress of overwhelm puts pressure on our systems and closes off the channels by which we most naturally glean information. And while looking at others' facial expressions might provide *some* helpful information for us, we can often sense how

others are feeling without observing this information. Facial expressions can be almost incidental for us.

We may find that, although we can often acutely sense how someone else is feeling, we might then struggle with what to *do* with that information, or how to respond, particularly when we may sense an incongruence between the external presentation and internal state of the person. This can be especially challenging to navigate in more casual or small talk–type interactions. As we struggle to manage and interpret all the information coming at us at once, we may naturally experience difficulty with knowing how to proceed in social interactions.

Communication Layer Cake

Many of us find that we thrive in a particular area of communication but experience difficulty in others. For some autistic folks, there may be a preference for communication around areas that are practical and concrete. On the other hand, other autistic folks may enjoy small talk because it tends to follow a formulaic set of rules, expectations, and even scripts. For example, if your neighbor says "Hi, how are you?" a common automatic response might be "Good, how are you?" Some find the rules, structure, and patterns of small talk to be comfortable to navigate.

Or we may struggle in the area of small talk because it feels entirely outside of our natural way of relating. When attempting small talk, I actually find it difficult to keep up with the conversation and often compare it to the feeling of trying to do long division in my head while in front of an audience.

But getting down into the deeper layers of communication and connection, those might come much more naturally. If we imagine communication as a layer cake, small talk would be at the very top. Under that would be what I would call the "social layer" of communication, which is a layer deeper than general small talk, where there might be a bit more personal sharing, but still maintaining the formality and slight distance. Below that is the "deep dive," which is a sharing of a much more accurate representation of our

internal states and authentic selves. I have a sense that even beyond the deep dive, there is yet a deeper layer of communication. One that accesses the essence of who we are as people.

At the "essence level," or "energetic level," there may be communication with words or entirely without. We may find that this is an area where, especially among autistic people with whom we resonate, we may communicate energetically, with a transfer of *knowing* that transcends words and outward language. Have you experienced this kind of connection?

Thinking of your own experience, in what layer(s) of communication do you feel most at home? Spending more time within the layers of communication that feel most natural for us can help us maintain connections in ways that preserve our energy.

Modes of Communication

When our energy is low, we may find that our primary form of communication, such as speaking, may become difficult, and utilizing an alternative form of communication, like typing, can be helpful. Some autistic folks find it helpful to create cards with pre-written phrases on them to express needs in moments when speaking may become difficult. It can also be helpful to know when to take a break and step away from speaking or communicating, if we're able, as we begin to become overwhelmed or our energy levels begin to drop.

We may also find that certain modes of interaction feel more comfortable than others, such as spending time in person versus talking on the phone, or texting versus video chat. Some autistic folks may find phone calls or video calls particularly draining, and so may gravitate toward texting or typing.

Mindfulness Moment

- What kinds of communication feel best for you (talking, typing, etc.)?

- Do you notice that your preferences change based on how much energy you have? If so, how?

- When your energy begins to drop, is there a mode of communication that you prefer to switch to, or is it helpful to take a step back from communication entirely to conserve your energy?

- Which modalities of communication feel best for you? (In person, phone, text, email, messaging?) What about each modality do you like or dislike?

- Can you make a plan with yourself to utilize the forms and modes of communication that feel best and are most preserving of your energy?

Up next, we'll continue the conversation about communication as we dive into self-advocacy and how we can work toward ensuring our needs are met.

Chapter 11

Self-Advocacy
Getting What You Need

Self-advocacy is the practice of identifying our needs and then communicating those needs to others so that the needs can be met. Self-advocacy can also include expressing a feeling, letting someone know how something they said or did might have affected you, setting boundaries, and saying "no." You may find that some aspects of self-advocacy are easier or more difficult than others. For example, you may find that expressing a need feels manageable, but that saying no or setting a boundary feels difficult, or even impossible.

The first step in self-advocacy is resting firmly in the knowledge that your own needs are just as valid as everyone else's. That they *matter* just as much as everyone else's, even though they may look different. As many in our community possess a strong sense of fairness and social justice, we may have an easier time advocating for others than for ourselves. But advocating for ourselves is just as necessary.

Why Is Advocating for Ourselves So Difficult?

Self-advocacy can be an area in which we struggle for a few reasons. One, we may not want to feel like we are being a bother or inconveniencing someone else by expressing a need. When setting a boundary, we might feel hesitant due to wanting to be polite or not

wanting to hurt someone else's feelings. And there may be a hesitation to say no when a request is made of us because we might want to be a good friend, relative, or neighbor, and be of help even if it would require energy that we simply don't have. We might find that difficulty saying no leads us to take on too many responsibilities or causes us to find ourselves in situations that aren't healthy or comfortable for us.

Sometimes difficulty with self-advocacy can occur if we are super sensitive to the emotional states of other people. Many in our community also experience "rejection sensitive dysphoria" (RSD), which can be a feeling of distress experienced not only with literal rejection, but also if we perceive that someone else has a negative feeling toward us (Dodson 2016). Folks who experience RSD might take extra care to avoid potentially experiencing rejection or negativity from others and, as a result, might find self-advocacy difficult.

If we ask for a need to be met and sense any hint of a feeling of inconvenience or frustration on the other person's part, it can easily create discomfort around asking for what we need. We may find that we avoid asking for what we need to avoid experiencing—and absorbing into our systems—the negative emotions, energy, or reactions from the other person.

Identifying Barriers to Self-Advocacy

As we work to find our voices for self-advocacy, it can be helpful to identify any thoughts, challenges, or mindsets that may be standing in our way. One challenge can be simply putting our needs into words. We may spend years unconsciously accommodating ourselves without even realizing it, and so we might not be able to immediately identify or name the needs that are present for us. For example, we may automatically ensure that we have more personal space while at a social gathering or within a crowded environment, but not be consciously aware that this need is due to sensory discomfort.

Are there any accommodations you've been making for yourself all along that you are now more consciously aware of, which you can more readily put into words? Sometimes, we need to sit with things for a moment to find the words to explain them to ourselves before we bring that information to others. Taking this moment to gather our thoughts can help ensure we have the best chance of being understood.

Another barrier to self-advocacy can be a fear that our need might be invalidated or dismissed. This can particularly occur around sensory considerations, as much of our struggle can be invisible. In a given environment, we might be overloaded by sensory elements that a nonautistic person might not even notice. We might be spending all of our energy to just exist among the sensory factors we feel bombarded by, "white-knuckling" our way through, while others around us might feel perfectly fine. This is why we may have heard "It's not that loud" or "It's not that crowded," causing us to second-guess ourselves or wonder if we are being "too sensitive." Do we hesitate to express our needs due to fear of experiencing this invalidation again, or the fear that no matter how much we express or explain our needs, others still won't understand?

We might also make an effort to hide our struggles or discomfort because sharing those struggles could potentially invite attention—or a feeling of intrusion that we don't want. We might have experienced others trying to offer well-meaning support that actually added to our overwhelm or placed us in the position of spending energy to reassure the other person. Or they might have offered us the kind of support that *they* would have found helpful, but that doesn't necessarily work for us, which can leave us feeling more isolated. For example, someone might see us struggling in a moment of sensory overload, but since that may be outside of their lived experience, they might try to be supportive by talking to us or giving us a hug, potentially further contributing to our overwhelm. And although we may sense and appreciate their sentiment of care and wanting to help, this disconnect can also highlight a divide between ourselves and others—and serve as a reminder that the understanding we seek often feels out of our reach. In our self-advocacy process, there are so many thoughts and feelings

that can come up and stand in our way. It can be helpful to understand where these thoughts come from.

The Past Informs the Present

How our needs and emotions were received by others, especially in our early days, can shape our ability to self-advocate in adulthood. In general, how did your caregivers respond to your needs while growing up? Were they validated and tended to with love and care? Or were they met with less-than-caring responses, leaving your needs unmet and leaving you potentially feeling like your emotions were unacceptable or not welcome?

As a child, were you allowed and encouraged to advocate for yourself? Or were you expected to comply with the authority of adults, no matter how you felt? Many folks within our community have experienced behaviorist approaches or compliance-based practices during childhood, which can dampen one's ability to determine and advocate for one's own needs. If you were encouraged to comply with adults, no matter how you were feeling, it can disconnect you from your own inner sense of self, needs, and interoceptive awareness. This is why I am so happy that many occupational therapists are increasingly drawing from interoceptive awareness as a foundation for self-advocacy and social skills when working with autistic children. Tuning in to our own interoceptive awareness and inner voice can help us determine what feels right for us, what needs are present, and how we authentically want to proceed.

What about during school years or early adulthood? How were your needs responded to by friends, family, or others? Our past experiences inform our present comfort with self-advocacy. If we've had any negative experiences around expressing needs, there could be a fear that if we express a need again, we might receive a negative response *and* our need will *still* go unmet. This experience can easily diminish our ability to self-advocate. Can you identify any barriers that might be present in your own self-advocacy process?

Mindfulness Moment

There can be a lot of old messages that play in our minds related to advocating for ourselves. Now that you have identified the barriers that may be in place, I invite you to take a moment to take a deep breath or two, and think of a need you'd like to express or a boundary you'd like to set.

Just take a moment to sit with the *knowing* that this need or boundary you would like to express is valid, important, and worthy. Notice if you feel any different once you've connected to this knowing. Do you feel stronger, more courageous, or more confident in the potential to self-advocate? You can also practice taking this moment to sit with your need and its importance right before you advocate for yourself in a real-life situation.

Self-Advocacy Role Models

Another barrier that can sometimes stand in the way of self-advocacy is that it may be unfamiliar territory for us. Self-advocacy may not be something we've been expressly taught, and so its practice can at first feel shaky and unfamiliar. For some, self-advocacy can seem new because we may not have seen self-advocacy demonstrated by the adults in our lives while growing up. Did you have any have role models for self-advocacy? What did you observe from the adults in your life when it came to asking for their own needs to be met, setting boundaries, or simply saying "No?"

When learning something new, it can be so helpful to have a model to use as a base for our own practices. Think about whether there is anyone in your life who is a great model of self-advocacy— do you know anyone who is great at saying no to things, setting boundaries, or asking for what they need? This could even be a

character from a book or movie whom you admire or with whom you identify. Maybe they confidently set boundaries, say no to things, or ask for what they need with all the confidence in the world. Are there any elements of that person's practice of self-advocacy that you think would work for you? Think of the elements you could borrow for yourself or try out as you are finding your footing, until you settle into a style of self-advocacy that feels comfortable and right for you.

Masking as a Tool

Self-advocacy is also a great opportunity to explore the nuances of the masking we employ. I have found that masking generally falls into two categories: the masking we do to *hide* who we are and what we need, and the masking we do that can actually help us to *express* who we are and what we need. The type of masking that helps us express ourselves can include taking on elements of someone we admire or who possesses qualities that we might want to develop within ourselves. We might want to "borrow" or adopt some of the great qualities of our self-advocacy role models until we settle into practices that feel most right for us.

Finding Your Self-Advocacy Style

As you borrow and try out different aspects of self-advocacy from different role models, or try out new ideas, you may find that you prefer a particular style of self-advocacy. Is it quick and direct? Does it involve a more educational approach? Do you prefer to include a bit of humor? In the beginning, we may try on different ways of going about making requests and setting boundaries until we find one that fits and feels most right for us. It can take a bit of trial, error, and exploration.

Also, self-advocacy is like a muscle, and it's so normal if it feels a bit more difficult and awkward at first. Our voices may come out shaky, or we may have difficulty finding our words. We might also

find that when we speak up, it surprises those around us, because they might not have heard us advocate for ourselves before. We may find we receive a mix of responses, both positive and negative.

New things can feel scary but tend to get easier with time as our confidence and self-certainty grows. As we reach a more solid understanding of our needs, increased confidence in expressing them, and the experience of having our needs met, we can develop a foundation of self-advocacy skills and confidence that help to make future self-advocacy feel much more natural and attainable.

Identifying Safe People

Self-advocacy is an act of strength and courage, but it can also be one of vulnerability as well. There can be something so inherently vulnerable about self-advocacy because to express our needs, we may be necessarily sharing aspects of ourselves that we might have otherwise kept private. That might include a trait that makes us different, a discomfort due to a sensory sensitivity that the people around us can't relate to, a way of connecting or communicating that might seem like a foreign language to others. What happens if we advocate for ourselves and don't get the most positive or supportive response?

Self-advocacy can open a window to seeing how others will respond to us when we express a need or set a boundary. How a person responds to your self-advocacy efforts can tell you a lot about their ability to be a *safe* person in your life. A safe person would be someone who you feel listens to you with openness, curiosity, and kindness. Even if they may not be able to accommodate your needs, the important thing is that you are received with respect. Some signs that someone could be *less* safe include that they might be dismissive about what you share with them or that they might respond unkindly.

There may be times when, even if we self-advocate or explain our needs or requests to the best of our abilities, we still do not feel heard or respected. In this case, sometimes *privacy*,

boundaries, and space can be the most helpful forms of self-advo-cacy. Space can include physical, emotional, and energetic distance if needed. You may also think about how *much* information or how much of your vulnerable self you want to share with someone who might not feel safe or receptive. If you are around a person who feels *less* safe, how do you feel in your body, your emotions, and your energy? How can you identify times when you may be feeling the need to step back or create a boundary?

The dynamics we address in this chapter relate to situations where abuse is not present, but if you are experiencing abuse or violence, here is the contact information for the National Domestic Violence Hotline (US): 1-800-799-SAFE (7233), or thehotline.org. Outside the US, visit findahelpline.com to locate resources near you.

On the opposite side of the coin, what does a *safe* person feel like? A safe person could be someone who listens with gentle empathy and openness. They might start from a place of not understanding *yet*, but demonstrate a willingness and commitment to learning more. Someone who meets your differences or responds to you expressing your needs with curiosity and care. When with a safe person, you might feel a lightness, comfort, or ease. It's as if your nervous system settles into a place of calm where you can rest in the knowing that you are safe and supported. Taking a moment to check in with yourself to see how you feel in your body, mind, and energy can be such a helpful tool to determine how safe and comfortable you feel when it comes to sharing your needs—or any aspect of yourself—in any given relationship or interaction.

How Much Information?

How much information do you need to disclose to ask for what you need? What specifics do you feel comfortable sharing? In some situations, you might feel comfortable sharing your autistic iden-tity, but in others, it might feel too vulnerable, and you might want

to disclose just your specific need, like a sensory accommodation. This option can be helpful in a new environment, where it might take a little bit of time to determine how safe or comfortable you feel with the people around you.

Sometimes, due to having been misunderstood in the past, we may have a tendency to "overexplain" ourselves—why we do what we do, or why we need what we need. Sometimes, though, more information isn't necessarily better—or more helpful. So feel free to think about how much is necessary to disclose in any given situation. In the United States, the Americans with Disabilities Act of 1990 (ADA) requires employers to provide "reasonable accommodations" in the workplace, but to receive accommodations, a disability needs to be disclosed (US Department of Labor n.d.). Is there a way in which you would feel most comfortable disclosing the information needed to access accommodations?

"I Need a Minute"

"I need a minute" is one of my go-to phrases for self-advocacy because it can be applicable in so many different situations. Someone asks you a question or makes a request of you, and you need extra time to think? "I need a minute; I'll get back to you." If you're finding yourself overwhelmed in a work situation, family event, or social gathering and need to take a walk? "I need a minute." This one little phrase is so handy because it has so many uses. So often, we experience the pressure to respond right away in social situations, while it might take a bit longer to process the information and formulate our thoughts. When the pressure to respond right away is removed, it can allow us the space and time we need to connect with ourselves and our inner voices about what we may be thinking or feeling. It can give us time to tune in to the two most important questions: "How am I feeling?" and "What do I need right now?"

Maintaining a Connection to Your Inner Voice

Taking the time to really check in with ourselves and our inner voices can be an incredibly effective tool for self-advocacy. Do you ever just have a gut feeling about something, or a subtle *knowing* that something feels off about a situation, even though there aren't any visible clues that would suggest anything is wrong? There are some things that look great on paper, but there might be a small voice telling you it's not a great idea. Taking a little time to check in with your inner voice before making a decision, or sometimes giving a response to a big question or request, can help you to determine what you feel is best for you. You can spend this time in meditation, taking a walk, or contemplating while washing the dishes. Once you have checked in with yourself and how you feel, then take a little *more* time to translate your feelings into language that feels right to you, which you can then use to express your thoughts and feelings. To easily remember this process, think of it in three basic phases: Check in, translate, express.

The Heads-Up

Sometimes it can be helpful to offer a quick heads-up to the person you're with by telling them about a need or an accommodation that might be helpful for you *later*. For example, if you're spending time with a friend and you know that after a while, you might get tired and need a rest from speaking, or might need to take a break to take a walk, you might find it helpful to let them know that at the start of your time together. That way, there is a little bit of a plan in place in case you do get tired or overwhelmed, and it helps to alleviate the pressure we can sometimes feel to *push through* when we start running out of energy. With a safe person in your life who is kind and receptive, would you feel comfortable letting them

know some ways they might be able to tell when you are struggling or overwhelmed, and in what ways they can best support you in these moments? This information can also help them better understand you and your needs.

Sometimes it might take a moment for others to understand just how important accommodations can be for us. Our world may be so different from theirs that they might not have any idea that there are often specific challenges or sensory considerations present for us, but once they *do* understand, they may well be receptive to supporting our needs. Sometimes, just building this understanding and insight can go a long way in bridging the gap in understanding and moving toward our needs being met. With a safe person, the sharing of vulnerability can often facilitate deeper and more authentic connection. Is there anyone in your life who feels like a safe and supportive person for you?

The Shorthand

There may be times in burnout when you receive a text, email, or phone call from a friend or loved one who is reaching out. You might like to respond, but feel that even responding to a text message would take energy you don't have. You may feel the need to explain why you don't have the energy to get together, or why it might have taken a long time to respond, which can feel so daunting. One idea is to prearrange a quick codeword or emoji for when you are low on energy but would like still like to respond to let them know you received their message, are thinking of them, and that you'll circle back when you have more energy. It could be a simple cloud emoji to let them know your battery is low, but that you'll respond when you're feeling more restored. Having this shorthand in place ahead of time allows you to respond without the pressure to offer a long explanation or overthink a response, while still conveying helpful information.

You Get to Choose

You don't have to answer every question asked of you, and you don't have to agree to every request made of you. Of course, there are some situations in life where we have to do whatever needs to be done, such as meeting caregiver responsibilities, ensuring our income, or taking care of our health. But there are times when we may be asked a question that we don't feel great about answering—whether because it feels like an intrusion or because we are being asked to comment on something on which we haven't quite yet formulated our thoughts. How do you feel when that happens? When you tune in to yourself, how do you recognize a question you *do* feel comfortable answering versus one that you want to either decline to respond to or defer until you've had more time to gather your thoughts?

Sometimes it can be difficult to think of a response in the moment, as we might be overwhelmed or caught off guard. For this reason, you may want to have a few scripts prepared for when you find yourself faced with a question you either don't feel comfortable answering or don't want to answer *right now*. Scripts can be so helpful because they offer us ready-made sentences to convey our thoughts. I compare using scripts to buying bread versus *making* bread. Similar to making bread, when we want to create a sentence to convey our thoughts, we have to gather all the ingredients (words) and put them together from scratch. This can consume a ton of our time and energy. Using scripts is like buying bread from the store. It's already made, we just have to select the one we want, which helps us to conserve our energy.

When responding to questions you're not sure if you're comfortable answering, here are some scripts you can try:

- "Why you do ask?" Sometimes the context of why someone is asking a question can give us important information that helps us formulate our answer. In the case of questions which may feel intrusive or too personal, it can offer a bit of deflection, as well as a moment for the asker to reflect on whether they really need the

answer. For questions that may be outright rude or intrusive, remember that no response *is* a response.

- "That's a great question. Let me think about that and get back to you." This can be a great option for when someone asks a question that you feel is important and requires a thoughtful response, but you need more time to gather your thoughts to express an answer in a way that feels right to you.

- Are there any other scripts that would be helpful for you when you are asked a question that you might want to give more thought to answering?

Scripts are also useful when requests are made of us. We may find that we have a tendency to quickly agree to requests, often because we want to make the other person happy or avoid disappointing them. This isn't always in our best interest because we may find ourselves initially agreeing to requests, and then, once we have had a little bit of time to think about it, we start to realize why it may not be a good idea, or that it may require more of us than we have to give in the moment. So, before you answer a request, feel free to take some time and think about it. Sit with the question "Do I have enough energy in my system to manage this?" If you need to delay your answer, here are some scripts you can use:

- "Let me think about that and get back to you." With this answer, you are not committing to a time frame in which to give a response.

- "I'll look at my schedule and can let you know by the end of the day/week." With this answer, you can set the time frame you'd like to give yourself to think more about the request that is being made, how taxing it might be of your energy, and whether or not you have that energy to spare. It can also remove the pressure to respond quickly because you have the whole time frame to offer a response.

- "Let me check in with you about this later/tomorrow/ next week. I may have a few questions about [whatever it is]." This answer not only gives you more time to think about whether or not you want to meet the request, but it also lets the asker know that you will need to gather more information before you commit or not. It also gives you a chance to think of any questions you may have, and think about a comfortable way of asking for any clarifying information.

When the Answer Is "No"

Saying no can feel particularly challenging because we may feel a responsibility to be helpful or avoid disappointing anyone. You may have heard that "'No' is a complete sentence," and it is! But in case you are looking for responses that are a bit longer or feel a bit softer, here are some possibilities:

- "I don't have the energy/bandwidth for that at the moment."

- "I'm currently at capacity."

- "I can't take on anything new at the moment."

- "That's not something I can manage in the immediate future."

- "My schedule is currently full/maxed out."

- "No thank you." This one lends itself to injecting a bit of humor if you are so inclined.

- "I am totally maxed out and cannot."

Is It a "No" or a "Not Right Now"?

There may be times when we are asked to so something that we would like to do, but we are not able to do it at the current moment. In these instances, you may not want to say no, but rather express that it's a "not right now" and leave the door open for the future. I find this approach helpful while in burnout because when our energy is limited, we will likely want to minimize any new commitments we take on, but we also know that once we start to feel better and our energy begins to return, we might like to meet the request—whether it's a new professional possibility, dinner with a friend, visiting a family member, or an opportunity to help a neighbor.

So, what are some ways to say "Not right now" but that you would like to in the future? First, ask yourself how much time you need between now and when you meet this request. What has to happen for you during this time to make honoring this request possible? Is it rest, some time alone, a day or two with nothing on your schedule, time to exercise? What would help to restore your energy to a place where you feel comfortably capable of doing what is being asked of you? Once you have a sense of how much time you may need, and how you might need to feel to be able to revisit the idea, here are a few possible scripts for expressing yourself:

- "I'm taking a breather for a moment but will circle back to you next week."

- "My plate is full at the moment—can you send me an email next week, and we can get something on the calendar for later this month?"

Are there any additional scripts that feel right for you? Feel free to inject your own personality, unique way of speaking, favorite movie lines, or even humor into your arsenal of scripts.

Mindfulness Moment

Now that you've had a moment to explore self-advocacy, look at some of the barriers that may be in the way, and think about some situations where self-advocacy might be needed, let's put it all together for an exercise in asking for what you need!

Think of a need or challenge that you may have—this could include a sensory concern, the feeling of being overscheduled, or the need to interact differently in particular social situations.

What kind of support or accommodation would be most helpful in alleviating this challenge or meeting this need? Could it include a sensory support, a break, reduced eye contact, or adjusting your schedule in some way?

Finally, can you think of a script that feels right for you to comfortably convey this need? It could even be something brief like "I need more space" or "I need to not talk for a while."

Take a moment to prepare this script. Sit with it and see if it feels right and authentic for you, and then make any adjustments as needed. Feel free to write it down in your journal or phone, and practice it as many times as you need to before bringing it into a real-life self-advocacy situation.

You can utilize this formula any time self-advocacy may be needed: identify the need, identify the accommodation, and create the script.

Next up, we'll look ahead to finding your people and building your best autistic life.

Chapter 12

The Path Forward

Finding Your People and Living Your Best Autistic Life

It has been so monumental in my experience as an autistic adult to connect with other autistic people. Individually, out there in the world, we can easily feel a sense of isolation, a feeling of being far away from others even when physically among people, or a deep sense of longing or loneliness. We might even find at times that we experience loneliness *more* when we are around other people, as we might not be able to access our inner worlds during those times, and still may find it difficult to resonate or connect with those around us on a meaningful level. Finding other autistic folks who share a similar way of thinking, communicating, and *being* can feel like being welcomed home.

Among autistic people with whom we relate, there can be an easy feeling of peace, a beautiful lightness, and an ability to freely be ourselves. With our shared way of being, we may sense we have a common language and culture. It's as if we resonate at a similar frequency; we can experience a more effortless transfer of energy and flow of communication. When connecting with our people, we may feel understood in a way we've never been understood before. Just this sense of being truly seen, even if only by *one* person who gets us, can feel so hopeful and life-changing.

Among ourselves, there can be a deep sense of sameness and resonance, relief, and the quiet understanding of "I'm like you, and you're like me." We can experience profound connection and community through the knowing that what makes you and I different from others is what makes us similar to each other. It can feel like magic.

In fact, recent research articles titled "A Certain Magic..." (Watts et al. 2024; Schneid and Raz 2020) and "I Never Realized Everybody Felt as Happy as I Do When I'm Around Autistic People" (Crompton et al. 2020) have tapped into what many autistic folks have known all along—that something magical happens when autistic people connect with each other. As described by Schneid and Raz (2020, 5), "A certain magic is created, like, electricity in the air." The power of finding our people—and the mutual understanding and support we can bring to each other—can be incredibly validating and healing.

Connecting with other autistic people can provide opportunities for the parts of ourselves that long to be seen and understood to finally be honored and acknowledged. We may find that our communication with other autistics is unique and quite different from the way we might connect with nonautistic folks. Among ourselves, we may communicate through a blend of energy, as well as a shorthand use of language. Do you notice that your interactions with other autistic people take a different shape than they do with neurotypical folks? What are your own observations?

Spending time with other autistic people can also be wonderful because we may value similar types of interactions. Nonautistic folks may favor particular ways of interacting that, for them, bring enjoyable energy exchanges. Sometimes, when *we* try to interact in these ways, it may not be our preferred way of interacting, and so instead of a mutual exchange of energy, our energy goes outward in one direction, acting as a drain on our batteries. Connecting with other autistic people with whom we share a resonance allows us to spend time speaking our native language, experiencing beautiful and restorative exchanges of energy. This time spent within our natural way of being can bring us such a lightness and joy.

Forming connections within our community can also help strengthen our positive sense of autistic identity. Among ourselves, we may mask less, if at all. We can find acceptance and even delight in what makes us different. Seeing our traits and quirks reflected back in others can help us feel less alone. A sense of belonging to a greater community can help us build confidence and pride in who we are. We are interconnected in a constellation of wonderful people who share our energetic makeup and can offer each other mutual understanding and support.

Outside of the immediate autistic community, we may also find kinship in nonautistic neurodivergent folks, as we may share traits or interests in common. We may also have friends and loved ones who are neurotypical who share similar interests, and who may be kind and supportive, and who value us for our authentic selves. Who makes up *your* community? And with whom are you able to best share caring and mutual support?

When navigating the nonautistic world, we may that find we suppress natural aspects of ourselves. At times, this can feel as if we are attempting to push down helium balloons that are trying to float upward toward the sky. When we find our people—or simply find peace in solitude—we may feel that we can finally stop struggling to push down these balloons, and allow them to freely and joyfully *float* upward. Here is an exercise for you to try.

Mindfulness Moment

Take a moment to visualize balloons that represent any aspects of your authentic self that may be wanting to be free and fly high—aspects that may be kept at bay through masking or being afraid to be seen.

- What color or colors are these balloons?
- How many are there?
- What shape(s) are they?

- What aspects of your beautiful authentic self do they represent?

Take a moment to really see these balloons and any aspect of yourself which you want to feel freer to be more authentic.

Imagine yourself holding onto these balloons by the cords, which have been keeping them tethered to the ground. And now—let them go.

Watch them as they float upward and upward toward the sky. You can follow them along on their path, staying with them as they float up above buildings, treetops, and toward the clouds.

Follow them as high and as far as you would like them to go. Do they drift onwards to visit faraway lands? Where would you like to go?

Spend a moment floating with them in the atmosphere. Honor each balloon, and each part of yourself which it represents, floating freely.

Notice the beautiful sunlight as it warms each aspect of your authentic self, which is now joyfully and buoyantly soaring. Imagine this light bringing healing to the aspects of yourself that need it most.

Take a moment and just stay in this warmth. Linger in this peaceful and celebratory moment for as long as you like, taking slow, deep breaths and bathing in this beautiful sunlight and fresh air.

When you are ready, slowly allow yourself to come back, bringing with you all the gifts from this flight. Feel free to note down any observations in your journal to carry with you.

Cultivating a Life That Works for You

As you recover from autistic burnout, you may be thinking of the road ahead—things you'd like to do, what you want your life to look like, connections you hope to make. The most important thing you will carry with you on this journey is your own self-knowledge and your connection to who you are. This insight and connection will help you take the best care of yourself to prevent future burnouts, as well as to identify any early signs that a burnout may be starting, so that you can implement your trusty self-care practices.

Beyond autistic burnout, your own self-knowledge can also help to lay the foundation for cultivating a life that works for you—not just to avoid burnout, but to *thrive*. Where do you want to go from here? Let's now take a moment to look ahead and to dream. Drawing from all of the elements that coalesce to support your needs—self-knowledge, sensory considerations, energy preservation, self-care tools, self-advocacy, connection, and community—I now invite you to put them all together, and to first start with a dream of a life that brings you vitality.

This daydreaming process can be helpful in clarifying your goals and intentions. When envisioning the life you want, I encourage you start big—imagine everything you could possibly want, in the best of all possible worlds. Starting big in this process helps us to connect with our authentic wants and needs, just to illustrate them for our own purposes. Once you gather this information about what you ultimately want most, then you can start to determine what elements within that dream are possible.

For example, in your dream life, you might want a job that is fully remote with option to travel for work. In reality, this might not be fully possible, but *some* aspect of the dream may be attainable—is there a possible work situation that could involve hybrid remote work, with the option to have short periods of working while traveling? Does this dream of fully remote work indicate that what you really value is freedom or perhaps a desire to more fully experience and explore the world? Our dreams can tell us so much about what is important to us. Connecting with the knowledge of what we want can help us to carve out the elements within the

dream that we might be able to incorporate into our lives. And now, for one final exercise.

Mindfulness Moment

Take a moment to envision the life you most want, that would best meet your needs.

- What would the flow of this life look like? Would it be fast-paced with constant activity and excitement? Or would it be slower and calmer, with a more peaceful rhythm, to find space in which to breathe?

- What would your work life look like? Would you work on-site or remotely or a combination thereof?

- Would you work with people, animals, or on your own?

- What would your ideal schedule look like? Understanding your natural energy patterns and rhythms, how would you most efficiently spend and preserve your energy?

- What are your ideal sensory environments? And what sensory tools would you keep available to utilize for your sensory comfort?

- What would your relationships look like? Would you have a large circle of friends or a few close and trusted folks within your inner circle?

- What about family? Do you envision spending lots of time with your family of origin, creating a family of your own, or being close to a chosen family of friends?

- What does your community look like? What kinds of people or groups resonate most with you?

- Consider how you would like to incorporate elements like nature, creativity, music, special interests, and favorite subjects. How can you make time to include what brings you the most joy?

- And finally, think about your own relationship to your beautiful self—how can you best maintain your connection to your own inner voice, honoring the truth of what it is sharing with you, to help you care for yourself as if you are your own dearest friend?

You know what to do! Spend some time reflecting on these questions and writing about them in your journal to keep with you and refer back to as you cultivate a thriving life that best meets your needs.

Reaching Out

In the midst of the Big Burnout, I remember a renewed feeling of hope as I started to make sense of my experiences and give them a name. As the caring support from others in the autistic community was so instrumental in my own burnout recovery, I remember at that time, hoping to maybe *someday* be able to walk with and offer support to others who were experiencing burnout as well. At that time, I barely had the energy to return a text message, and so the thought of reaching out to be of any help to *any*one seemed so far away. And it may feel that way now for you too, friend. Remember, if all you do with this day is get through it, that is entirely enough. But I have found that with the return of energy

and movement beyond burnout, connecting with and extending support to others where possible is a source of great joy and healing as well.

As we become our more authentic selves, it's as if we're connecting conduits together—creating channels for energy and joy to naturally, freely, and fully flow, bringing through what is most right for us. We become more in alignment and may find that we are now suddenly connecting to others—and aspects of life which resonate with us most. We may feel that we are awakening, finally, as our true and vibrant selves.

Take the greatest of care of yourself during this time, and if you may have the energy a while from now, you might find you'd like to reach out and offer care and support to someone else. In the world of music, when one tuning fork is struck near another tuning fork of the same note, the vibrations move through the air and cause the other one to sound as well. Our energy can impact those around us, and when we resonate with each other, something magical is created that is greater than the sum of our parts as individuals. We are all so connected. And there is so much love and joy for you in this world.

Conclusion

And now, dear friend and reader, we have reached the end of this journey together, but you can carry all these tools with you to continue your path on your own. My wish is that you will make it an ongoing practice to check in with yourself with all the greatest of love and respect that you deserve. By honoring who you are, everything that makes you the person you are, you help bring all the elements together to help your light shine brightest. It has been an honor to be part of your journey. Wishing you wonder and light along the path.

References

Abbott, R., and H. Lavretsky. 2013. "Tai Chi and Qigong for the Treatment and Prevention of Mental Disorders." *Psychiatric Clinics of North America* 36 (1): 109–119.

American Psychiatric Association [APA]. 2013. *Desk Reference to the Diagnostic Criteria from DSM-5*. Arlington, VA: American Psychiatric Association.

Attwood, T. 2019. "Good Mental Health for Autistic Girls and Women (Taken from Full Video)." Yellow Ladybugs, April 29. Video, 39 min., 18 sec. https://www.youtube.com/watch?v=-n6IWTRVGeg.

Baron-Cohen, S. 2002. "The Extreme Male Brain Theory of Autism." *Trends in Cognitive Sciences* 6 (6): 248–254. https://www.sciencedirect.com/science/article/abs/pii/S1364661302019046.

Brach, T. 2021. "The Wise Heart of Radical Acceptance." Tara Brach. September 1. https://www.tarabrach.com/wise-heart-radical-acceptance/.

Brewer, R., R. Cook, and G. Bird. 2016. "Alexithymia: A General Deficit of Interoception." *Royal Society Open Science* 3 (10): 150664.

Chawla, V. 2023. "How Yoga Affects the Brain and Body to Reduce Stress." Stanford Lifestyle Medicine. October 3. https://longevity.stanford.edu/lifestyle/2023/10/03/how-yoga-affects-the-brain-and-body-to-reduce-stress/.

Cleveland Clinic. 2022. "Dopamine." Cleveland Clinic. https://my.clevelandclinic.org/health/articles/22581-dopamine.

Cohen, L. 2024. pers. comm. October 18.

Crompton, C. J., S. Hallett, D. Ropar, E. Flynn, and S. Fletcher-Watson. 2020. "'I Never Realised Everybody Felt as Happy as I Do When I Am Around Autistic People': A Thematic Analysis of Autistic Adults' Relationships with Autistic and Neurotypical Friends and Family." *Autism* 24 (6): 1438–1448.

Cuve, H. C., J. Murphy, H. Hobson, E. Ichijo, C. Catmur, and G. Bird. 2021. "Are Autistic and Alexithymic Traits Distinct? A Factor-Analytic and Network Approach." *Journal of Autism and Developmental Disorders* 52 (5): 2019–2034.

den Houting, J. 2019. "Why Everything You Know About Autism Is Wrong." TEDx Macquarie University, New South Wales, Australia. Video, 13 min., 21 sec. https://www.ted.com/talks/jac_den_houting_why_everything_you_know_about_autism_is_wrong/transcript?subtitle=en.

Dodson, W. W. 2016. "Emotional Regulation and Rejection Sensitivity." Children and Adults with Attention-Deficit/Hyperactivity Disorder [CHADD]. https://chadd.org/wp-content/uploads/2016/10/ATTN_10_16_EmotionalRegulation.pdf.

Glover Blackwell, A. 2017. "The Curb-Cut Effect." *Stanford Social Innovation Review*. https://ssir.org/articles/entry/the_curb_cut_effect.

Grandin, T. n.d. "Description and Schematic Details of the Squeeze Machine." Dr. Temple Grandin's Website. https://www.grandin.com/inc/intro-squeeze.html.

Grandin, T. 2006. *Thinking in Pictures, Expanded Edition: My Life with Autism*. New York: Vintage Books.

Greve, F. 2007. "Curb Ramps Liberate Americans with Disabilities—And Everyone Else." *McClatchy Newspapers*, June 11. https://www.mcclatchydc.com/news/article24460762.html.

Hannah, D. 2014. "Dan Rather's, 'Daryl Hannah: The Big Interview' Excerpt from June 23, 2014." Dan Rather Reports. Video, 1 min., 57 sec. https://www.youtube.com/watch?v=yUuoq8CWeeU.

Hellström, B., and U. M. Anderberg. 2003. "Pain Perception across the Menstrual Cycle Phases in Women with Chronic Pain." *Perceptual and Motor Skills* 96 (1): 201–211.

Jenrose. 2018. "Fork Theory." Jenrose.com. December 15. https://jenrose.com/fork-theory/.

Karp, G. 2011. "Gary Karp on 'The Curb Cut Effect.'" Excerpt of speech to the Federal Deposit Insurance Corporation. Washington, D.C. Video, 2 min., 32 sec. https://www.youtube.com/watch?v=iuIkFRZKfCU.

Linehan, M. 2020. *Building a Life Worth Living: A Memoir.* New York: Random House.

Mantzalas, J., A. L. Richdale, and C. Dissanayake. 2023. "Examining Subjective Understandings of Autistic Burnout Using Q Methodology: A Study Protocol." *PLoS One* 18 (5): e0285578.

Markram, K., and H. Markram. 2010. "The Intense World Theory—A Unifying Theory of the Neurobiology of Autism." *Frontiers in Human Neuroscience* 4.

Mayo Clinic. 2024. "Acupuncture." Mayo Foundation for Medical Education and Research (MFMER), April 20. https://www.mayoclinic.org/tests-procedures/acupuncture/about/pac-20392763.

Milton, D. E. M. 2012. "On the Ontological Status of Autism: The 'Double Empathy Problem.'" *Disability and Society* 27 (6): 883–887.

Miserandino, C. 2003. "The Spoon Theory." But You Don't Look Sick? https://butyoudontlooksick.com/articles/written-by-christine/the-spoon-theory/.

Murray, D., M. Lesser, and W. Lawson. 2005. "Attention, Monotropism, and the Diagnostic Criteria for Autism." *Autism* 9 (2): 139–156.

Olkin, R. 2022. "Conceptualizing Disability: The Three Models of Disability." American Psychological Association. March 29. https://www.apa.org/ed/precollege/psychology-teacher-network/introductory-psychology/disability-models.

Polyvagal Institute. n.d. "What is Polyvagal Theory?" Polyvagal Institute. https://www.polyvagalinstitute.org/whatispolyvagaltheory.

Raymaker, D. M., A. R. Teo, N. A. Steckler, B. Lentz, M. Scharer, A. Delos Santos, et al. 2020. "'Having All of Your Internal Resources Exhausted Beyond Measure and Being Left with No Clean-Up Crew': Defining Autistic Burnout." *Autism Adulthood* 2 (2): 132–143.

Richeson, N. E., J. A. Spross, K. Lutz, and C. Peng. 2010. "Effects of Reiki on Anxiety, Depression, Pain, and Physiological Factors in Community-Dwelling Older Adults." *Research in Gerontological Nursing* 3 (3): 187–199.

Rivera, L. 2024. "Autism NeuroDivergence & Sensory Processing— My Personal AuDHD (Autistic and ADHD) Experience" Neurodivergent Rebel. August 2. https://neurodivergentrebel.com/2024/08/02/autism-neurodivergence-sensory-processing-my-personal-audhd-autistic-and-adhd-experience/.

Schneid, I., and A. E. Raz. 2020. "The Mask of Autism: Social Camouflaging and Impression Management as Coping/Normalization from the Perspectives of Autistic Adults." *Social Science and Medicine* 248: 112826.

Silberman, S. 2015. *Neurotribes: The Legacy of Autism and the Future of Neurodiversity*. New York: Avery.

Solomon, A. 2013. "Depression, the Secret We Share." TEDxMet, October. Video, 29 min., 7 sec. https://www.ted.com/talks/andrew_solomon_depression_the_secret_we_share?language=enanddelay=0sandsubtitle=en.

Stillman, W. 2006. *Autism and the God Connection: Redefining the Autistic Experience Through Extraordinary Accounts of Spiritual Giftedness*. Naperville, IL: Sourcebooks.

Toudal, M., and T. Attwood. 2025. *Energy Accounting: Stress Management and Mental Health Monitoring for Autism and Related Conditions*. Philadelphia: Jessica Kingsley Publishers.

United States Centers for Disease Control and Prevention. 2025. "Data and Statistics on Autism Spectrum Disorder." CDC. May 27. https://www.cdc.gov/autism/data-research/index.html.

United States Department of Labor. n.d. "Youth, Disclosure, and the Workplace Why, When, What, and How." Office of Disability Employment Policy. https://www.dol.gov/agencies/odep/publications/fact-sheets/youth-disclosure-and-the-workplace-why-when-what-and-how.

Usui, M. n.d. "The Five Reiki Principles." International School of Reiki. https://isoreiki.com/reiki-manuals/reiki-level-one-manual/module-one/the-reiki-principles/.

Watts, G., C. Crompton, C. Grainger, J. Long, M. Botha, M. Somerville, and E. Cage. 2024. "'A Certain Magic'—Autistic Adults' Experiences of Interacting with Other Autistic People and Its Relation to Quality of Life: A Systematic Review and Thematic Meta-Synthesis." *Autism*: 13623613241255811.

Sharon Kaye O'Connor, LCSW, is a psychotherapist, educator, consultant, and writer in New York, NY. She is coauthor of the book, *Academic and Student Affairs in Collaboration*. In addition to traditional psychotherapy, Sharon is an ordained Spiritualist minister, and has trained in holistic modalities including Reiki, breathwork, energy healing, and meditation.

As an autistic clinician, Sharon writes and teaches extensively about autism—from an autistic perspective—with the mission of translating the experience into further understanding and support for the autistic community.

Foreword writer **William Stillman** is an award-winning author of ten books on autism and special needs parenting, including *Demystifying the Autistic Experience*, *Empowered Autism Parenting*, and his groundbreaking work *Autism and the God Connection*, among others. His books have been featured on *The Glenn Beck Show* and the NBC hit series *Parenthood*. Stillman has also served on several autism advisory boards, including AUTCOM (the Autism National Committee).

Real change *is* possible

For more than fifty years, New Harbinger has published proven-effective self-help books and pioneering workbooks to help readers of all ages and backgrounds improve mental health and well-being, and achieve lasting personal growth. In addition, our spirituality books offer profound guidance for deepening awareness and cultivating healing, self-discovery, and fulfillment.

Founded by psychologist Matthew McKay and Patrick Fanning, New Harbinger is proud to be an independent, employee-owned company. Our books reflect our core values of integrity, innovation, commitment, sustainability, compassion, and trust. Written by leaders in the field and recommended by therapists worldwide, New Harbinger books are practical, accessible, and provide real tools for real change.

newharbingerpublications

MORE BOOKS from
NEW HARBINGER PUBLICATIONS

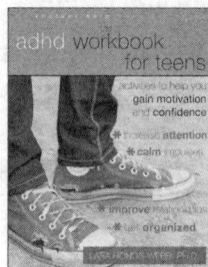

Did you know there are **free tools** you can download for this book?

Free tools are things like **worksheets**, **guided meditation exercises**, and **more** that will help you get the most out of your book.

You can download free tools for this book— whether you bought or borrowed it, in any format, from any source—from the New Harbinger website. All you need is a NewHarbinger.com account. Just use the URL provided in this book to view the free tools that are available for it. Then, click on the "download" button for the free tool you want, and follow the prompts that appear to log in to your NewHarbinger.com account and download the material.

You can also save the free tools for this book to your **Free Tools Library** so you can access them again anytime, just by logging in to your account! Just look for this button on the book's free tools page.

+ Save this to my free tools library

Did you know there are **free tools** you can download for this book?

Free tools are things like **worksheets**, **guided meditation exercises**, and **more** that will help you get the most out of your book.

You can download free tools for this book— whether you bought or borrowed it, in any format, from any source—from the New Harbinger website. All you need is a NewHarbinger.com account. Just use the URL provided in this book to view the free tools that are available for it. Then, click on the "download" button for the free tool you want, and follow the prompts that appear to log in to your NewHarbinger.com account and download the material.

You can also save the free tools for this book to your **Free Tools Library** so you can access them again anytime, just by logging in to your account! Just look for this button on the book's free tools page.

+ Save this to my free tools library

If you need help accessing or downloading free tools, visit **newharbinger.com/faq** or contact us at **customerservice@newharbinger.com**.

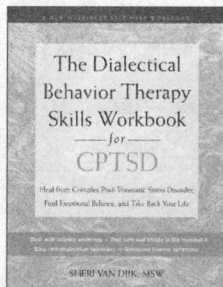